YX 7/01 ✓ 7/01

SHAKESPEARE MADE EASY

MODERN ENGLISH VERSION
SIDE-BY-SIDE WITH FULL ORIGINAL TEXT

Hamlet

EDITED AND RENDERED INTO MODERN ENGLISH BY
Alan Durband

BARRON'S

First U.S. edition published 1986 by
Barron's Educational Series, Inc.

Hutchinson & Co. (Publishers) Ltd
An imprint of the Hutchinson Publishing Group
17–21 Conway Street, London W1P 6JD

Hutchinson Publishing Group (Australia) Pty Ltd
PO Box 496, 16–22 Church Street, Hawthorne,
Melbourne, Victoria 3122

Hutchinson Group (NZ) Ltd
32–34 View Road, PO Box 40–086, Glenfield, Auckland 10

Hutchinson Group (SA) (Pty) Ltd
PO Box 337, Bergvlei 2012, South Africa

First published 1986
© Alan Durband 1986

All inquiries should be addressed to:
Barron's Educational Series, Inc.
250 Wireless Boulevard
Hauppauge, New York 11788

International Standard Book No. 0–8120–3638–7

Library of Congress Catalog No. 85-22952

Library of Congress Cataloging in Publication Data
Shakespeare, William, 1564-1616.
    Hamlet.

    (Shakespeare made easy)
    Summary: Presents the original text of Shakespeare's
play side by side with a modern version, discusses the
author and the theater of his time, and provides quizzes
and other study activities.

    1. Shakespeare, William, 1564-1616. Hamlet.
2. Shakespeare, William, 1564-1616—Study and teaching. [1. Shakespeare, William, 1564-1616. Hamlet. 2.
Shakespeare, William, 1564-1616—Study and teaching.
3. Plays] I. Durband, Alan. II. Title. III. Series: Shakespeare, William, 1564-1616. Shakespeare made easy.
PR2807. A25D87 1986   822.3'3   85-22952
ISBN 0-8120-3638-7

PRINTED IN THE UNITED STATES
30 29 28 27 26 25 24 23 22

'Reade him, therefore; and againe, and againe: And if then you do not like him, surely you are in some danger, not to understand him. . . .'

John Hemming
Henry Condell

Preface to the 1623 Folio Edition

Shakespeare Made Easy

Titles in the series

Hamlet
Henry IV, Part I
Julius Caesar
King Lear
Macbeth
The Merchant of Venice
A Midsummer Night's Dream
Romeo and Juliet
The Tempest
Twelfth Night

Contents

Introduction   **6**

William Shakespeare: life, plays, theater, verse   8
Hamlet: date, sources, text   15

HAMLET

Original text and modern version   17

Activities   **312**

Characters   312
Textual questions   320
Examination questions   325
One-word-answer quiz   327
What's missing?   329

Introduction

Shakespeare Made Easy is intended for readers approaching the plays for the first time, who find the language of Elizabethan poetic drama an initial obstacle to understanding and enjoyment. In the past, the only answer to the problem has been to grapple with the difficulties with the aid of explanatory footnotes (often missing when they are most needed) and a stern teacher. Generations of students have complained that "Shakespeare was ruined for me at school."

Usually a fuller appreciation of Shakespeare's plays comes in later life, when the mind has matured and language skills are more developed. Often the desire to read Shakespeare for pleasure and enrichment follows from a visit to the theater, where excellence of acting and production can bring to life qualities which sometimes lie dormant on the printed page.

Shakespeare Made Easy can never be a substitute for the original plays. It cannot possibly convey the full meaning of Shakespeare's poetic expression, which is untranslatable. *Shakespeare Made Easy* concentrates on the dramatic aspect, enabling the novice to become familiar with the plot and characters, and to experience one facet of Shakespeare's genius. To know and understand the central issues of each play is a sound starting point for further exploration and development.

Discretion can be used in choosing the best method to employ. One way is to read the original Shakespeare first, ignoring the modern translation or using it only when interest or understanding flags. Another way is to read the translation first, to establish confidence and familiarity with plots and characters.

Either way, cross-reference can be illuminating. The modern text can explain "what is being said" if Shakespeare's language is particularly complex or his expression antiquated. The Shakespeare text will show the reader of the modern paraphrase how much more can be expressed in poetry than in prose.

The use of *Shakespeare Made Easy* means that the newcomer need never be overcome by textual difficulties. From first to last, a measure of understanding is at hand – the key is provided for what has been a locked door to many students in the past. And as understanding grows, so an awareness develops of the potential of language as a vehicle for philosophic and moral expression, beauty, and the abidingly memorable.

Even professional Shakespearean scholars can never hope to arrive at a complete understanding of the plays. Each critic, researcher, actor, or producer merely adds a little to the work that has already been done, or makes fresh interpretations of the texts for new generations. For everyone, Shakespearean appreciation is a journey. *Shakespeare Made Easy* is intended to help with the first steps.

William Shakespeare

His life

William Shakespeare was born in Stratford-on-Avon, Warwickshire, on April 23, 1564, the son of a prosperous wool and leather merchant. Very little is known of his early life. From parish records we know that he married Ann Hathaway in 1582, when he was eighteen and she was twenty-six. They had three children, the eldest of whom died in childhood.

Between his marriage and the next thing we know about him there is a gap of ten years. Probably he became a member of a traveling company of actors. By 1592 he had settled in London, and had earned a reputation as an actor and playwright.

Theaters were then in their infancy. The first (called *The Theatre*) was built by the actor James Burbage in 1576, in Shoreditch, then a suburb of London. Two more followed as the taste for theater grew: *The Curtain* in 1577 and *The Rose* in 1587. The demand for new plays naturally increased. Shakespeare probably earned a living adapting old plays and working in collaboration with others on new ones. Today we would call him a "free lance," since he was not permanently attached to one theater.

In 1594, a new company of actors, The Lord Chamberlain's Men, was formed, and Shakespeare was one of the shareholders. He remained a member throughout his working life. The Company was regrouped in 1603, and renamed The King's Men, with James I as their patron.

Shakespeare and his fellow actors prospered. In 1598 they built their own theater, *The Globe*, which broke away from the traditional rectangular shape of the inn and its yard (the early home of traveling bands of actors). Shakespeare described it in *Henry V* as "this wooden O," because it was circular.

Many other theaters were built by investors eager to profit from the new enthusiasm for drama. *The Hope, The Fortune, The Red Bull*, and *The Swan* were all open-air "public" theaters. There were also many "private" (or indoor) theaters, one of which (*The Blackfriars*) was purchased by Shakespeare and his friends because the child actors who performed there were dangerous competitors (Shakespeare denounces them in *Hamlet*).

After writing some thirty-seven plays (the exact number is something which scholars argue about), Shakespeare retired to his native Stratford, wealthy and respected. He died on his birthday in 1616.

His plays

Shakespeare's plays were not all published in his lifetime. None of them comes to us exactly as he wrote it.

In Elizabethan times, plays were not regarded as either literature or good reading matter. They were written quickly (often by more than one writer), performed perhaps ten or twelve times, and then discarded. Fourteen of Shakespeare's plays were first printed in Quarto (17cm × 21cm) volumes, not all with his name as the author. Some were authorized (the "good" Quartos) and probably were printed from prompt copies provided by the theater. Others were pirated (the "bad" Quartos) by booksellers who may have employed shorthand writers, or bought actors' copies after the run of the play had ended.

In 1623, seven years after Shakespeare's death, John Hemming and Henry Condell (fellow actors and shareholders in The King's Men) published a collected edition of Shakespeare's works – thirty-six plays in all – in a Folio (21cm × 34cm) edition. From their introduction it would seem that they used Shakespeare's original manuscripts ("we have scarce received from him a blot in his papers") but the Folio volumes that still survive are not all exactly alike, nor are the plays printed as we know them today, with act and scene divisions and stage directions.

A modern edition of a Shakespeare play is the result of a great deal of scholarly research and editorial skill over several centuries. The aim is always to publish a text (based on the good and bad Quartos and the Folio editions) that most closely resembles what Shakespeare intended. Misprints have added to the problems, so some words and lines are pure guesswork. This explains why some versions of Shakespeare's plays differ from others.

His theater

The first playhouse built as such in Elizabethan London, constructed in 1576, was *The Theatre*. Its cofounders were John Brayne, an investor, and James Burbage, a carpenter turned actor. Like the six or seven "public" (or outdoor) theaters which followed it over the next thirty years, it was situated outside the city, to avoid conflict with the authorities. They disapproved of players and playgoing, partly on moral and political grounds, and partly because of the danger of spreading the plague. (There were two major epidemics during Shakespeare's lifetime, and on each occasion the theaters were closed for lengthy periods.)

The Theatre was a financial success, and Shakespeare's company performed there until 1598, when a dispute over the lease of the land forced Burbage to take down the building. It was recreated in Southwark, as *The Globe*, with Shakespeare and several of his fellow actors as the principal shareholders.

By modern standards, *The Globe* was small. Externally, the octagonal building measured less than thirty meters across, but in spite of this it could accommodate an audience of between two and three thousand people. (The largest of the three theaters at the National Theatre complex in London today seats 1160.)

Performances were advertised by means of playbills posted around the city, and they took place during the hours of daylight when the weather was suitable. A flag flew to show that all was well, to save playgoers a wasted journey.

At the entrance, a doorkeeper collected one penny (about 60 cents today) for admission to the "pit" – a name taken from the

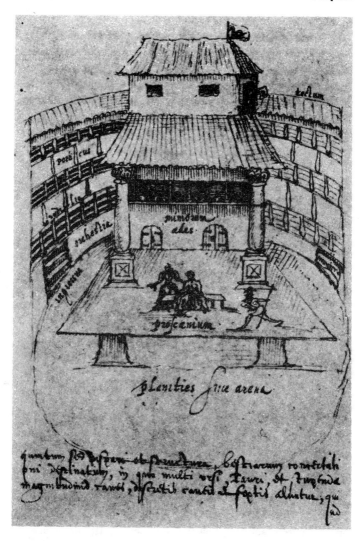

Interior of the Swan Theatre – from a pen and ink drawing made in 1596 (Mansell Collection)

old inn-yards, where bearbaiting and cockfighting were popular sports. This was the minimum charge for seeing a play. The "groundlings," as they were called, simply stood around the three sides of the stage, in the open air. Those who were better off could pay extra for a seat under cover. Stairs led from the pit to three tiers of galleries round the walls. The higher one went, the more one paid. The best seats cost one shilling, (or $7 today). In theaters owned by speculators like Francis Langley and Philip Henslowe, half the gallery takings went to the landlord.

A full house might consist of 800 groundlings and 1500 in the galleries, with a dozen more exclusive seats on the stage itself for the gentry. A new play might run for between six and sixteen performances; the average was about ten. As there were no breaks between scenes, and no intermissions, most plays could be performed in two hours. A trumpet sounded three times before the play began.

The acting company assembled in the Tiring House at the rear of the stage. This was where they "attired" (or dressed) themselves – not in costumes representing the period of the play, but in Elizabethan doublet and hose. All performances were therefore in modern dress, though no expense was spared to make the stage costumes lavish. The entire company was male. By law actresses were not allowed, and female roles were performed by boys.

Access to the stage from the Tiring House was through two doors, one on each side of the stage. Because there was no front curtain, every entrance had to have its corresponding exit, so an actor killed on stage had to be carried off. There was no scenery: the audience used its imagination, guided by the spoken word. Storms and night scenes might well be performed on sunny days in mid-afternoon; the Elizabethan playgoer relied entirely on the playwrights' descriptive skills to establish the dramatic atmosphere.

Once on stage, the actors and their expensive clothes were protected from sudden showers by a canopy, the underside of which was painted blue, and spangled with stars to represent the heavens. A trapdoor in the stage made ghostly entrances and the gravedigging scene in *Hamlet* possible. Behind the main stage, in between the two entrance doors, there was a curtained area, concealing a small inner stage, useful for bedroom scenes. Above this was a balcony, which served for castle walls (as in *Henry V*) or a domestic balcony (as in the famous scene in *Romeo and Juliet*).

The acting style in Elizabethan times was probably more declamatory than we favor today, but the close proximity of the audience also made a degree of intimacy possible. In those days soliloquies and asides seemed quite natural. Act and scene divisions did not exist (those in printed versions of the play today have been added by editors), but Shakespeare often indicates a scene ending by a rhyming couplet.

A company such as The King's Men at *The Globe* would consist of around twenty-five actors, half of whom might be shareholders, and the rest part-timers engaged for a particular play. Amongst the shareholders in *The Globe* were several specialists – William Kempe, for example, was a renowned comedian and Robert Armin was a singer and dancer. Playwrights wrote parts to suit the actors who were available, and devised ways of overcoming the absence of women. Shakespeare often has his heroines dress as young men, and physical contact between lovers was formal compared with the realism we expect today.

His verse

Shakespeare wrote his plays mostly in blank verse: that is, unrhymed lines consisting of ten syllables, alternately stressed and unstressed. The technical term for this form is the "iambic pentameter." When Shakespeare first began to write for the stage, it was fashionable to maintain this regular beat from the first line of the play till the last.

Shakespeare conformed at first, and then experimented. Some of his early plays contain whole scenes in rhyming couplets – in *Romeo and Juliet*, for example, there is extensive use of rhyme, and as if to show his versatility, Shakespeare even inserts a sonnet into the dialogue.

But as he matured, he sought greater freedom of expression than rhyme allowed. Rhyme is still used to indicate a scene-ending, or to stress lines which he wishes the audience to remember. Generally, though, Shakespeare moved towards the rhythms of everyday speech. This gave him many dramatic advantages, which he fully and subtly exploits in terms of atmosphere, character, emotion, stress and pace.

It is Shakespeare's poetic imagery, however, that most distinguishes his verse from that of lesser playwrights. It enables him to stretch the imagination, express complex thought patterns in memorable language, and convey a number of associated ideas in a compressed and economical form. A study of Shakespeare's imagery – especially in his later plays – is often the key to a full understanding of his meaning and purposes.

At the other extreme is prose. Shakespeare normally reserves it for servants, clowns, commoners, and pedestrian matters such as lists, messages and letters.

Hamlet

Date

The exact date of composition of *Hamlet* is conjectural. It was entered in the Stationers' Register in 1602, but it was acted in one form or another as early as 1599.

Sources

An earlier play than Shakespeare's, based on the *Hamlet* story, is known to have existed as early as 1589, and Shakespeare may well have performed in it in 1594. No copy has survived. Contemporary evidence suggests the author was Thomas Kyd, who also wrote *The Spanish Tragedy*, another play involving murder, a ghost, revenge and insanity.

The story of Hamlet is older still. A Danish historian, Saxo Grammaticus, tells it as a folk story in his *History of Denmark*, first published in 1514; and Francois de Belleforest retold it in French in *Tragic Histories*, first published in 1576.

These sources provided Shakespeare with his scaffolding and raw materials. The masterpiece that resulted is the product of his own unique genius.

Text

A great deal of scholarly detective work has been done to unravel the unique complexity of the text of *Hamlet*. There are three main versions: an unauthorized Quarto of 1603; a second Quarto of 1604, said to be "according to the true and perfect copy" and almost twice as long; and the Folio edition of 1623, in which more than 70 lines are introduced, some 225 others removed, and many extra words and exclamations printed that may well have been spoken by actors in performance for dramatic effect. Spread across these versions (and three more Quartos in Shakespeare's lifetime which followed the text of Q2) there are the usual errors of typesetting and transcription to be taken into account, plus variations in act and scene divisions after Act 2 Scene 2.

There is therefore no text of *Hamlet* which has absolute authority over another, and every edition including this one is based on editorial research and personal choice.

Hamlet

Original text and modern version

The characters

Hamlet Prince of Denmark
Claudius King of Denmark, and Hamlet's uncle
Gertrude the Queen; Hamlet's mother, and recently remarried
The ghost of the late King, Hamlet's father
Polonius an elderly Councillor of State
Laertes his son
Ophelia his daughter
Horatio Hamlet's friend
Rosencrantz } courtiers, and formerly fellow students of
Guildenstern } Hamlet
Fortinbras Prince of Norway
Voltemand }
Cornelius } Danish councillors and ambassadors to Norway
Marcellus }
Barnardo } members of the King's guard
Francisco }
Osric a fashionable courtier
Reynaldo Polonius's servant
A gravedigger
A gravedigger's mate
A captain in Fortinbras's army
Players members of a touring company
Ambassadors from England
A gentleman of the Danish court
A priest
Sailors
Lords, Ladies, Soldiers, Messengers and Attendants

Scene: Elsinore
         In and around the Court of the King of Denmark

Act one

Scene 1

Elsinore. A platform before the castle. Enter **Barnardo** *and* **Francisco,** *two Sentinels.*

Barnardo Who's there?

Francisco Nay, answer me. Stand and unfold yourself.

Barnardo Long live the King!

Francisco Barnardo?

5 **Barnardo** He.

Francisco You come most carefully upon your hour.

Barnardo 'Tis now struck twelve. Get thee to bed, Francisco.

Francisco For this relief much thanks. 'Tis bitter cold,
And I am sick at heart.

10 **Barnardo** Have you had quiet guard?

Francisco Not a mouse stirring.

Barnardo Well, good night.
If you do meet Horatio and Marcellus,
The rivals of my watch, bid them make haste.

15 **Francisco** I think I hear them.

[*Enter* **Horatio** *and* **Marcellus**]

Stand ho! Who's there?

Horatio Friends to this ground.

Act one

Scene 1

Elsinore in Denmark: a platform on the castle walls. It is midnight, and **Francisco**, *a sentry, is waiting to go off duty.* **Barnardo** *approaches him in the dark.*

Barnardo   Who's there?

Francisco   [*raising his spear*]   No: answer *me*! Halt and identify yourself!

Barnardo   [*giving the password*]   Long live the King!

Francisco   [*lowering his weapon*]   Barnardo?

Barnardo   Yes.

Francisco   You're on the dot.

Barnardo   It's turned twelve. Off to bed, Francisco.

Francisco   Many thanks for coming. It's bitterly cold. I'm fed up.

Barnardo   All quiet tonight?

Francisco   Not so much as a mouse.

Barnardo   Well, good night. If you should meet Horatio and Marcellus, the other men on duty, tell them to hurry.   [*He starts his patrol*]

Francisco   I think I can hear them.

   [**Horatio** *and* **Marcellus** *enter*]

   Halt! Who goes there?

Horatio   Friends.

Marcellus   And liegemen to the Dane.

Francisco   Give you good night.

20 **Marcellus**   Oh, farewell honest soldier. Who hath relieved
  you?

Francisco   Barnardo hath my place. Give you good
  night.   [*Exit*]

Marcellus   Holla, Barnardo!

25 **Barnardo**   Say, what, is Horatio there?

Horatio   A piece of him.

Barnardo   Welcome, Horatio. Welcome, good Marcellus.

Horatio   What, has this thing appeared again tonight?

Barnardo   I have seen nothing.

30 **Marcellus**   Horatio says 'tis but our fantasy,
  And will not let belief take hold of him,
  Touching this dreaded sight twice seen of us.
  Therefore I have entreated him along
  With us to watch the minutes of this night,
35 That if again this apparition come,
  He may approve our eyes and speak to it.

Horatio   Tush, tush, 'twill not appear.

Barnardo   Sit down awhile,
  And let us once again assail your ears,
40 That are so fortified against our story,
  What we two nights have seen.

Horatio   Well, sit we down.
  And let us hear Barnardo speak of this.

Barnardo   Last night of all,
45 When yond same star that's westward from the pole,

Marcellus   And loyal subjects of the King of Denmark.

Francisco   [*preparing to leave*]   Good night to you.

Marcellus   Good night, worthy soldier. Who relieved you?

Francisco   Barnardo took my place. Good night.

[*He goes*]

Marcellus   [*calling*]   Hello, Barnardo!

Barnado   [*replying from a short distance*]   Hey, what? Is Horatio there?

Horatio   [*offering his hand to shake*]   Some of him!

Barnardo   Welcome, Horatio. Welcome, Marcellus.

Horatio   Well, has this thing appeared again tonight?

Barnardo   I've seen nothing.

Marcellus   Horatio says it's only our imaginations, and won't believe in the scary sight that we've seen twice. That's why I've got him to join us on tonight's watch, so that if this ghost comes again he can confirm that our eyes haven't deceived us, and speak to it.

Horatio   [*scornfully*]   Really, now! It won't appear.

Barnardo   Sit down a moment, and let's tell you again, in spite of your skepticism, what we've seen these past two nights.

Horatio   Well, sit then, and let's hear Barnardo tell his story.

Barnardo   Last night, when the star that's to the west of the

Had made his course t'illume that part of heaven
Where now it burns, Marcellus and myself,
The bell then beating one –

[Enter **Ghost**]

Marcellus   Peace, break thee off. Look where it comes again.

50 **Barnardo**   In the same figure like the King that's dead.

Marcellus   Thou art a scholar. Speak to it, Horatio.

Barnardo   Looks it not like the King? Mark it, Horatio.

Horatio   Most like. It harrows me with fear and wonder.

Barnardo   It would be spoke to.

55 **Marcellus**   Question it, Horatio.

Horatio   What art thou that usurp'st this time of night,
Together with that fair and warlike form
To which the majesty of buried Denmark
Did sometimes march? By heaven, I charge thee speak.

60 **Marcellus**   It is offended.

Barnardo   See, it stalks away.

Horatio   Stay, speak, speak, I charge thee speak!

[Exit **Ghost**]

Marcellus   'Tis gone and will not answer.

Barnardo   How now, Horatio! You tremble and look pale.
65   Is not this something more than fantasy?
What think you on't?

Horatio   Before my God, I might not this believe
Without the sensible and true avouch
Of mine own eyes.

24

North star had moved to where it's shining now, Marcellus
and myself – the bell having struck one –

[*The* **Ghost** *enters*]

Marcellus   Sh! Say no more. Look – here it comes again!

Barnardo   As before, looking like the dead King!

Marcellus   You know what to say; speak to it, Horatio.

Barnardo   Doesn't it look like the King? See, Horatio!

Horatio   Very like. It chills me with fear and astonishment.

Barnardo   It wishes to be spoken to.

Marcellus   Ask it something, Horatio.

Horatio   Who are you, to intrude upon us at this time of night,
dressed in the armor the late King used to wear? In
heaven's name: reply!

[*The* **Ghost** *turns to go*]

Marcellus   It has taken offense.

Barnardo   Look – it's walking stiffly away.

Horatio   Stop! Reply! Reply! I demand a reply!

[*The* **Ghost** *leaves*]

Marcellus   It's gone and won't answer.

Barnardo   Well, Horatio? You are trembling, and look pale.
Isn't this something more than mere imagination? What do
you think about it?

Horatio   As God's my witness, I wouldn't have believed this
without seeing it for myself.

70 **Marcellus**   Is it not like the King?

Horatio   As thou art to thyself:
　　Such was the very armour he had on
　　When he th'ambitious Norway combated.
　　So frowned he once, when in an angry parle
75　He smote the sledded Polacks on the ice.
　　'Tis strange.

Marcellus   Thus twice before, and jump at this dead hour,
　　With martial stalk hath he gone by our watch.

Horatio   In what particular thought to work I know not,
80　But in the gross and scope of my opinion,
　　This bodes some strange eruption to our state.

Marcellus   Good now, sit down, and tell me, he that knows,
　　Why this same strict and most observant watch
　　So nightly toils the subject of the land,
85　And why such daily cast of brazen cannon
　　And foreign mart for implements of war,
　　Why such impress of shipwrights, whose sore task
　　Does not divide the Sunday from the week:
　　What might be toward that this sweaty haste
90　Doth make the night joint-labourer with the day?
　　Who is't that can inform me?

Horatio   That can I.
　　At least the whisper goes so. Our last King,
　　Whose image even but now appeared to us,
95　Was as you know by Fortinbras of Norway,
　　Thereto pricked on by a most emulate pride,
　　Dared to the combat; in which our valiant Hamlet
　　(For so this side of our known world esteemed him)
　　Did slay this Fortinbras, who by a sealed compact
100　Well ratified by law and heraldry
　　Did forfeit, with his life, all those his lands

26

Marcellus   Isn't it like the King?

Horatio   As you are to yourself. That was exactly the armor he was wearing when he fought old Fortinbras of Norway. He wore that very frown when, after fierce fighting, he defeated the Polish soldiers on their sledges as they crossed the ice. It's strange.

Marcellus   Likewise twice before, at the dead of night – this time precisely – he has passed us on our watch, walking with that military gait.

Horatio   I don't know what to think. But overall, this points to some violent disorder in our society.

Marcellus   Right then: sit down and tell me – whoever can – why this strict and careful guard duty burdens our fellow countrymen every night. Why is there so much manufacturing of brass cannons, and international trade in armaments? Why are shipwrights being conscripted to work strenuous seven-day weeks? What's the threat that accounts for all this feverish round-the-clock activity?

Horatio   I can explain. At any rate, this is how it's rumored. Our previous King, whose ghost has just appeared to us, was, as you know, dared to single combat by Fortinbras of Norway, who was prompted by an arrogant pride. Our valiant King Hamlet – for such the western world regarded him – killed this Fortinbras, who thereby forfeited to his conqueror (according to the terms of a formal legal agreement) all the lands he possessed. Our King had

Which he stood seized of to the conqueror;
Against the which a moiety competent
Was gaged by our King, which had returned
105   To the inheritance of Fortinbras,
Had he been vanquisher; as, by the same cov'nant
And carriage of the article designed,
His fell to Hamlet. Now, sir, young Fortinbras,
Of unimproved mettle, hot and full,
110   Hath in the skirts of Norway here and there
Sharked up a list of lawless resolutes
For food and diet to some enterprise
That hath a stomach in't; which is no other,
As it doth well appear unto our state,
115   But to recover of us by strong hand
And terms compulsatory those foresaid lands
So by his father lost. And this, I take it,
Is the main motive of our preparations,
The source of this our watch, and the chief head
120   Of this post-haste and rummage in the land.

Barnardo   I think it be no other but e'en so.
Well may it sort that this portentous figure
Comes armed through our watch so like the King
That was and is the question of these wars.

125   **Horatio**   A mote it is to trouble the mind's eye.
In the most high and palmy state of Rome,
A little ere the mightiest Julius fell,
The graves stood tenantless and the sheeted dead
Did squeak and gibber in the Roman streets;
130   As stars with trains of fire, and dews of blood,
Disasters in the sun; and the moist star,
Upon whose influence Neptune's empire stands,
Was sick almost to doomsday with eclipse.
And even the like precurse of feared events,
135   As harbingers preceding still the fates

28

matched this with a territory of equal size, which would
have reverted to Fortinbras had he won: just as, on the
same contractual basis, Fortinbras's stake fell to Hamlet.
Now, sir, his son, young Fortinbras, as yet untested but
spoiling for a fight, has recruited a gang of desperadoes
from various places in the Norwegian provinces: cannon
fodder for an enterprise of some daring, which is obviously
nothing less than the recovery by armed force of the
aforesaid lands lost by his father. And this, as I understand
it, is the main reason for our preparations, the explanation
for our guard duty, and the origin of all this hectic activity
throughout the country.

Barnardo   I'm sure you are right. It's consistent with this
specter visiting us on sentry duty dressed in armor, and
looking very like the King who was, and still is, the central
issue of the war.

Horatio   It nags the mind. When Rome was at its greatest, just
before the mighty Julius Caesar was assassinated, graves
opened and corpses in their shrouds shrieked dementedly in
the streets of Rome. Comets with fiery blood-red tails came
as omens from the sun; and the moon, which governs the
tides, was almost totally extinguished. Similar dire warnings
predicting future calamities have been given to our country

And prologue to the omen coming on,
Have heaven and earth together demonstrated
Unto our climatures and countrymen.

[*Enter* **Ghost**]

But soft, behold. Lo, where it comes again.
140   I'll cross it though it blast me. [**Ghost** *spreads its arms*]
                          Stay, illusion:
If thou hast any sound or use of voice,
Speak to me.
If there be any good thing to be done
145   That may to thee do ease, and grace to me,
Speak to me;
If thou art privy to thy country's fate,
Which, happily, foreknowing may avoid,
Oh speak!
150   Or if thou hast uphoarded in thy life
Extorted treasure in the womb of earth,
For which, they say, you spirits oft walk in death,
Speak of it. Stay and speak! [*The cock crows*]
                      Stop it, Marcellus.

155 **Marcellus**   Shall I strike at it with my partisan?

Horatio   Do if it will not stand.

Barnardo   'Tis here.

Horatio   'Tis here.

[*Exit* **Ghost**]

Marcellus   'Tis gone.
160   We do it wrong, being so majestical,
To offer it the show of violence,
For it is as the air, invulnerable,
And our vain blows malicious mockery.

and our fellow countrymen, both in the heavens and here on earth.

[*The* **Ghost** *enters*]

But sh! Look! See where it comes again. I'll confront it, even though it might destroy me.

[*The* **Ghost** *spreads its arms wide, but* **Horatio** *addresses it boldly*]

Stop, ghost! If you can talk, speak to me!   [*The* **Ghost** *makes no reply*]   If there's some good deed you'd like done that might bring peace to you and grace to me, speak!   [*Again the* **Ghost** *is silent*]   If you know of something that may befall your country that can, perhaps, be avoided, oh speak!   [*The* **Ghost** *does not respond*]   Or if you've buried a hoard of ill-gotten treasure during your life, the reason (so they say) why you spirits often cannot rest after death, speak about it! Stay and speak!   [*A cock crows, signifying the approach of day. The* **Ghost** *turns away*]   Stop it, Marcellus!

Marcellus   Shall I strike out at it with my spear?

Horatio   Do, if it won't stay put.

Barnardo   [*pointing in one direction*]   It's here.

Horatio   [*pointing in another*]   No, it's here.

[*The* **Ghost** *departs*]

Marcellus   It has gone. It's wrong of us to threaten so regal a figure. It is like the air: you cannot hurt it. Our ineffective blows only demonstrate our hostility.

Barnardo   It was about to speak when the cock crew.

165 **Horatio**   And then it started like a guilty thing
Upon a fearful summons. I have heard
The cock, that is the trumpet to the morn,
Doth with his lofty and shrill-sounding throat
Awake the god of day, and at his warning,
170 Whether in sea or fire, in earth or air,
Th'extravagant and erring spirit hies
To his confine; and of the truth herein
This present object made probation.

Marcellus   It faded on the crowing of the cock.
175 Some say that ever 'gainst that season comes
Wherein our Saviour's birth is celebrated,
The bird of dawning singeth all night long;
And then, they say, no spirit dare stir abroad,
The nights are wholesome; then no planets strike,
180 No fairy takes, nor witch hath power to charm,
So hallowed and so gracious is that time.

Horatio   So have I heard and do in part believe it.
But look, the morn in russet mantle clad
Walks o'er the dew of yon high eastward hill.
185 Break we our watch up, and by my advice
Let us impart what we have seen tonight
Unto young Hamlet; for upon my life
This spirit, dumb to us, will speak to him.
Do you consent we shall acquaint him with it
190 As needful in our loves, fitting our duty?

Marcellus   Let's do't, I pray, and I this morning know
Where we shall find him most conveniently.

[Exeunt]

Barnardo   It was about to speak when the cock crowed.

Horatio   And then it was startled, like someone guilty responding to a challenge. I've heard it said that the cock, morning's trumpeter, wakes the god of day with its clarion call; and the wandering spirit far from home (whichever element it belongs to: the sea, or fire, or earth, or the air) hastens to its base when warned by the cockcrow. This specter we've seen proves the truth of the story.

Marcellus   It disappeared when the cock crowed. Some people say that before Christmas the cock crows all night long. And then, so they say, no spirit dares to roam. The nights are free from evil; the stars are not sinister; fairies make no mischief; witches cannot cast spells: that period is so holy and blessed.

Horatio   So I've heard, and I'm inclined to believe it.   [*He points*]   But look: rosy dawn rises over the hill there in the east. Let's disband. My advice is that we should tell young Hamlet what we've seen tonight. I'd wager my life that this spirit will talk to him though it won't speak to us. Do you agree that we should tell him of it, out of friendship as befits our duty?

Marcellus   Yes, let's do that. I know where we'll easily find him this morning.

[*They go*]

Scene 2

Flourish. Enter **Claudius** *the* **King of Denmark, Gertrude** *the* **Queen,** *Council, including* **Voltemand, Cornelius, Polonius** *and his son* **Laertes, Hamlet,** *with others*.

King   Though yet of Hamlet our dear brother's death
    The memory be green; and that it us befitted
    To bear our hearts in grief, and our whole kingdom
    To be contracted in one brow of woe;
5   Yet so far hath discretion fought with nature
    That we with wisest sorrow think on him,
    Together with remembrance of ourselves.
    Therefore our sometime sister, now our Queen,
    Th'imperial jointress of this warlike state,
10 Have we, as 'twere with a defeated joy,
    With an auspicious and a dropping eye,
    With mirth in funeral and with dirge in marriage,
    In equal scale weighing delight and dole,
    Taken to wife. Nor have we herein barred
15 Your better wisdoms, which have freely gone
    With this affair along. For all, our thanks.
    Now follows that you know: young Fortinbras,
    Holding a weak supposal of our worth,
    Or thinking by our late dear brother's death
20 Our state to be disjoint and out of frame,
    Colleagued with this dream of his advantage,
    He hath not failed to pester us with message
    Importing the surrender of those lands
    Lost by his father, with all bonds of law,
25 To our most valiant brother. So much for him.
    Now for ourself, and for this time of meeting,
    Thus much the business is: we have here writ
    To Norway, uncle of young Fortinbras –

Scene 2

*The King of Denmark's Court. A flourish of trumpets heralds
the entry of* **Claudius***, the new King, and his wife* **Gertrude***,
widow of the late* **King Hamlet***. They have recently married.
They are followed by the Council, including* **Voltemand***,*
Cornelius*, and* **Polonius***, who is accompanied by his son*
Laertes*.* **Hamlet** *(son of* **King Hamlet** *and* **Gertrude***) enters last.
He is dressed in mourning black.*

King Though the death of Hamlet, our dear brother-in-law, is
still a memory fresh in our minds – and though we rightly
mourned for him, with the entire kingdom sharing a
common grief – nevertheless, common sense has overcome
our natural feelings to the extent that we sorrow for him
level-headedly, remembering at the same time our own
interests and responsibilites. Therefore, we have married
our former sister-in-law, who is now our Queen and joint
ruler of our warlike country. We did so with (as it
were) a downhearted sort of happiness; with one eye
cheerful, the other sad: bringing joy to the funeral, and
sorrow to the marriage; delight and misery were equally
balanced. Nor have we disregarded your wise counsel; it has
been fully supportive and freely given. Thank you for
everything. Next, something you already know. Young
Fortinbras, holding us in low esteem – or thinking our
country is disordered and disorganized because of our dear
brother's death – in furtherance of his ambitious dreams,
has not failed to pester us with messages, demanding the
surrender of the lands which his father lost (all quite legally)
to our most valiant brother. So much for the deeds of
Fortinbras. As for our own response, and the reason for
summoning this meeting, this is how things are right
now.   [*He shows a letter to the Council*]   We have written
to the King of Norway, young Fortinbras's uncle – who,

30   Who, impotent and bedrid, scarcely hears
Of this his nephew's purpose – to suppress
His further gait herein, in that the levies,
The lists, and full proportions are all made
Out of his subject; and we here dispatch
You, good Cornelius, and you, Voltemand,
35   For bearers of this greeting to old Norway,
Giving to you no further personal power
To business with the King more than the scope
Of these dilated articles allow.
Farewell, and let your haste commend your duty.

40 **Corn., Volt.**   In that, and all things, will we show our duty.

King   We doubt it nothing. Heartily farewell.

[Exeunt **Voltemand** *and* **Cornelius**]

And now, Laertes, what's the news with you?
You told us of some suit; what is't, Laertes?
You cannot speak of reason to the Dane
45   And lose your voice. What wouldst thou beg, Laertes,
That shall not be my offer, not thy asking?
The head is not more native to the heart,
The hand more instrumental to the mouth,
Than is the throne of Denmark to thy father.
50   What wouldst thou have, Laertes?

Laertes   My dread lord,
Your leave and favour to return to France,
From whence though willingly I came to Denmark
To show my duty in your coronation,
55   Yet now I must confess, that duty done,
My thoughts and wishes bend again towards France
And bow them to your gracious leave and pardon.

King   Have you your father's leave? What says Polonius?

Polonius   He hath, my lord, wrung from me my slow leave

powerless and bedridden, hardly knows of his nephew's intentions – to stop him from proceeding further, because the conscripts, the regulars, and all the military forces consist entirely of his subjects. We here dispatch you, good Cornelius, and you, Voltemand, as the bearers of this greeting to the old King of Norway, giving you no further personal powers to negotiate with the King beyond what is described at length in these terms of reference.   [*He hands them an official document*]   Farewell, and make haste.

Corn., Volt.   In that, as in all things, we will perform our duty.

King   We do not doubt it. Our hearty farewell!

> [**Voltemand** *and* **Cornelius** *bow and leave hurriedly. The* **King** *turns to* **Polonius's** *son*]

And now, Laertes, what's your news? You mentioned some request. What is it, Laertes? You cannot ask anything reasonable of the King of Denmark and waste your breath. What would you beg, Laertes, that I will not freely grant you without your asking? The head could not be more closely related to the heart, nor the mouth more indebted to the hand, than the throne of Denmark is to your father. What is your wish, Laertes?

Laertes   My revered lord: your leave and permission to return to France. Though I willingly came to Denmark to show my loyalty at your coronation, I must now confess that, my duty done, my thoughts and wishes incline towards France again, subject to your gracious indulgence and consent.

King   Have you your father's permission? What does Polonius say?

Polonius   He has, my lord, extracted from me my grudging

60   By laboursome petition, and at last
        Upon his will I sealed my hard consent.
        I do beseech you give him leave to go.

King   Take thy fair hour, Laertes, time be thine,
        And thy best graces spend it at thy will.
65   But now, my cousin Hamlet, and my son –

Hamlet   [*aside*] A little more than kin, and less than kind.

King   How is it that the clouds still hang on you?

Hamlet   Not so, my lord, I am too much i'th'sun.

Queen   Good Hamlet, cast thy nighted colour off,
70   And let thine eye look like a friend on Denmark.
        Do not for ever with thy vailed lids
        Seek for thy noble father in the dust.
        Thou know'st 'tis common: all that lives must die,
        Passing through nature to eternity.

75 **Hamlet**   Ay, madam, it is common.

Queen   If it be,
        Why seems it so particular with thee?

Hamlet   Seems, madam? Nay, it is. I know not seems.
        'Tis not alone my inky cloak, good mother,
80   Nor customary suits of solemn black,
        Nor windy suspiration of forced breath,
        No, nor the fruitful river in the eye,
        Nor the dejected haviour of the visage,
        Together with all forms, moods, shapes of grief,
85   That can denote me truly. These indeed seem,
        For they are actions that a man might play;
        But I have that within which passes show,
        These but the trappings and the suits of woe.

King   'Tis sweet and commendable in your nature, Hamlet,
90   To give these mourning duties to your father,

consent through constant pleading. In the end, I reluctantly endorsed his wishes. I beseech you to give him leave to go.

King Enjoy yourself while you are young, Laertes; have your fling and use your talents as you think best. [**Laertes** *bows gratefully. The* **King** *turns to* **Hamlet**, *who has been wrapped in his own thoughts since his arrival*] But now my nephew Hamlet, and my son –

Hamlet [*aside*] Closely related in one sense, but not so in another . . .

King Why are you still under a cloud?

Hamlet Not so, my lord. I'm suffering from too much sun. [*It is no accident that "sun" and "son" sound the same*]

Queen Hamlet, dear: throw off your black mood, and look upon the King with a more friendly eye. Don't go round forever with downcast looks, as if you were seeking for your noble father in the dust. You know it's normal: everything that lives must die, passing through the stages of life to eternity.

Hamlet Yes, madam. It's normal.

Queen If it is, how come it seems so special in your case?

Hamlet *Seems*, madam? No, it *is*. I don't understand your *seems*. It's not simply my black mood, mother dear, or my traditional mourning clothes, or heavy sighs – no, nor is it copious tears, miserable looks, and all the related forms, expressions and appearances of grief – that can accurately convey my true feelings. These do indeed *seem*, because they are actions that a man can falsify. But I have something inside me that is beyond pretense. Those other things are only the frills and the formal dress of mourning.

King It's very sweet-natured and commendable of you, Hamlet, to mourn your father in this dutiful way.

But you must know your father lost a father,
That father lost, lost his; – and the survivor bound
In filial obligation for some term
To do obsequious sorrow. But to persever
95   In obstinate condolement is a course
Of impious stubbornness, 'tis unmanly grief,
It shows a will most incorrect to heaven,
A heart unfortified, a mind impatient,
An understanding simple and unschooled;
100   For what we know must be, and is as common
As any the most vulgar thing to sense –
Why should we in our peevish opposition
Take it to heart? Fie, 'tis a fault to heaven,
A fault against the dead, a fault to nature,
105   To reason most absurd; whose common theme
Is death of fathers, and who still hath cried
From the first corse till he that died today,
'This must be so.' We pray you throw to earth
This unprevailing woe, and think of us
110   As of a father; for let the world take note
You are the most immediate to our throne,
And with no less nobility of love
Than that which dearest father bears his son
Do I impart towards you. For your intent
115   In going back to school in Wittenberg,
It is most retrograde to our desire,
And we beseech you bend you to remain
Here in the cheer and comfort of our eye,
Our chiefest courtier, cousin, and our son.

120 **Queen**   Let not thy mother lose her prayers, Hamlet:
I pray thee stay with us, go not to Wittenberg.

Hamlet   I shall in all my best obey you, madam.

King   Why, 'tis a loving and a fair reply.
Be as ourself in Denmark. Madam, come.

But you must know that your father lost a father; that lost father in turn lost his; and the survivor was duty-bound as a son to go into a period of deep mourning. But to persist in obstinate grieving is a stubborn, irreligious course. It shows a willful disrespect to heaven; a weakness of will; an impatient mind; an ignorant and untrained intellect. Why should we, in our foolish perversity, take to heart what we know to be inevitable, and the most obvious thing there is? Tush: it's an offense against heaven, an offense to the dead, an offense to the natural order of things; an absurd contradiction to reason! Nature takes the death of fathers as a norm, and has consistently declared – from the first to die till the one who passed away today: ''This must be so!'' We beg you to bury your purposeless grief, and to think of us as you would a father. Let the world take note: you are next in succession to the throne and, with a love no less profound than that which a devoted father bears towards his son, I shall deal liberally with you. As for your intention of returning to Wittenberg University, that's the opposite of what we would wish. We entreat you to stay here, in the hospitality and comfort of our royal presence, as the highest-ranking member of our court, our kinsman, and our son.

Queen   Don't let your mother's prayers be in vain, Hamlet. I pray that you'll stay with us. Don't go to Wittenberg.

Hamlet   I shall obey you, madam, to the best of my ability.

King   Why, that's a loving and a courteous reply. Act royally in Denmark. [*To the* **Queen**]   Madam, come. Hamlet's

125   This gentle and unforced accord of Hamlet
         Sits smiling to my heart; in grace whereof
         No jocund health that Denmark drinks today
         But the great cannon to the clouds shall tell,
         And the King's rouse the heaven shall bruit again,
130   Re-speaking earthly thunder. Come away.

[Flourish. Exeunt all but **Hamlet**]

Hamlet O that this too too solid flesh would melt,
         Thaw and resolve itself into a dew,
         Or that the Everlasting had not fixed
         His canon 'gainst self-slaughter. O God! God!
135   How weary, stale, flat, and unprofitable
         Seem to me all the uses of this world!
         Fie on't, ah fie! 'Tis an unweeded garden
         That grows to seed; things rank and gross in nature
         Possess it merely. That it should come to this!
140   But two months dead – nay, not so much, not two –
         So excellent a king, that was to this
         Hyperion to a satyr; so loving to my mother
         That he might not beteem the winds of heaven
         Visit her face too roughly. Heaven and earth!
145   Must I remember? Why, she would hang on him
         As if increase of appetite had grown
         By what it fed on; and yet within a month –
         Let me not think on't! Frailty, thy name is woman!
         A little month, or ere those shoes were old
150   With which she followed my poor father's body,
         Like Niobe, all tears – why she, even she –
         O God! A beast that wants discourse of reason
         Would have mourned longer – married with my uncle,
         My father's brother – but no more like my father
155   Than I to Hercules. Within a month,

gentle and voluntary consent cheers my heart. To celebrate it, I'll drink no health today without firing a mighty cannon to inform the clouds; and the heavens will proclaim the King's toast again, reechoing the thunder from the earth below. Come, let's away.

[*Trumpets sound. Everyone leaves except* **Hamlet**]

Hamlet   If only my too solid flesh would melt, thaw, and turn itself into dew; or that the Almighty had not prohibited suicide! Oh, God, God!   [*He sighs heavily*] How weary, stale, boring and purposeless everything on this earth seems to be! A blight upon it! It's a neglected garden that's gone to seed; it's overwhelmed with repulsive weeds.   That it should come to this! Only two months dead – no not so much, not two! Such an excellent King! He was to this one   [*he nods in the direction of the departed* **Claudius**]   as the sun god is to a lascivious beast. He was so loving to my mother that he wouldn't allow the wind to blow too roughly on her face. Heaven and earth, must I remember? Why, she would cling to him as if she had an insatiable appetite for him. And yet, in less than a month . . . I mustn't think about it! Weakness and womanhood go together! A mere month: even before the shoes were old in which she followed my poor father's corpse, sobbing inconsolably, like Niobe – why, she, she of all women! – [*He breaks off, distractedly*]   Oh, God! a brainless beast would have mourned longer! She married my uncle! My father's brother, but no more like my father than I am to Hercules! Within a month, before those

Ere yet the salt of most unrighteous tears
Had left the flushing in her galled eyes,
She married. O most wicked speed! To post
With such dexterity to incestuous sheets!
160   It is not, nor it cannot come to good.
But break, my heart, for I must hold my tongue.

[*Enter* **Horatio**, **Marcellus**, *and* **Barnardo**]

Horatio   Hail to your lordship.

Hamlet   I am glad to see you well.
Horatio, or I do forget myself.

165 **Horatio**   The same, my lord, and your poor servant ever.

Hamlet   Sir, my good friend, I'll change that name with you.
And what make you from Wittenberg, Horatio? –
Marcellus?

Marcellus   My good lord.

170 **Hamlet**   I am very glad to see you.   [*To* **Barnardo**]   Good
even, sir.
But what in faith make you from Wittenberg?

Horatio   A truant disposition, good my lord.

Hamlet   I would not have your enemy say so,
175   Nor shall you do my ear that violence
To make it truster of your own report
Against yourself. I know you are no truant.
But what is your affair in Elsinore?
We'll teach you to drink deep ere you depart.

180 **Horatio**   My lord, I came to see your father's funeral.

deceitful tears had ceased to flow from her eyes red with
weeping, she married! Oh, such wicked speed! To hop so
nimbly into an incestuous bed!   [*In Hamlet's day, incest
included marriage with a husband's brother*]   It's not right,
and no good can come of it. But let my heart break: I must
hold my tongue.

[**Horatio, Marcellus** *and* **Barnardo** *enter*]

Horatio   Greetings to your lordship.

Hamlet   [*absently*]   I'm glad to see you well.
   [*Recognizing his visitors and cheering up*]   Horatio, if I'm
   not mistaken?

Horatio   Indeed, my lord; and your humble servant ever.

Hamlet   Sir, my good friend; your servant too.   [*They
   embrace*]   And what are you doing away from
   Wittenberg, Horatio?   [*He notices Horatio has
   companions*]   Marcellus!

Marcellus   [*bowing*]   My good lord.

Hamlet   I'm very glad to see you.   [*To* **Barnardo**]   Good
   evening, sir.   [*To* **Horatio** *again*]   But whatever
   brings you here from Wittenberg?

Horatio   A tendency to truancy, my good lord!

Hamlet   I wouldn't take that from your enemy – so I won't
   offend my ears by hearing you speak ill of yourself! I know
   you are no truant. What's your business in Elsinore?
   We'll teach you to drink deep before you depart!

Horatio   My lord, I came to see your father's funeral.

Hamlet   I prithee do not mock me, fellow-student.
I think it was to see my mother's wedding.

Horatio   Indeed, my lord, it followed hard upon.

Hamlet   Thrift, thrift, Horatio. The funeral baked meats
185   Did coldly furnish forth the marriage tables.
Would I had met my dearest foe in heaven
Or ever I had seen that day, Horatio!
My father – methinks I see my father –

Horatio   Where, my lord?

190   **Hamlet**   In my mind's eye, Horatio.

Horatio   I saw him once; he was a goodly king.

Hamlet   He was a man, take him for all in all:
I shall not look upon his like again.

Horatio   My lord, I think I saw him yesternight.

195   **Hamlet**   Saw? Who?

Horatio   My lord, the King your father.

Hamlet   The King my father?

Horatio   Season your admiration for a while
With an attent ear till I may deliver
200   Upon the witness of these gentlemen
This marvel to you.

Hamlet   For God's love, let me hear!

Horatio   Two nights together had these gentlemen,
Marcellus and Barnardo, on their watch
205   In the dead waste and middle of the night
Been thus encountered: a figure like your father
Armed at point exactly, cap-a-pe,
Appears before them, and with solemn march

Hamlet   Please don't make fun of me, fellow student. I think it was to see my mother's wedding . . .

Horatio   [*embarrassed*]   Indeed, my lord, it took place very soon afterwards.

Hamlet   Thrift, thrift, Horatio. The leftover meat pies from the funeral were served up cold for the wedding breakfast. Would that I'd met my worst enemy in heaven, Horatio, rather than that I'd seen that day. My father – I think I can see my father –

Horatio   [*startled*]   Where, my lord?

Hamlet   [*pointing to his own head*]   In my mind's eye, Horatio.

Horatio   I saw him once. He was a fine King.

Hamlet   He was a man, altogether perfect – I'll never see anyone like him again.

Horatio   My lord, I think I saw him last night.

Hamlet   Saw? Who?

Horatio   My lord, your father the King.

Hamlet   My father the King?

Horatio   Restrain your amazement and listen carefully till I've described this marvel to you, with these gentlemen as witnesses.

Hamlet   For the love of God, let me hear!

Horatio   For two nights in succession these gentlemen, Marcellus and Barnardo, while on their watch in the middle of the night, have been confronted thus: a figure like your father, armed correctly in every detail from head to foot, appears before them, and walks

Goes slow and stately by them; thrice he walked
210   By their oppressed and fear-surprised eyes
Within his truncheon's length, whilst they, distilled
Almost to jelly with the act of fear,
Stand dumb and speak not to him. This to me
In dreadful secrecy impart they did,
215   And I with them the third night kept the watch,
Where, as they had delivered, both in time,
Form of the thing, each word made true and good,
The apparition comes. I knew your father;
These hands are not more like.

220   **Hamlet**   But where was this?

Marcellus   My lord, upon the platform where we watch.

Hamlet   Did you not speak to it?

Horatio   My lord, I did,
But answer made it none. Yet once methought
225   It lifted up its head and did address
Itself to motion like as it would speak.
But even then the morning cock crew loud,
And at the sound it shrunk in haste away
And vanished from our sight.

230   **Hamlet**   'Tis very strange.

Horatio   As I do live, my honoured lord, 'tis true;
And we did think it writ down in our duty
To let you know of it.

Hamlet   Indeed, sirs; but this troubles me.
235   Hold you the watch tonight?

All   We do, my lord.

Hamlet   Armed, say you?

All   Armed, my lord.

past them solemnly at a slow and steady pace. Three
times he walked in front of their spellbound and
awestruck eyes, as close to them as the length of his
martial baton. Dissolved almost to a jelly with fear,
they stand dumb, and don't speak to him. They told
me about this in absolute secrecy, and I joined them
on watch on the third night, where, just as they'd
described – both in terms of time, and the appearance
of the thing, down to the last letter – the apparition
comes. I recognized your father. These hands are not
more similar.   [*He spreads his own out to show how
alike they are*]

Hamlet   But where was this?

Marcellus   My lord, upon the battlement where we
watched.

Hamlet   Didn't you speak to it?

Horatio   My lord, I did, but it didn't reply. But once, I
thought, it lifted up its head and made as if to speak.
Just then the morning cock crowed loudly, and at the
sound it shrank away in haste, and vanished from our
sight.

Hamlet   It's very strange.

Horatio   Upon my life, my honored lord, it's true. We
thought it our duty to let you know of it.

Hamlet   Of course, sirs. But this worries me. Are you on
watch tonight?

All   We are, my lord.

Hamlet   [*referring to the* **Ghost**]   Did you say armed?

All   Armed, my lord.

Hamlet From top to toe?

240 **All** My lord, from head to foot.

Hamlet Then saw you not his face?

Horatio Oh yes, my lord, he wore his beaver up.

Hamlet What looked he, frowningly?

Horatio A countenance more in sorrow than in anger.

245 **Hamlet** Pale, or red?

Horatio Nay, very pale.

Hamlet And fixed his eyes upon you?

Horatio Most constantly.

Hamlet I would I had been there.

250 **Horatio** It would have much amazed you.

Hamlet Very like.
Stayed it long?

Horatio While one with moderate haste might tell a hundred.

Mar., Bar. Longer, longer.

255 **Horatio** Not when I saw't.

Hamlet His beard was grizzled, no?

Horatio It was as I have seen it in his life,
A sable silvered.

Hamlet I will watch tonight.
260 Perchance 'twill walk again.

Horatio I warrant it will.

Hamlet If it assume my noble father's person,
I'll speak to it though hell itself should gape

Hamlet   From top to toe?

All   From head to foot, my lord.

Hamlet   Then you didn't see his face?

Horatio   Oh yes, my lord. He wore his visor up.

Hamlet   How did he look? Fiercely, like a warrior?

Horatio   His face showed more sorrow than anger.

Hamlet   Pale or red?

Horatio   Oh, very pale.

Hamlet   And looked hard at you?

Horatio   Throughout.

Hamlet   I wish I'd been there.

Horatio   It would have astounded you.

Hamlet   Very probably. Did it stay long?

Horatio   While you could count a hundred reasonably quickly.

Mar., Bar.   Longer, longer!

Horatio   Not when I saw it.

Hamlet   His beard was streaked with gray, hm?

Horatio   It was like I'd seen it during his life: black streaked with silver.

Hamlet   I'll watch tonight. Perhaps it will walk again.

Horatio   I'm sure it will.

Hamlet   If it comes looking like my noble father, I'll speak to it even if hell itself should open wide, and

And bid me hold my peace. I pray you all,
265   If you have hitherto concealed this sight,
Let it be tenable in your silence still;
And whatsomever else shall hap tonight,
Give it an understanding but no tongue.
I will requite your loves. So fare you well.
270   Upon the platform 'twixt eleven and twelve,
I'll visit you.

All   Our duty to your honour.

Hamlet   Your loves, as mine to you. Farewell.

[*Exeunt* **Horatio, Marcellus,** *and* **Barnardo**]

My father's spirit – in arms! All is not well.
275   I doubt some foul play. Would the night were come.
Till then sit still, my soul. Foul deeds will rise,
Though all the earth o'erwhelm them, to men's eyes.

[*Exit*]

Scene 3

Enter **Laertes** *and* **Ophelia**.

Laertes   My necessaries are embarked. Farewell.
And sister, as the winds give benefit
And convoy is assistant, do not sleep,
But let me hear from you.

5 **Ophelia**   Do you doubt that?

Laertes   For Hamlet, and the trifling of his favours,
Hold it a fashion and a toy in blood,

show the penalty for speaking. I would ask you all, if
you have kept this sighting secret up to now, to
continue to say nothing about it. And whatever else
should happen tonight, take it all in but don't report it.
I shall repay your loyalty. So, goodbye. I'll visit you on
the platform between eleven and twelve.

All   Be assured of our duty to your honor.

Hamlet   Your love even, as you have mine. Goodbye.

[**Horatio, Marcellus** *and* **Barnardo** *leave*]

The spirit of my father – in armor! All is not well. I
suspect foul play. I wish it were evening. Till then, be
patient, my soul. Evil deeds will surface, however
deeply they are buried.

[*He goes*]

Scene 3

The house of Polonius. **Laertes** *and his sister* **Ophelia** *enter.*

Laertes   My luggage is on board. Farewell. And sister,
whenever there's a ship ready to sail, don't rest till you've
written to me.

Ophelia   Can you doubt it?

Laertes   As for Hamlet, and his interest in you: regard it as of
no significance – as a youthful flirtation; an early flowering

A violet in the youth of primy nature,
Forward, not permanent, sweet, not lasting,
10   The perfume and suppliance of a minute,
No more.

Ophelia   No more but so?

Laertes   Think it no more.
For nature crescent does not grow alone
15   In thews and bulk, but as this temple waxes,
The inward service of the mind and soul
Grows wide withal. Perhaps he loves you now,
And now no soil nor cautel doth besmirch
The virtue of his will; but you must fear,
20   His greatness weighed, his will is not his own.
For he himself is subject to his birth:
He may not, as unvalued persons do,
Carve for himself, for on his choice depends
The safety and health of this whole state;
25   And therefore must his choice be circumscribed
Unto the voice and yielding of that body
Whereof he is the head. Then if he says he loves you,
It fits your wisdom so far to believe it
As he in his particular act and place
30   May give his saying deed; which is no further
Than the main voice of Denmark goes withal.
Then weigh what loss your honour may sustain
If with too credent ear you list his songs,
Or lose your heart, or your chaste treasure open
35   To his unmastered importunity.
Fear it, Ophelia, fear it, my dear sister,
And keep you in the rear of your affection
Out of the shot and danger of desire.
The chariest maid is prodigal enough
40   If she unmask her beauty to the moon.
Virtue itself scapes not calumnious strokes;

of nature in its springtime; fast-blooming, therefore not
enduring; pleasing, but not lasting; the fragrance of a
passing moment's fancy. Nothing more.

Ophelia Nothing more than that?

Laertes Regard it as nothing more. Because maturity is not
merely a matter of physical development; as we grow, so
too does responsibility in the mind and the soul. Perhaps he
loves you now, and his intentions are entirely honorable.
But you must bear in mind, taking his high rank into
account, that he is not his own master. He is subject to the
responsibilities of his birth. He cannot please himself like
ordinary folk. The safety and well-being of the whole
country depends upon his choice. Therefore he can only act
with the approval and consent of those whom he rules. So if
he says he loves you, you would be wise to believe it only to
the extent that a man of his rank *can* turn his words into
deeds – which is no further than what popular opinion
would approve of. So measure the loss to your honor if
you put too much faith in his love songs, or if you fall
in love with him, or if you yield your virginity to his
self-indulgent entreaties. Fear it, Ophelia; fear it, my dear
sister, and stay out of harm's way by controlling your
affections. A good girl keeps herself to herself. Virtue is no
protection against scandal-mongering. Too often beauty is

The canker galls the infants of the spring
Too oft before their buttons be disclosed,
And in the morn and liquid dew of youth
45   Contagious blastments are most imminent.
Be wary then: best safety lies in fear.
Youth to itself rebels, though none else near.

Ophelia   I shall the effect of this good lesson keep
As watchman to my heart. But good my brother,
50   Do not as some ungracious pastors do,
Show me the steep and thorny way to heaven,
Whiles like a puffed and reckless libertine
Himself the primrose path of dalliance treads,
And recks not his own rede.

55   **Laertes**   Oh fear me not.

[*Enter* **Polonius**]

I stay too long. But here my father comes.
A double blessing is a double grace:
Occasion smiles upon a second leave.

Polonius   Yet here, Laertes? Aboard, aboard for shame.
60   The wind sits in the shoulder of your sail,
And you are stayed for. There, my blessing with thee.
And these few precepts in thy memory
Look thou character. Give thy thoughts no tongue,
Nor any unproportioned thought his act.
65   Be thou familiar, but by no means vulgar;
The friends thou hast, and their adoption tried,
Grapple them unto thy soul with hoops of steel,
But do not dull thy palm with entertainment
Of each new-hatched, unfledged comrade. Beware
70   Of entrance to a quarrel, but being in,
Bear't that th'opposed may beware of thee.
Give every man thy ear, but few thy voice;
Take each man's censure, but reserve thy judgment.

56

ruined in its early stages: the bright promise of youth is
particularly prone to corruption. So beware: safety lies in
fearing the worst. Young people are hot-blooded by nature.

Ophelia   I'll take the significance of this worthy lesson to
heart. But, dear brother, don't be like one of those ungodly
preachers: showing me the hard and uncomfortable way to
heaven while like a bloated and reckless sinner you yourself
take the easy path of wanton pleasure, disregarding your
own advice.

Laertes   Don't worry about me.

[**Polonius**, *their father, enters*]

I should be off. Here comes my father. Two farewell
blessings are twice as good as one: a fortunate opportunity
for a second leave-taking!

Polonius   Still here, Laertes? Get aboard, aboard: shame on
you! The wind's just right and they are waiting for you.   [*He
places his hands on* **Laertes'** *head*]   There, take my blessing
with you, and see that these few maxims are imprinted in
your memory . . . Never say what you are thinking, nor put
hasty thoughts into action. Be friendly but don't cheapen
yourself. Those friends you have who've proved themselves
by experience, grasp them to your soul with bands of steel.
But don't offer the hand of friendship to every new-made,
unproven, back-slapping acquaintance. Beware of starting a
quarrel, but once you are involved, see that your opponent
gets more than he bargained for. Hear all, but say little. Take
each man's opinion, but keep your own judgment to

Costly thy habit as thy purse can buy,
75   But not expressed in fancy; rich, not gaudy;
For the apparel oft proclaims the man,
And they in France of the best rank and station
Are of a most select and generous chief in that.
Neither a borrower nor a lender be,
80   For loan oft loses both itself and friend,
And borrowing dulls the edge of husbandry.
This above all: to thine own self be true,
And it must follow as the night the day
Thou canst not then be false to any man.
85   Farewell: my blessing season this in thee!

Laertes   Most humbly do I take my leave, my lord.

Polonius   The time invests you; go, your servants tend.

Laertes   Farewell, Ophelia, and remember well
What I have said to you.

90 **Ophelia**   'Tis in my memory locked,
And you yourself shall keep the key of it.

Laertes   Farewell.

[*Exit* **Laertes**]

Polonius   What is't, Ophelia, he hath said to you?

Ophelia   So please you, something touching the Lord
95   Hamlet.

Polonius   Marry, well bethought!
'Tis told me he hath very oft of late
Given private time to you, and you yourself
Have of your audience been most free and bounteous.
100   If it be so – as so 'tis put on me,
And that in way of caution – I must tell you

yourself. Dress as well as you can afford; but don't go to extremes of fashion — good quality rather than loudness — because you can usually tell a man by the style of his clothes, and French nobles are particularly discriminating in this respect. Be neither a borrower nor a lender. A loan often loses both the money and the friend, and borrowing makes a man a spendthrift. This above all else: be consistent; then it follows as surely as night follows day that you cannot deceive any man. Farewell. May my blessing help you accomplish all this.

Laertes [*bowing*] I take my leave of you most humbly, my lord.

Polonius Time is pressing. Go, your servants are waiting.

Laertes Farewell, Ophelia, and don't forget what I have said to you.

Ophelia It's locked in my memory, and you yourself shall keep the key.

Laertes Farewell.

[*He goes*]

Polonius What has he said to you, Ophelia?

Ophelia With respect, something concerning the Lord Hamlet.

Polonius Indeed. A timely thought. I'm told he has often seen you privately lately, and that you yourself have been liberal and generous in your availability. If this is so — as people are keen to tell me by way of warning — I must tell you that you

You do not understand yourself so clearly
As it behoves my daughter and your honour.
What is between you? Give me up the truth.

105 **Ophelia**   He hath, my lord, of late made many tenders
Of his affection to me.

Polonius   Affection? Pooh! You speak like a green girl,
Unsifted in such perilous circumstance.
Do you believe his tenders, as you call them?

110 **Ophelia**   I do not know, my lord, what I should think.

Polonius   Marry, I will teach you. Think yourself a baby
That you have ta'en these tenders for true pay
Which are not sterling. Tender yourself more dearly
Or – not to crack the wind of the poor phrase,
115   Running it thus – you'll tender me a fool.

Ophelia   My lord, he hath importuned me with love
In honourable fashion.

Polonius   Ay, fashion you may call it. Go to, go to.

Ophelia   And hath given countenance to his speech, my lord,
120   With almost all the holy vows of heaven.

Polonius   Ay, springes to catch woodcocks! I do know,
When the blood burns, how prodigal the soul
Lends the tongue vows. These blazes, daughter,
Giving more light than heat, extinct in both,
125   Even in their promise as it is a-making,
You must not take for fire. From this time
Be something scanter of your maiden presence,
Set your entreatments at a higher rate
Than a command to parley. For Lord Hamlet,
130   Believe so much in him that he is young,
And with a larger tether may he walk
Than may be given you. In few, Ophelia,
Do not believe his vows; for they are brokers

don't understand yourself as clearly as is becoming to my daughter, and your honor. What's between you? Tell me the truth.

Ophelia   He has, my lord, tendered his affection for me frequently of late.

Polonius   Affection? Pooh, you speak like an immature girl, inexperienced in such dangerous matters! Do you believe his tenders, as you call them?

Ophelia   I don't know what I should think, my lord.

Polonius   Well then, I'll teach you. Consider yourself a baby to have taken these tenders for real currency, when they're counterfeit. Tender yourself at a higher rate or – at the risk of straining the expression, using it like this – you'll tender me a love child.

Ophelia   [*shocked*]   My lord, he has wooed me in an honorable fashion.

Polonius   [*scornfully*]   Yes, fashion you may well call it! Really, now!

Ophelia   And he has backed his words, my lord, with almost all the holy vows of heaven.

Polonius   Yes. Traps to catch stupid birds! I know how glibly promises are made when passion is roused. You mustn't mistake these flare-ups, daughter, that give more light than heat, and that disappear the very moment the promises are made, for fire. From now on, be more sparing of your maidenly presence. Don't yield at the first request for a meeting. As for Lord Hamlet, believe him only inasmuch as he is young, with greater freedom of action than you have. In short, Ophelia, do not believe his vows. They are not

Not of that dye which their investments show,
135 But mere implorators of unholy suits,
Breathing like sanctified and pious bawds
The better to beguile. This is for all.
I would not, in plain terms, from this time forth
Have you so slander any moment leisure
140 As to give words or talk with the Lord Hamlet.
Look to't, I charge you. Come your ways.

Ophelia   I shall obey, my lord.

[*Exeunt*]

Scene 4

The platform. Enter **Hamlet, Horatio,** *and* **Marcellus**.

Hamlet   The air bites shrewdly, it is very cold.

Horatio   It is a nipping and an eager air.

Hamlet   What hour now?

Horatio   I think it lacks of twelve.

5 **Marcellus**   No, it is struck.

Horatio   Indeed? I heard it not.
It then draws near the season
Wherein the spirit held his wont to walk.

[*A flourish of trumpets, and two pieces of ordnance go off*]

What does this mean, my lord?

10 **Hamlet**   The King doth wake tonight and takes his rouse,

spokesmen in their true colors, but merely pleaders on behalf of sin, sounding like saintly and pious go-betweens, the better to deceive. This is final. In plain words, from now on I don't want you to misuse your leisure time by talking to the Lord Hamlet. Those are my orders: do as I say. Come along.

Ophelia   I shall obey, my lord.

[*They go*]

Scene 4

The castle walls. Enter **Hamlet, Horatio** *and* **Marcellus.**

Hamlet   The wind bites keenly. It's very cold.

Horatio   It's a sharp and bitter wind.

Hamlet   What's the time?

Horatio   Not yet midnight.

Marcellus   No, it has struck.

Horatio   Indeed? I didn't hear it. It's approaching the time when the Ghost usually walks.

[*A flourish of trumpets is heard from inside the castle. Two cannon are fired*]

What does this mean, my lord?

Hamlet   The King is celebrating tonight: drinking deep, making

Keeps wassail, and the swagg'ring upspring reels;
And, as he drains his draughts of Rhenish down,
The kettle-drum and trumpet thus bray out
The triumph of his pledge.

15 Horatio   Is it a custom?

Hamlet   Ay marry is't,
But to my mind, though I am native here
And to the manner born, it is a custom
More honoured in the breach than the observance.
20   This heavy-headed revel east and west
Makes us traduced and taxed of other nations –
They clepe us drunkards, and with swinish phrase
Soil our addition; and indeed it takes
From our achievements, though performed at height,
25   The pith and marrow of our attribute.
So, oft it chances in particular men
That for some vicious mole of nature in them,
As in their birth, wherein they are not guilty
(Since nature cannot choose his origin),
30   By the o'ergrowth of some complexion,
Oft breaking down the pales and forts of reason,
Or by some habit, that too much o'erleavens
The form of plausive manners – that these men,
Carrying, I say, the stamp of one defect,
35   Being Nature's livery or Fortune's star,
His virtues else, be they as pure as grace,
As infinite as man may undergo,
Shall in the general censure take corruption
From that particular fault. The dram of evil
40   Doth all the noble substance of a doubt
To his own scandal.

[*Enter* **Ghost**]

Horatio   Look, my lord, it comes.

merry, and rollicking to wild dances. And as he drains his
tankards of Rhenish wine, kettledrums and trumpets blare
out in celebration of his toasts.

Horatio   Is it a custom?

Hamlet   It certainly is. But in my opinion, though I'm a Dane
and born to it, it's a tradition far better broken than
observed. This drunken revelry makes us maligned and put
to shame by other nations. They call us drunkards, and
besmirch our reputation by alluding to us as swine. Indeed,
it diminishes our considerable achievements and loses us
esteem. Particular individuals are often affected in the same
way. Because of some constitutional defect (such as
something inherited, which isn't their fault, since one
cannot choose one's ancestors; or some dominant
character trait that leads to irrational conduct; or some
behavior-pattern that offends convention) these men
(suffering as I say from being marked by one defect, a
blemish of Nature or bad luck), no matter what their other
virtues (even if they are pristinely pure and as plentiful as is
humanly possible), will be corrupted, as far as public opinion
is concerned, by that one single fault. That small speck of
evil often outweighs all the good in a man, to his own
discredit.

[*The* **Ghost** *enters*]

Horatio   Look, my lord. Here it is.

Hamlet   Angels and ministers of grace defend us!
Be thou a spirit of health or goblin damned,
45   Bring with thee airs from heaven or blasts from hell,
Be thy intents wicked or charitable,
Thou com'st in such a questionable shape
That I will speak to thee. I'll call thee Hamlet,
King, father, royal Dane. O, answer me!
50   Let me not burst in ignorance, but tell
Why thy canonized bones, hearsed in death,
Have burst their cerements; why the sepulchre
Wherein we saw thee quietly inurned
Hath op'd his ponderous and marble jaws
55   To cast thee up again. What may this mean,
That thou, dead corse, again in complete steel
Revisits thus the glimpses of the moon,
Making night hideous and we fools of nature
So horridly to shake our disposition
60   With thoughts beyond the reaches of our souls?
Say why is this? Wherefore? What should we do?

[**Ghost** *beckons*]

Horatio   It beckons you to go away with it,
As if it some impartment did desire
To you alone.

65 **Marcellus**   Look with what courteous action
It waves you to a more removed ground.
But do not go with it.

Horatio   No, by no means.

Hamlet   It will not speak. Then I will follow it.

70 **Horatio**   Do not, my lord.

Hamlet   Why, what should be the fear?
I do not set my life at a pin's fee,
And for my soul, what can it do to that,

Hamlet   [*crossing himself*]   Angels and God's messengers
defend us!   [*To the* **Ghost**]   Whether you are a good angel
or a devil, bringing with you heavenly breezes or hellish
blasts; whether your intentions are wicked or benevolent;
you come in a form so easy to question that I'll speak to you.
I'll call you Hamlet, King, father, royal Dane! Oh, answer me!
Do not let me burst with ignorance, but tell me why your
bones, buried with all sacred rites, and coffined in death,
have burst from their shroud; and why the tomb in which
we saw you quietly buried has opened its weighty marble
doors to cast you up again. What can it mean when you,
dead corpse, revisit us again in full armor, by moonlight;
making night terrifying, and we simple mortals rack our
brains distressfully with thoughts about realms beyond our
ken? Tell us the reason! Why? What do you want us to do?

[*The* **Ghost** *beckons to* **Hamlet**]

Horatio   It beckons you to go away with it, as if it wants to
say something to you alone.

Marcellus   See how courteously it waves you towards a more
distant place. But don't go with it!

Horatio   No, by no means.

Hamlet   It will not speak. Therefore I'll follow it.

Horatio   Don't, my lord!

Hamlet   Why, what's to fear? I don't value my life as highly as
a pin; and as for my soul, what can it do to that, being

Being a thing immortal as itself?
75   It waves me forth again. I'll follow it.

Horatio   What if it tempt you toward the flood, my lord,
Or to the dreadful summit of the cliff
That beetles o'er his base into the sea,
And there assume some other horrible form
80   Which might deprive your sovereignty of reason
And draw you into madness? Think of it:
The very place puts toys of desperation,
Without more motive, into every brain
That looks so many fathoms to the sea
85   And hears it roar beneath.

Hamlet   It waves me still.
Go on, I'll follow thee.

Marcellus   You shall not go, my lord.

Hamlet   Hold off your hands.

90   **Horatio**   Be ruled; you shall not go.

Hamlet   My fate cries out
And makes each petty artery in this body
As hardy as the Nemean lion's nerve.
Still am I called. Unhand me, gentlemen.
95   By heaven, I'll make a ghost of him that lets me.
I say away! Go on, I'll follow thee.

[*Exeunt* **Ghost** *and* **Hamlet**]

Horatio   He waxes desperate with imagination.

Marcellus   Let's follow. 'Tis not fit thus to obey him.

Horatio   Have after. To what issue will this come?

100   **Marcellus**   Something is rotten in the state of Denmark.

Horatio   Heaven will direct it.

something as immortal as itself? It waves me on again. I'll
follow it.

Horatio   What if it tempts you towards the ocean, my
lord, or to the fearful precipice that overhangs the sea,
and there assumes some other horrible form that could
deprive you of your reason, and make you mad? Think
of it. The very situation in itself puts desperate
thoughts into every brain that sees the sea from such
a height, and hears it roar below.

Hamlet   It's still waving me on.   [*To the* **Ghost**]   Go
on. I'll follow you.

Marcellus   [*restraining him*]   You shall not go, my lord!

Hamlet   Take your hands away!

Horatio   Do as we say. You shall not go!

Hamlet   [*struggling*]   My fate cries out, and the
smallest artery in my body has the courage of the lion slain
by Hercules!   [*He turns to the* **Ghost** *again*]   Still it calls
me! Let me go, gentlemen! By heaven, I'll make a ghost of
anyone who tries to stop me!   [*Reaching for his sword*]
Get away, I say!   [*To the* **Ghost**]   Go on – I'll follow you!

[*The* **Ghost** *leaves, followed by* **Hamlet**]

Horatio   He's going crazy in his fantasies!

Marcellus   Let's follow. It wouldn't be right to obey him.

Horatio   Let's pursue him. What will come of this?

Marcellus   There's something foul going on in the state
of Denmark.

Horatio   [*resignedly*]   Heaven will sort it out.

Marcellus   Nay, let's follow him.

[Exeunt]

Scene 5

Enter **Ghost** *and* **Hamlet**.

Hamlet   Whither wilt thou lead me? Speak, I'll go no further.

Ghost   Mark me.

Hamlet   I will.

Ghost   My hour is almost come
5   When I to sulph'rous and tormenting flames
    Must render up myself.

Hamlet   Alas, poor ghost.

Ghost   Pity me not, but lend thy serious hearing
    To what I shall unfold.

10 **Hamlet**   Speak, I am bound to hear.

Ghost   So art thou to revenge when thou shalt hear.

Hamlet   What?

Ghost   I am thy father's spirit,
    Doomed for a certain term to walk the night,
15   And for the day confined to fast in fires,
    Till the foul crimes done in my days of nature
    Are burnt and purged away. But that I am forbid
    To tell the secrets of my prison-house,
    I could a tale unfold whose lightest word

70

Marcellus   No – let's follow him!

[*They leave in pursuit*]

Scene 5

At a distance along the battlements. Enter the **Ghost** *and* **Hamlet.**

Hamlet   Where are you leading me? Answer – I'll go no further.

Ghost   Listen.

Hamlet   I will.

Ghost   Daybreak is almost here, when I must give myself up to the infernal and tormenting flames.   [*He refers to purgatory*]

Hamlet   Alas, poor ghost!

Ghost   Don't pity me, but give your full attention to what I shall reveal.

Hamlet   Speak. I have no choice but to hear.

Ghost   So are you also bound to revenge, when you shall hear.

Hamlet   What?

Ghost   I am your father's ghost; doomed for a certain period to walk at night, and during the daytime to fast in fires, till the wicked sins done during my lifetime are burnt and purged away. If I were not forbidden to reveal the secrets of my prison, I could tell you a tale whose simplest word

71

20   Would harrow up thy soul, freeze thy young blood,
      Make thy two eyes like stars start from their spheres,
      Thy knotted and combined locks to part,
      And each particular hair to stand on end
      Like quills upon the fretful porpentine.
25   But this eternal blazon must not be
      To ears of flesh and blood. List, list, o, list!
      If thou didst ever thy dear father love –

Hamlet   O, God!

Ghost   Revenge his foul and most unnatural murder.

30 **Hamlet**   Murder!

Ghost   Murder most foul, as in the best it is,
      But this most foul, strange and unnatural.

Hamlet   Haste me to know't, that I with wings as swift
      As meditation or the thoughts of love
35   May sweep to my revenge.

Ghost   I find thee apt;
      And duller shouldst thou be than the fat weed
      That roots itself in ease on Lethe wharf,
      Wouldst thou not stir in this. Now, Hamlet, hear.
40   'Tis given out that, sleeping in my orchard,
      A serpent stung me; so the whole ear of Denmark
      Is by a forged process of my death
      Rankly abused; but know, thou noble youth,
      The serpent that did sting thy father's life
45   Now wears his crown.

Hamlet   O my prophetic soul! My uncle!

Ghost   Ay, that incestuous, that adulterate beast,
      With witchcraft of his wit, with traitorous gifts –
      O wicked wit, and gifts that have the power
50   So to seduce! – won to his shameful lust

would terrify your soul, freeze your young blood, make your two eyes protrude from their sockets, your tousled hair to straighten out, and every individual hair to stand on end like quills upon a frightened porcupine. But this revelation of the afterlife is not for ears of flesh and blood. Listen, listen, oh, listen! If you ever loved your father –

Hamlet   Oh, God!

Ghost   – revenge his foul and most unnatural murder.

Hamlet   Murder!

Ghost   Murder most foul, as it always is: but this one exceptionally foul, remarkable, and against nature.

Hamlet   Tell me quickly, so that with speed swifter than thinking or the thoughts of love I may sweep to my revenge!

Ghost   Well said. You'd be as languid as the drowsy poppies that root in comfort on the banks of Lethe   [*the legendary river of forgetfulness*]   if this did not arouse you. Now, Hamlet, listen. The official story is that, sleeping in my garden, a snake bit me: so everyone in Denmark is vilely misled by a lying account of my death. Know this, noble youth: the serpent that stung your father's life away now wears his crown!

Hamlet   As I suspected! My uncle!

Ghost   Yes: that incestuous, that adulterous beast, with clever witchcraft, with traitorous skills – oh, such wicked cleverness, and such seductive skills! – he satisfied his

The will of my most seeming-virtuous Queen.
O Hamlet, what a falling off was there,
From me, whose love was of that dignity
That it went hand in hand even with the vow
55   I made to her in marriage; and to decline
Upon a wretch whose natural gifts were poor
To those of mine!
But virtue, as it never will be moved,
Though lewdness court it in a shape of heaven,
60   So lust, though to a radiant angel linked,
Will sate itself in a celestial bed
And prey on garbage.
But soft! Methinks I scent the morning air:
Brief let me be. Sleeping within my orchard,
65   My custom always of the afternoon,
Upon my secure hour thy uncle stole
With juice of cursed hebenon in a vial,
And in the porches of my ears did pour
The leperous distilment; whose effect
70   Holds such an enmity with blood of man
That swift as quicksilver it courses through
The natural gates and alleys of the body,
And with a sudden vigour it doth posset
And curd, like eager droppings into milk,
75   The thin and wholesome blood. So did it mine,
And a most instant tetter barked about,
Most lazar-like, with vile and loathsome crust
All my smooth body.
Thus was I, sleeping, by a brother's hand
80   Of life, of crown, of queen at once dispatched,
Cut off even in the blossoms of my sin,
Unhouseled, disappointed, unaneled,
No reck'ning made, but sent to my account
With all my imperfections on my head.
85   O horrible! O horrible! Most horrible!

shameful lust by infatuating my apparently virtuous Queen. Oh, Hamlet, what a fall from grace that was! To go from me, whose love was of such high quality that it kept total faith with the vow I made to her in marriage – and to descend to a wretch whose merits were poor compared to those of mine. But just as virtue can never be seduced, even when tempted by lewdness in a saintly disguise, so lust – though it takes on the form of a radiant angel – will gratify its appetite in a holy bed, finding its victims amongst the depraved. But stay: I think I can smell the morning air. Let me be brief. Sleeping in my garden, my custom always in the afternoon, during my hour of relaxation your uncle stole upon me, with poisonous sap in a vial. In my ears he poured the leprous essence, whose effect is so injurious to man's blood that swift as quicksilver it runs through the veins, and with a sudden force it thickens and curdles the healthy blood like acid dropping into milk. It did this to mine, and immediately my skin erupted like that of a leper, with a vile and loathsome crust all over my smooth body. Thus, as I slept, I was deprived by my brother of my life, my crown, and my queen, all at once; slain in the midst of my daily trespasses; without benefit of the last rites; totally unprepared; sent to my final reckoning with all my sins upon

If thou has nature in thee, bear it not,
Let not the royal bed of Denmark be
A couch for luxury and damned incest.
But howsoever thou pursuest this act,
90   Taint not thy mind nor let thy soul contrive
Against thy mother aught. Leave her to heaven,
And to those thorns that in her bosom lodge
To prick and sting her. Fare thee well at once:
The glow-worm shows the matin to be near
95   And 'gins to pale his uneffectual fire.
Adieu, adieu, adieu. Remember me.

                                                        [*Exit*]

Hamlet   O all you host of heaven! O earth! What else?
And shall I couple hell? O fie! Hold, hold, my heart,
And you, my sinews, grow not instant old,
100   But bear me stiffly up. Remember thee?
Ay, thou poor ghost, whiles memory holds a seat
In this distracted globe. Remember thee?
Yea, from the table of my memory
I'll wipe away all trivial fond records,
105   All saws of books, all forms, all pressures past
That youth and observation copied there,
And thy commandment all alone shall live
Within the book and volume of my brain,
Unmixed with baser matter. Yes, by heaven!
110   O most pernicious woman!
O villain, villain, smiling damned villain!
My tables. Meet it is I set it down
That one may smile, and smile, and be a villain –
At least I am sure it may be so in Denmark.   [*Writes*]
115   So, uncle, there you are. Now to my word.
It is 'Adieu, adieu, remember me.'
I have sworn't.

my head. Oh, how horrible, horrible, most horrible! If you have any natural feelings in you, do not tolerate it. Do not let the royal bed of Denmark be a couch for lust and damnable incest! But however you decide to proceed, do not poison your mind nor take any action against your mother. Leave her to heaven and to the stings of her own conscience. A quick farewell. The glowworm's ineffective fire begins to fade, showing that morning is near. Adieu, adieu, adieu. Remember me!

[*The* **Ghost** *vanishes*]

Hamlet   Oh, you angels! Oh, earth!   [*He realizes that the* **Ghost***'s origins are in doubt*]   What else? Shall I call on *hell*, too?   [*He chokes at the thought, and puts his hand to his chest*]   Do not break, my heart; and you, my sinews, do not suddenly grow old, but keep me firmly on my feet. Remember you? Yes, you poor ghost − while I still have memory in my demented head! Remember you? Yes, I'll forget all trivial, frivolous memories; all bookish wisdom; all past impressions based on youthful experience and observation! Your command alone shall be filed away in my brain, unmixed with less important matters. Yes, by heaven!   [*He winces again as ugly memories return*]   Oh, that most wicked woman! Oh, that villain; that villain, that smiling, damned villain!   [*He fumbles in his pockets*]   My notebook. I really must make a note, that a man can smile, and smile, yet be a villain − at least I'm sure that's true in Denmark.   [*He scribbles as he speaks*]   So, uncle,   [*as he puts the book away*]   there you are!   [*Resolutely*]   Now to my slogan: it is ''Adieu, adieu, remember me.'' I have given my oath!

[*Enter* **Horatio** *and* **Marcellus**]

Horatio   My lord, my lord.

Marcellus   Lord Hamlet.

120 **Horatio**   Heavens secure him.

Hamlet   [*aside*]   So be it.

Marcellus   Hillo, ho, ho, my lord.

Hamlet   Hillo, ho, ho, boy. Come, bird come.

Marcellus   How is't, my noble lord?

125 **Horatio**   What news, my lord?

Hamlet   O, wonderful!

Horatio   Good my lord, tell it.

Hamlet   No, you will reveal it.

Horatio   Not I, my lord, by heaven.

130 **Marcellus**   Nor I, my lord.

Hamlet   How say you then, would heart of man once think
it –
But you'll be secret?

Hor., Mar.   Ay, by heaven.

135 **Hamlet**   There's never a villain dwelling in all Denmark
But he's an arrant knave.

Horatio   There needs no ghost, my lord, come from the grave
To tell us this.

Hamlet   Why, right, you are i'th'right.
140 And so without more circumstance at all,
I hold it fit that we shake hands and part,

[**Horatio** *and* **Marcellus** *call him as they approach*]

Horatio   My lord, my lord!

Marcellus   Lord Hamlet!

Horatio   Heaven protect him!

Hamlet   [*to himself*]   So be it.

Marcellus   [*calling him like a falconer*]   Hello, ho, ho, my lord!

Hamlet   [*responding similarly*]   Hello, ho, ho, boy!   [*He whistles*]   Come, bird, come!

Marcellus   Are you all right, my noble lord?

Horatio   What news, my lord?

Hamlet   [*excitedly*]   Oh, astounding!

Horatio   My good lord, tell it.

Hamlet   No, you'll reveal it.

Horatio   I won't, my lord, I swear by heaven.

Marcellus   Nor will I, my lord.

Hamlet   [*beginning as if he meant to tell*]   What do you say, then . . . Would anyone ever think that . . .   [*He breaks off*]   But you will keep a secret?

Hor., Mar.   Yes, by heaven.

Hamlet   [*he draws them towards him and whispers confidentially*]   There's not a single villain living in all Denmark who isn't a thoroughgoing rogue . . .

Horatio   There's no need for a ghost to come from the grave to tell us that, my lord.

Hamlet   How right! You're absolutely right! And so without more ado I think it's best if we shake hands and part; you in

79

You as your business and desires shall point you –
For every man hath business and desire,
Such as it is; and for my own poor part,
145   I will go pray.

Horatio   These are but wild and whirling words, my lord.

Hamlet   I am sorry they offend you, heartily –
Yes faith, heartily.

Horatio   There's no offence, my lord.

150   **Hamlet**   Yes by Saint Patrick but there is, Horatio,
And much offence too. Touching this vision here,
It is an honest ghost, that let me tell you.
For your desire to know what is between us,
O'ermaster't as you may. And now, good friends,
155   As you are friends, scholars, and soldiers,
Give me one poor request.

Horatio   What is't, my lord? We will.

Hamlet   Never make known what you have seen tonight.

Hor., Mar.   My lord, we will not.

160   **Hamlet**   Nay, but swear't.

Horatio   In faith, my lord, not I.

Marcellus   Nor I, my lord, in faith.

Hamlet   Upon my sword.

Marcellus   We have sworn, my lord, already.

165   **Hamlet**   Indeed, upon my sword, indeed.

Ghost   [*beneath*]   Swear.

Hamlet   Ah ha, boy, say'st thou so? Art thou there,

80

whatever direction your business and pleasure direct
you – because every man has business and pleasure, such
as it is – and for my own poor part, I'll go pray.

Horatio   Your words are wild and hysterical, my lord.

Hamlet   I'm sorry they offend you, really I am. Yes, indeed. I
really am.

Horatio   No offense, my lord.

Hamlet   Yes by Saint Patrick, but there *is*, Horatio – and much
offense, too. As for this vision here, it's a genuine ghost, let
me tell you that. As for your desire to know what we have
said to each other, suppress it as best you can. And now,
good friends: as you *are* friends, scholars, and soldiers,
grant me one small request.

Horatio   What is it, my lord? We will.

Hamlet   Never to reveal what you have seen tonight.

Hor., Mar.   My lord, we won't.

Hamlet   No, but swear to it.

Horatio   Honestly, my lord, I won't tell.

Marcellus   Nor I, my lord, in all faith.

Hamlet   Swear upon my sword.   [*He raises it*]

Marcellus   We have sworn already, my lord.

Hamlet   [*insisting*]   Indeed. But upon my sword.   [*He will not
be denied*]   Indeed.

[*The* **Ghost***'s voice is heard from below*]

Ghost   Swear.

Hamlet   Aha, boy. Do you say so too? Are you there, old

truepenny?
Come on, you hear this fellow in the cellarage.
Consent to swear.

170 **Horatio**   Propose the oath, my lord.

Hamlet   Never to speak of this that you have seen.
Swear by my sword.

Ghost   Swear. [*They swear*]

175 **Hamlet**   Hic et ubique? Then we'll shift our ground.
Come hither, gentlemen,
And lay your hands again upon my sword.
Swear by my sword
Never to speak of this that you have heard.

180 **Ghost**   Swear by his sword. [*They swear*]

Hamlet   Well said, old mole. Canst work i'th'earth so fast?
A worthy pioneer! Once more remove, good friends.

Horatio   O, day and night, but this is wondrous strange.

Hamlet   And therefore as a stranger give it welcome.
185 There are more things in heaven and earth, Horatio,
Than are dreamt of in your philosophy.
But come,
Here, as before, never, so help you mercy,
How strange or odd so e'er I bear myself –
190 As I perchance hereafter shall think meet
To put an antic disposition on –
That you, at such time seeing me, never shall,
With arms encumbered thus, or this head-shake,
Or by pronouncing of some doubtful phrase,
195 As 'Well, we know', or 'We could and if we would',

faithful? [*To* **Horatio** *and* **Marcellus** *again*] Come on: you
can hear this fellow down in the cellar. Agree to swear.

Horatio Propose the oath, my lord.

Hamlet Never to speak of what you have seen. Swear by my
sword. [*He stretches it out so that they can lay their hands
on it*]

Ghost [*from a different area*] Swear.

[**Horatio** *and* **Marcellus** *do so*]

Hamlet Here and everywhere? Then we'll shift our ground.
Come here, gentlemen, and lay your hands on my sword
again. Swear by my sword never to speak of what you have
heard.

Ghost [*from a different area*] Swear by his sword.

[*They swear*]

Hamlet Well said, old mole! Can you tunnel through the earth
so fast? What a skillful miner! Let's move once more, good
friends.

Horatio Oh, day and night! This is very strange.

Hamlet And therefore as it is a stranger, welcome it. There
are more things in heaven and earth, Horatio, than
philosophy realizes. But come. [*He places the sword again
for them to swear upon*] Here, as before: swear that you
will never, so help you God, however strange or odd I might
sometimes behave – because I may perhaps think it best to
feign insanity – that if you see me at such a time you never
will – by means of arms folded like this [*he demonstrates*]
– or a shake of the head like this [*he shows them*] –
or by uttering some cryptic phrase such as "Well, *we*
know . . ." or "We could if we so wished . . ."

Or 'If we list to speak', or 'There be and if there might',
Or such ambiguous giving out, to note
That you know aught of me – this do swear,
So grace and mercy at your most need help you.

200 **Ghost**   Swear.   [*They swear*]

Hamlet   Rest, rest, perturbed spirit! So, gentlemen,
With all my love I do commend me to you;
And what so poor a man as Hamlet is
May do t'express his love and friending to you,
205   God willing, shall not lack. Let us go in together.
And still your fingers on your lips, I pray.
The time is out of joint. O, cursed spite,
That ever I was born to set it right!
Nay, come, let's go together.

[*Exeunt*]

or ''If we chose to speak . . .'' or ''There are those who could say more . . .'' or other similar ambiguous hints – give any indication that you know the truth about me. Swear this, upon God's mercy in your hour of need!

Ghost   Swear!

[*They swear for the third time*]

Hamlet   Rest, rest, troubled spirit!   [*To* **Horatio** *and* **Marcellus**]   So, gentlemen, my fondest regards to you. And whatever a man may do who's as poor as Hamlet, to show his love and friendship to you, God willing you shall not lack it. Let us go in together. And don't forget – your fingers on your lips, please.   [*He makes a ''keep mum'' sign*]   Everything's in a mess. What cursed bad luck that I should be chosen to put things right!   [**Horatio** *and* **Marcellus** *stand aside to let him go first*]   No. Come, let's go together.

[*They go inside*]

Act two

Scene 1

Enter **Polonius** *and* **Reynaldo**.

Polonius Give him this money and these notes, Reynaldo.

Reynaldo I will, my lord.

Polonius You shall do marvellous wisely, good Reynaldo,
Before you visit him, to make inquire
5 Of his behaviour.

Reynaldo My lord, I did intend it.

Polonius Marry, well said, very well said. Look you, sir,
Inquire me first what Danskers are in Paris,
And how, and who, what means, and where they keep,
10 What company, at what expense; and finding
By this encompassment and drift of question
That they do know my son, come you more nearer
Than your particular demands will touch it.
Take you as 'twere some distant knowledge of him,
15 As thus, 'I know his father, and his friends,
And in part him.' Do you mark this, Reynaldo?

Reynaldo Ay, very well, my lord.

Polonius 'And in part him. But,' you may say, 'not well;
But if't be he I mean, he's very wild,
20 Addicted so and so' – and there put on him
What forgeries you please – marry, none so rank
As may dishonour him – take heed of that –
But, sir, such wanton, wild, and usual slips
As are companions noted and most known
25 To youth and liberty.

Act two

Scene 1

The apartment of Polonius. Enter **Polonius** *and his servant* **Reynaldo**. *They are discussing* **Laertes**, *who has gone to Paris.*

Polonius   Give him this money and these notes, Reynaldo.

Reynaldo   I will, my lord.

Polonius   You'd certainly be very wise, good Reynaldo, to make inquiries about his behavior before you visit him.

Reynaldo   My lord, I intended to.

Polonius   Indeed; well said, very well said. And look here, sir, do find out first what Danes there are in Paris, and how they came to be there, and who they are, and what means they have, and where they lodge, and what company they keep, and how much they spend. Discovering by means of this roundabout and vague sort of questioning that they know my son, you'll get nearer to the real point than you could by being straightforward. Pretend you have some distant knowledge of him, saying for example ''I know his father, and his friends, and to some extent him.'' Are you noting this, Reynaldo?

Reynaldo   Yes, very carefully, my lord.

Polonius   – ''And to some extent him. But'' – you might say – ''not well. But if he's the one I mean, he's very wild; addicted to so-and-so.'' There you can make up whatever you like. Mind you, nothing so bad that it dishonors him. Watch that. But, sir, the sort of frivolous, wild, and commonplace misdemeanors that are usually regarded as going hand-in-hand with youth and liberty.

Reynaldo   As gaming, my lord?

Polonius   Ay, or drinking, fencing, swearing,
Quarrelling, drabbing – you may go so far.

30 **Reynaldo**   My lord, that would dishonour him.

Polonius   'Faith no, as you may season it in the charge.
You must not put another scandal on him,
That he is open to incontinency;
That's not my meaning. But breathe his faults so quaintly
35 That they may seem the taints of liberty,
The flash and outbreak of a fiery mind,
A savageness in unreclaimed blood,
Of general assault.

Reynaldo   But my good lord –

40 **Polonius**   Wherefore should you do this?

Reynaldo   Ay, my lord, I would know that.

Polonius   Marry, sir, here's my drift,
And I believe it is a fetch of warrant.
45 You laying these slight sullies on my son,
As 'twere a thing a little soiled i'th'working,
Mark you,
Your party in converse, him you would sound,
Having ever seen in the prenominate crimes
50 The youth you breathe of guilty, be assured
He closes with you in this consequence
'Good sir,' or so, or 'friend,' or 'gentleman,'
According to the phrase or the addition
Of man and country.

55 **Reynaldo**   Very good, my lord.

Polonius   And then, sir, does a this – a does – what was I

Reynaldo   Such as gambling, my lord?

Polonius   Yes, or drinking, fencing, swearing, quarreling, or whoring. You can go that far.

Reynaldo   My lord, that would dishonor him!

Polonius   Truly, no, because you can tone it down in the telling. You mustn't scandalize him in another way by saying he is guilty of being a libertine. That's not my meaning. But touch upon his faults so artfully that they may appear to be blemishes caused by freedom; the impetuosity of a lively mind; a wildness that comes from a lack of discipline, to which most men are subject.

Reynaldo   But my good lord –

Polonius   Why should you do this?

Reynaldo   Yes, my lord; I'd like to know that.

Polonius   Well, sir, here's my scheme, and I believe it's a fair device. Your attributing these slight defects to my son – a bit of shop-soiling as it were – well now, the man you are chatting to – the fellow you wish to interrogate – knowing the young man you are talking about to be guilty of the aforementioned imperfections, you can be sure he'll naturally agree with you, like this: ''Dear sir,'' or something similar – or ''friend'' – or ''gentleman'' – according to whatever is the correct form of address of the man and his country.

Reynaldo   Very good, my lord.

Polonius   And then, sir, he does this. He – [**Polonius** *has lost*

89

about to say? By the mass, I was about to say something.
Where did I leave?

Reynaldo   At 'closes in the consequence.'

60 **Polonius**   At 'closes in the consequence,' ay, marry.
He closes thus: 'I know the gentleman,
I saw him yesterday,' or 'th'other day,'
Or then, or then, with such or such, 'and as you say,
There was a gaming,' 'there o'ertook in's rouse,'
65 'There falling out at tennis,' or perchance
'I saw him enter such a house of sale' –
Videlicet a brothel, or so forth.
See you now,
Your bait of falsehood takes this carp of truth;
70 And thus do we of wisdom and of reach,
With windlasses and with assays of bias,
By indirections find directions out.
So by my former lecture and advice
Shall you my son. You have me, have you not?

75 **Reynaldo**   My lord, I have.

Polonius   God be wi' you, fare you well.

Reynaldo   Good my lord.

Polonius   Observe his inclination in yourself.

Reynaldo   I shall, my lord.

80 **Polonius**   And let him ply his music.

Reynaldo   Well, my lord.

[*Exit*]

[*Enter* **Ophelia**]

his train of thought]   What was I about to say? Confound it, I was about to say something. Where did I leave off?

Reynaldo   At "he confides in you like this . . ."

Polonius   At "he confides in you like this"? Yes indeed! He confides thus: "I know that gentleman. I saw him yesterday," or "the other day" – or at such a time, or such a time, with such-and-such – "and as you say, there he was, gambling"; "there he was, drunk"; "there he was, squabbling at tennis"; or maybe, "I saw him enter this place of business" – namely, a brothel – and so forth. D'you see? Your use of falsehood as a bait means you catch a big fish – the truth. That's the way we men of brains and understanding, with roundabout methods and devious inquiries, find out the real truth by indirect means. You'll achieve this with my son if you employ my aforesaid lesson and advice. You have my meaning, have you not?

Reynaldo   My lord, I have.

Polonius   Goodbye. Fare you well.

Reynaldo   Thank you, my lord.

Polonius   [*calling him back*]   Keep your eye on him.

Reynaldo   I shall, my lord.

Polonius   And let him have his fling!

Reynaldo   Surely, my lord.

[*He bows and leaves*]

[**Ophelia** *enters, distressed*]

Polonius   Farewell. How now, Ophelia, what's the matter?

Ophelia   Oh, my lord, my lord, I have been so affrighted.

Polonius   With what, i'th'name of God?

85 **Ophelia**   My lord, as I was sewing in my chamber,
Lord Hamlet, with his doublet all unbraced,
No hat upon his head, his stockings fouled,
Ungartered and down-gyved to his ankle,
Pale as his shirt, his knees knocking each other,
90 And with a look so piteous in purport
As if he had been loosed out of hell
To speak of horrors, he comes before me.

Polonius   Mad for thy love?

95 **Ophelia**   My lord, I do not know,
But truly I do fear it.

Polonius   What said he?

Ophelia   He took me by the wrist and held me hard.
Then goes he to the length of all his arm,
And with his other hand thus o'er his brow
100 He falls to such perusal of my face
As he would draw it. Long stayed he so.
At last, a little shaking of mine arm,
And thrice his head thus waving up and down,
He raised a sigh so piteous and profound
105 As it did seem to shatter all his bulk
And end his being. That done, he lets me go,
And with his head over his shoulder turned
He seemed to find his way without his eyes,
For out o'doors he went without their helps,
110 And to the last bended their light on me.

Polonius   Come, go with me, I will go seek the King.
This is the very ecstasy of love,

Polonius   Farewell.   [*Seeing his daughter*]   Well now, Ophelia. What's the matter?

Ophelia   Oh, my lord, my lord. I've been so frightened!

Polonius   What with, in God's name?

Ophelia   My lord, as I was sewing in my room, Lord Hamlet confronted me with his clothing all unbuttoned; without a hat; his stockings dirty, lacking garters, and fallen round his ankles; pale as his shirt; his knees knocking together; and with a haunted look as if he'd been let out of hell to describe its horrors.

Polonius   Mad for love of you?

Ophelia   My lord, I do not know, but frankly I'm afraid he is.

Polonius   What did he say?

Ophelia   He took me by the wrist and gripped me hard. Then he stretched out his arm, and with his other hand like this across his brow he studied my face as intently as if he intended to draw it. He stayed like that a long time. Finally, after shaking my arm a little and nodding his head up and down three times like this   [*she nods slowly and solemnly*]   he sighed so piteously and profoundly it seemed to shatter his entire body and end his life. Having done that, he let me go, and with his head turned back over his shoulder he seemed to find his way without using his eyes, because he went outside without their help, and to the last kept them fixed on me.

Polonius   Come along with me. I'll find the King. This is love at

Whose violent property fordoes itself
And leads the will to desperate undertakings
115   As oft as any passion under heaven
That does afflict our natures. I am sorry –
What, have you given him any hard words of late?

Ophelia   No, my good lord, but as you did command,
I did repel his letters and denied
120   His access to me.

Polonius   That hath made him mad.
I am sorry that with better heed and judgment
I had not quoted him. I feared he did but trifle
And meant to wrack thee. But beshrew my jealousy!
125   By heaven, it is as proper to our age
To cast beyond ourselves in our opinions
As it is common for the younger sort
To lack discretion. Come, go we to the King.
This must be known, which, being kept close, might move
130   More grief to hide than hate to utter love.
Come.

[*Exeunt*]

Scene 2

Flourish. Enter **King** *and* **Queen**, **Rosencrantz** *and*
Guildenstern, *with Attendants.*

King   Welcome, dear Rosencrantz and Guildenstern!
Moreover that we much did long to see you,
The need we have to use you did provoke
Our hasty sending. Something have you heard

its most extreme. Its violent nature leads to suicide as often as any passion that ever afflicted mankind. I'm sorry – [*He breaks off*]   Now have you spoken harshly to him recently?

Ophelia   No, my good lord, but as you ordered, I returned his letters and refused to let him visit me.

Polonius   This has unhinged his mind. I'm sorry I hadn't sized him up more accurately. I was afraid he was only trifling and meant to ruin you. Bother my suspicious nature! By heaven, it's as characteristic of the older generation to be mistrustful as it is for young ones to be naive. Come, let us go to the King. This must be reported. Secrecy might cause more grief than disclosure will give offense. Come.

[*They leave*]

Scene 2

The King's Court. A flourish of trumpets announces the entrance of the **King** *and* **Queen, Rosencrantz** *and* **Guildenstern** *(once fellow students of Hamlet) and Attendants.*

King   Welcome, dear Rosencrantz and Guildenstern. Besides longing to see you, we sent for you in haste because we needed your services. You've heard a little about Hamlet's

5   Of Hamlet's transformation – so I call it,
Since nor th'exterior nor the inward man
Resembles that it was. What it should be,
More than his father's death, that thus hath put him
So much from th'understanding of himself
10   I cannot dream of. I entreat you both
That, being of so young days brought up with him,
And since so neighboured to his youth and haviour,
That you vouchsafe your rest here in our court
Some little time, so by your companies
15   To draw him on to pleasures and to gather,
So much as from occasion you may glean,
Whether aught to us unknown afflicts him thus
That, opened, lies within our remedy.

Queen   Good gentlemen, he hath much talked of you,
20   And sure I am, two men there is not living
To whom he more adheres. If it will please you
To show us so much gentry and good will
As to expend your time with us awhile
For the supply and profit of our hope,
25   Your visitation shall receive such thanks
As fits a king's remembrance.

Rosencrantz   Both your Majesties
Might, by the sovereign power you have of us,
Put your dread pleasures more into command
30   Than to entreaty.

Guildenstern   But we both obey,
And here give up ourselves in the full bent
To lay our service freely at your feet
To be commanded.

35 **King**   Thanks, Rosencrantz and gentle Guildenstern.

Queen   Thanks, Guildenstern and gentle Rosencrantz.

transformation; I call it that since he's not the man he was physically or mentally. I can't imagine what has disturbed him like this, other than his father's death. I'd ask you both, having been brought up with him since childhood, and ever since been intimately acquainted with his lifestyle and habits, to agree to stay here in our court for a while, so that by your companionship you can get him to enjoy things again – and discover, as far as opportunity allows, whether there is something we don't know about that's causing his affliction, which we can put right once it's revealed.

Queen   Good gentlemen, he has talked about you a great deal, and I'm quite sure there are no two men alive with whom he is more intimate. If you would be kind enough to show us so much courtesy and goodwill as to spend your time with us for a while, in pursuance of our hopes, your stay will be royally rewarded.

Rosencrantz   As our sovereign rulers, both your Majesties might *order* us to fulfill your respected wishes rather than request us.

Guildenstern   But we both obey, and offer ourselves to the utmost of our abilities as your loyal servants, ready to be commanded.

King   Thanks, Rosencrantz and kind Guildenstern.

Queen   Thanks, Guildenstern and kind Rosencrantz. I would

And I beseech you instantly to visit
My too much changed son. Go, some of you,
And bring these gentlemen where Hamlet is.

40 **Guildenstern**   Heavens make our presence and our practices
Pleasant and helpful to him.

Queen   Ay, amen.

[*Exeunt* **Rosencrantz** *and* **Guildenstern**]

[*Enter* **Polonius**]

Polonius   The ambassadors from Norway, my good lord,
Are joyfully returned.

45 **King**   Thou still hast been the father of good news.

Polonius   Have I, my lord? I assure my good liege
I hold my duty as I hold my soul,
Both to my God and to my gracious King;
And I do think – or else this brain of mine
50 Hunts not the trail of policy so sure
As it hath used to do – that I have found
The very cause of Hamlet's lunacy.

King   O, speak of that: that I do long to hear.

Polonius   Give first admittance to th'ambassadors.
55 My news shall be the fruit to that great feast.

King   Thyself do grace to them and bring them in.

[*Exit* **Polonius**]

He tells me, my dear Gertrude, he hath found
The head and source of all your son's distemper.

Queen   I doubt it is no other but the main,
60 His father's death and our o'er-hasty marriage.

ask you to visit my too-much-altered son immediately.   [*To Attendants*]   Go, one of you, and take these gentlemen to where Hamlet is.

Guildenstern   Pray heaven that our presence and our endeavors will be pleasing and helpful to him.

Queen   Amen to that.

[**Rosencrantz** *and* **Guildenstern** *bow and leave with an* **Attendant**]

[**Polonius** *enters and addresses the* **King**]

Polonius   I'm glad to say the ambassadors from Norway have returned, my good lord.

King   You have always been the bearer of good news.

Polonius   Have I, my lord? I assure your majesty that my duty and my soul are dedicated alike to my God and to my gracious King. And I think – unless this brain of mine isn't as shrewd as it once was – that I have found the actual cause of Hamlet's lunacy.

King   Oh, more about that – I'm longing to hear.

Polonius   First, admit the ambassadors. My news will be the dessert to follow their great feast.

King   Do the honors yourself and bring them in.

[**Polonius** *goes*]

[*Turning to his wife*]   He tells me, my dear Gertrude, that he has found the origin of your son's disorder.

Queen   I have no doubt it's none other than the obvious one: his father's death and our over-hasty marriage.

King   Well, we shall sift him.

[*Enter* **Polonius, Voltemand,** *and* **Cornelius**]

                                                Welcome, my good friends.
Say, Voltemand, what from our brother Norway?

Voltemand   Most fair return of greetings and desires.
Upon our first, he sent out to suppress
65   His nephew's levies, which to him appeared
To be a preparation 'gainst the Polack;
But better looked into, he truly found
It was against your highness. Whereat grieved,
That so his sickness, age, and impotence
70   Was falsely borne in hand, sends out arrests
On Fortinbras; which he, in brief, obeys,
Receives rebuke from Norway, and, in fine,
Makes vow before his uncle never more
To give th'assay of arms against your Majesty.
75   Whereon old Norway, overcome with joy,
Gives him three thousand crowns in annual fee
And his commission to employ those soldiers
So levied, as before, against the Polack,
With an entreaty, herein further shown,   [*Giving a paper*]
80   That it might please you to give quiet pass
Through your dominions for this enterprise,
On such regards of safety and allowance
As therein are set down.

King   It likes us well;
85   And at our more considered time we'll read,
Answer, and think upon this business.
Meantime, we thank you for your well-took labour.
Go to your rest; at night we'll feast together.
Most welcome home.

                                 [*Exeunt* **Voltemand** *and* **Cornelius**]

King   Well, we'll question him.

[**Polonius** *enters, with* **Voltemand** *and* **Cornelius**]

Welcome, my good friends. Voltemand, tell us what
message you have from our brother the King of Norway.

Voltemand   A most favorable response to your greetings and
requests. As soon as we broached the matter, he sent
orders out to disband the army levied by his nephew, which
he had taken to be a preparation against the King of Poland.
When he looked into it more carefully, he found that it was
indeed directed against your Highness. Whereupon, grieved
that he'd been misled in his sickness, old age, and
powerlessness, he sent Fortinbras orders restraining him. In
brief, he obeys; is rebuked by the King; and, specifically,
vows in front of his uncle never again to challenge your
Majesty. At this, the old King, overcome with joy, gives
Fortinbras an annuity of three thousand crowns and a
commission to employ against Poland the soldiers he'd
levied earlier, together with a request, the details of which
are here   [*he passes a document to the* **King**]   that it might
please your Majesty to give safe passage through your
dominions for this expedition, with such precautions and
terms as are therein set down.

King   I'm pleased with that, and when we have more time
we'll read, answer, and think about this business.
Meantime, we thank you for your successful efforts. Take
some rest; tonight we'll feast together. Welcome back.

[**Voltemand** *and* **Cornelius** *leave*]

90 **Polonius**   This business is well ended.
My liege and madam, to expostulate
What majesty should be, what duty is,
Why day is day, night night, and time is time,
Were nothing but to waste night, day, and time.
95 Therefore, since brevity is the soul of wit,
And tediousness the limbs and outward flourishes,
I will be brief. Your noble son is mad.
Mad call I it, for to define true madness,
What is't but to be nothing else but mad?
100 But let that go.

Queen   More matter with less art.

Polonius   Madam, I swear I use no art at all.
That he is mad 'tis true; 'tis true 'tis pity;
And pity 'tis 'tis true. A foolish figure!
105 But farewell it, for I will use no art.
Mad let us grant him then. And now remains
That we find out the cause of this effect,
Or rather say the cause of this defect,
For this effect defective comes by cause:
110 Thus it remains; and the remainder thus:
Perpend,
I have a daughter – have whilst she is mine –
Who in her duty and obedience, mark,
Hath given me this. Now gather and surmise.
115 [*Reads*]   *To the celestial and my soul's idol, the most beautified*
Ophelia – That's an ill phrase, a vile phrase, 'beautified' is a
vile phrase. But you shall hear thus: *in her excellent white*
bosom, these, etc.

Queen   Came this from Hamlet to her?

120 **Polonius**   Good madam, stay awhile, I will be faithful.

Doubt that the stars are fire,
Doubt that the sun doth move,

102

Polonius   A happy outcome. My King and Queen: to debate
what kingship should be, what duty is, why day is day
and night is night and time is time, would be only to waste
night, day, and time. Therefore, since conciseness is the
essence of good expression, and longwindedness is only
external ornamentation, I will be brief. Your noble son is
mad. I call it mad because to define true madness,
wouldn't one have to be mad oneself? But let that pass . . .

Queen   [*bored by the old man's verbosity*]   More content, and
less style!

Polonius   Madam, I swear I'm using none at all. That he is
mad, is true. That it's true is a pity. And it's a pity that it's
true. Rather subtle: but I'll let it go, because I won't indulge
in wordplay. So, let's grant that he is mad. It now remains
that we find out the cause of this effect – or rather, the
cause of this *defect*, since this effect must have a defective
source. Therefore it remains . . . [*He loses his thread*]   This
is what remains therefore: take note. I have a daughter –
that is, until she marries – who in her dutifulness and
obedience – mark what I say – has given me this.   [*He
shows Hamlet's letter*]   Now draw your own conclusion.
[*He clears his throat importantly and reads*]

*To the celestial – and my soul's – idol, the most beautified
Ophelia –*

That's a bad word. A vile word. ''Beautified'' is a vile word.
But there's more, thus:

– this letter is sent to her excellent white bosom, etc. etc.

Queen   Did this come to her from Hamlet?

Polonius   Good madam, be patient. I'll reveal all.

Doubt that the stars are fire;
Doubt that the sun does move;

> *Doubt truth to be a liar,*
> *But never doubt I love.*

125 *Oh dear Ophelia, I am ill at these numbers. I have not art to*
reckon my groans. But that I love thee best, oh, most best,
believe it. Adieu. Thine evermore, most dear lady, whilst this
machine is to him, Hamlet.

This in obedience hath my daughter shown me,
130 And, more above, hath his solicitings,
As they fell out by time, by means, and place,
All given to mine ear.

King But how hath she received his love?

Polonius What do you think of me?

135 **King** As of a man faithful and honourable.

Polonius I would fain prove so. But what might you think,
When I had seen this hot love on the wing –
As I perceived it, I must tell you that,
Before my daughter told me – what might you
140 Or my dear Majesty your queen here think
If I had played the desk or table-book,
Or given my heart a winking mute and dumb,
Or looked upon this love with idle sight –
What might you think? No, I went round to work,
145 And my young mistress thus I did bespeak:
'Lord Hamlet is a prince out of thy star.
This must not be.' And then I prescripts gave her,
That she should lock herself from his resort,
Admit no messengers, receive no tokens;
150 Which done, she took the fruits of my advice,
And he, repelled – a short tale to make –
Fell into a sadness, then into a fast,
Thence to a watch, thence into a weakness,
Thence to a lightness, and, by this declension,

Doubt truth to be a liar,
But never doubt I love.

Oh, dear Ophelia, I'm bad at poetry. I have no skill in verse
to express my sufferings. But that I love you more than
anyone else, much more, believe me! Adieu. Yours ever,
most dear lady, as long as I live, Hamlet.

My daughter has shown me this out of obedience, and in
addition she has told me of his courtship as it proceeded:
the means employed and where they met.

King   How has she responded to his love?

Polonius   How do you regard me?

King   As a faithful and honorable man.

Polonius   And so I would wish to be. What would you have
thought, when I saw this passionate love affair taking
off – and I recognized it, I must tell you that, before my
daughter told me – what would you have thought, or my
dear Majesty your Queen here have thought, if I'd been a
go-between, or if I'd suppressed my conscience, or looked
upon their love without attaching much importance to it?
What would you have thought? No. I got down to work, and
said this to my young madam: ''Lord Hamlet is a prince out
of your class. This must stop.'' And then I gave her orders:
to lock herself away from him, admit no messengers,
receive no love tokens. Having done this, she went further
in following my advice, and he, rejected – to cut a long story
short – fell into a depression; then couldn't eat; then
couldn't sleep; then went into a decline; then went

105

155 Into the madness wherein now he raves
And all we mourn for.

King   Do you think 'tis this?

Queen It may be; very like.

Polonius Hath there been such a time – I would fain know
160   that –
That I have positively said ''Tis so,'
When it proved otherwise?

King   Not that I know.

Polonius [*points to his head and shoulder*] Take this from this
165   if this be otherwise:

If circumstances lead me, I will find
Where truth is hid, though it were hid indeed
Within the centre.

King   How may we try it further?

170 **Polonius** You know sometimes he walks four hours together
Here in the lobby.

Queen   So he does indeed.

Polonius At such a time I'll loose my daughter to him.
Be you and I behind an arras then.
175   Mark the encounter: if he love her not,
And be not from his reason fall'n thereon,
Let me be no assistant for a state,
But keep a farm and carters.

King   We will try it.

[*Enter* **Hamlet,** *reading a book*]

180 **Queen** But look where sadly the poor wretch comes reading.

106

delirious; and, by this process, reached the madness which he's now suffering from, which we all mourn.

King   [*to* **Gertrude**]   Do you think this is it?

Queen   It could be. Very probably.

Polonius   Has there ever been a time, I'd like to know, when I've positively said, ''This is so,'' when it has proved otherwise?

King   Not that I know.

Polonius   [*pointing to his head and shoulders*]   Take this from this if I'm not right. Given the evidence, I'll find out the truth, even if it's hidden in the center of the earth.

King   How can we test it out further?

Polonius   You know that he sometimes walks four hours on end here in the lobby?

Queen   So he does indeed.

Polonius   At such a time I'll put my daughter in his way. You and I will be behind the wall tapestry, watching the encounter. If he doesn't love her, and hasn't lost his reason because of it, let me cease to be a minister of state and run a farm and wagons!

King   We'll try it.

[**Hamlet** *enters, reading a book*]

Queen   Look how sadly the poor wretch comes, reading.

Polonius   Away, I do beseech you both, away.
I'll board him presently. Oh, give me leave.

[*Exeunt* **King** *and* **Queen** *and Attendants*]

How does my good Lord Hamlet?

Hamlet   Well, God-a-mercy.

185 **Polonius**   Do you know me, my lord?

Hamlet   Excellent well. You are a fishmonger.

Polonius   Not I, my lord.

Hamlet   Then I would you were so honest a man.

Polonius   Honest, my lord?

190 **Hamlet**   Ay sir. To be honest, as this world goes, is to be one
man picked out of ten thousand.

Polonius   That's very true, my lord.

Hamlet   For if the sun breed maggots in a dead dog, being a
good kissing carrion – Have you a daughter?

195 **Polonius**   I have, my lord.

Hamlet   Let her not walk i'th'sun. Conception is a blessing,
but as your daughter may conceive – friend, look to't.

Polonius   [*aside*] How say you by that? Still harping on my
daughter. Yet he knew you not at first; he said I was a
200 fishmonger. He is far gone. And truly in my youth I suffered
much extremity for love, very near this. I'll speak to him
again. What do you read, my lord?

Hamlet   Words, words, words.

Polonius   Go away, both of you, please; away; I'll approach him immediately. If you'd be so kind . . .

[*The* **King, Queen** *and Attendants leave hurriedly*]

How is my good Lord Hamlet?

Hamlet   Well, God have mercy on you.

Polonius   Do you know me, my lord?

Hamlet   Extremely well. You are a fishmonger.

Polonius   Not I, my lord.

Hamlet   Then I wish you were such an honest man.

Polonius   Honest, my lord?

Hamlet   Yes, sir. To be honest, as this world goes, is to be one man in ten thousand.

Polonius   That's very true, my lord.

Hamlet   [*reading from his book*]   ''Because if the sun can beget maggots in the carcass of a dead dog, it being an excellent breeding ground . . .''   [*To* **Polonius**]   Have you got a daughter?

Polonius   I have, my lord.

Hamlet   Don't let her walk in the sun. Conception is a blessing, but since your daughter may conceive – watch it, friend!

Polonius   [*aside*]   How about that! Always harping on my daughter! Yet he didn't know me at first. He said I was a fishmonger. He's far gone. And in my youth, to tell the truth, I suffered extremely in the cause of love, very like this. I'll speak to him again.   [*To* **Hamlet**]   What are you reading, my lord?

Hamlet   Words, words, words.

Polonius   What is the matter, my lord?

Hamlet   Between who?

Polonius   I mean the matter that you read, my lord.

Hamlet   Slanders, sir. For the satirical rogue says here that
old men have grey beards, that their faces are wrinkled, their
eyes purging thick amber and plumtree gum, and that they
205   have a plentiful lack of wit, together with most weak
hams – all which, sir, though I most powerfully and potently
believe, yet I hold it not honesty to have it thus set down.
For you yourself, sir, shall grow old as I am – if like a crab
you could go backward.

210   **Polonius**   [*aside*] Though this be madness, yet there is method
in't. Will you walk out of the air, my lord?

Hamlet   Into my grave?

Polonius   Indeed, that's out of the air. [*Aside*] How pregnant
sometimes his replies are – a happiness that often madness
215   hits on, which reason and sanity could not so prosperously
be delivered of. I will leave him and suddenly contrive the
means of meeting between him and my daughter. My lord, I
will take my leave of you.

Hamlet   You cannot, sir, take from me anything that I will
220   not more willingly part withal – except my life, except my
life, except my life.

Polonius   Fare you well, my lord.

Hamlet   These tedious old fools!

[*Enter* **Rosencrantz** *and* **Guildenstern**]

Polonius   You go to seek the Lord Hamlet. There he is.

Polonius   What's the matter, my lord?   [*He means the subject matter*]

Hamlet   Between who?   [**Hamlet** *deliberately takes "matter" to mean "quarrel"*]

Polonius   I mean the matter you are reading, my lord.

Hamlet   Slanders, sir. The satirical rogue says here   [*tapping the book*]   that old men have gray beards; that their faces are wrinkled; their eyes oozing thick discharge; and that they have a considerable lack of brains, together with very weak thighs. All of which, sir, I most fervently believe, though I don't think it's decent to have it written down like this. As for yourself, sir, you'll grow old, like me – if you could go backwards, like a crab.

Polonius   [*aside*]   Though this is madness, there's sense in it.   [*To* **Hamlet**]   Will you come in out of the air, sir?

Hamlet   Into my grave?

Polonius   Indeed, that *is* "out of the air."   [*Aside*]   How quick-witted his replies sometimes are! It's a skill that madness often possesses, which sanity couldn't get away with. I'll leave him, and immediately arrange a means whereby he and my daughter shall meet.   [*To* **Hamlet**]   My lord, I'll take my leave of you.

Hamlet   You cannot, sir, take from me anything that I would not part with more willingly. Except my life . . . except my life . . . except my life . . .

Polonius   Farewell, my lord.

Hamlet   [*aside*]   These tedious old fools!

[**Rosencrantz** *and* **Guildenstern** *enter*]

Polonius   You are seeking the Lord Hamlet? There he is.

225 **Rosencrantz**   God save you, sir.

[*Exit* **Polonius**]

Guildenstern   My honoured lord.

Rosencrantz   My most dear lord.

Hamlet   My excellent good friends. How dost thou,
Guildenstern? Ah, Rosencrantz. Good lads, how do you
230   both?

Rosencrantz   As the indifferent children of the earth.

Guildenstern   Happy in that we are not over-happy: on
Fortune's cap we are not the very button.

Hamlet   Nor the soles of her shoes?

235 **Rosencrantz**   Neither, my lord.

Hamlet   Then you live about her waist, or in the middle of
her favours?

Guildenstern   Faith, her privates we.

Hamlet   In the secret parts of Fortune? Oh most true, she
240   is a strumpet. What news?

Rosencrantz   None, my lord, but the world's grown honest.

Hamlet   Then is doomsday near. But your news is not true.
Let me question more in particular. What have you, my
good friends, deserved at the hands of Fortune that she sends
245   you to prison hither?

Guildenstern   Prison, my lord?

Hamlet   Denmark's a prison.

Rosencrantz   Then is the world one.

Rosencrantz   God save you, sir.

[**Polonius** *leaves*]

Guildenstern   [*bowing*]   My honored lord.

Rosencrantz   [*bowing*]   My most dear lord.

Hamlet   My excellent good friends! How are you, Guildenstern? Ah, Rosencrantz? Good lads, how are you both?

Rosencrantz   So-so.

Guildenstern   Happy in that we aren't *too* happy. On Fortune's cap, we aren't the button on the top!

Hamlet   Nor the soles of her shoes?

Rosencrantz   Neither, my lord.

Hamlet   Then you are living round about her waist, or in the middle of her favors?

Guildenstern   Faith, we're her privates!

Hamlet   In the secret parts of Lady Fortune? Oh, how true – she's a wanton! What news?

Rosencrantz   None, my lord, except that the world has reformed itself.

Hamlet   Doomsday must be near. But your news isn't true. Let me question you more specifically. What bad luck, my good friends, has brought you here to prison?

Guildenstern   Prison, my lord?

Hamlet   Denmark's a prison.

Rosencrantz   Then the world is one too.

Hamlet   A goodly one, in which there are many confines,
250   wards, and dungeons, Denmark being one o'th'worst.

Rosencrantz   We think not so, my lord.

Hamlet   Why, then 'tis none to you; for there is nothing either
good or bad but thinking makes it so. To me it is a prison.

Rosencrantz   Why, then your ambition makes it one: 'tis too
255   narrow for your mind.

Hamlet   O, God, I could be bounded in a nutshell and count
myself a king of infinite space – were it not that I have bad
dreams.

Guildenstern   Which dreams indeed are ambition; for the very
260   substance of the ambitious is merely the shadow of a dream.

Hamlet   A dream itself is but a shadow.

Rosencrantz   Truly, and I hold ambition of so airy and light a
quality that it is but a shadow's shadow.

Hamlet   Then are our beggars bodies, and our monarchs and
265   outstretched heroes the beggars' shadows. Shall we to th'
court? For by my fay, I cannot reason.

Both   We'll wait upon you.

Hamlet   No such matter. I will not sort you with the rest of
my servants; for, to speak to you like an honest man, I
270   am most dreadfully attended. But in the beaten way of
friendship, what make you at Elsinore?

Rosencrantz   To visit you, my lord, no other occasion.

Hamlet   Beggar that I am, I am even poor in thanks, but I
thank you. And sure, dear friends, my thanks are too dear a
275   halfpenny. Were you not sent for? Is it your own inclining?
Is it a free visitation? Come, come, deal justly with me.
Come, come. Nay, speak.

114

Hamlet   A sizeable one, in which there are many jails, cells, and dungeons, Denmark being one of the worst.

Rosencrantz   We don't think so, my lord.

Hamlet   Well, then, it isn't one to you. Things aren't either good or bad – they are what you think they are. To me, it's a prison.

Rosencrantz   Why then, your ambition makes it one. It's too limiting for your mind.

Hamlet   Oh, God, I could be confined to a nutshell and regard myself as a king of infinite space – if it were not that I have bad dreams.

Guildenstern   Those dreams are, in fact, ambition: what an ambitious man attains is what he dreams about.

Hamlet   A dream itself is only a shadow.

Rosencrantz   Truly, and I regard ambition as being so insubstantial that it's only a shadow's shadow.

Hamlet   In that case our unambitious beggars are "bodies," and our monarchs and ambitious heroes are the beggars' "shadows." Shall we go to law about it? Because, faith, I can't fathom this out.

Ros., Guild.   We'll escort you.

Hamlet   No way. I won't have you classed as my servants. Quite frankly, I'm very badly looked after. But not to beat about the bush, what are you doing in Elsinore?

Rosencrantz   To visit you, my lord. No other reason.

Hamlet   Being a beggar, I'm even short of thanks: but I thank you. Actually, dear friends, my thanks aren't worth so much as a halfpenny. Were you sent for, perhaps? Have you come because you want to? Are there no strings attached? Come, come, play fair with me. Come, come. Speak now.

Guildenstern   What should we say, my lord?

Hamlet   Why, anything. But to the purpose. You were sent
280   for, and there is a kind of confession in your looks, which
your modesties have not craft enough to colour. I know the
good King and Queen have sent for you.

Rosencrantz   To what end, my lord?

Hamlet   That, you must teach me. But let me conjure you, by
285   the rights of our fellowship, by the consonancy of our youth,
by the obligation of our ever-preserved love, and by what
more dear a better proposer can charge you withal, be even
and direct with me whether you were sent for or no.

Rosencrantz   [*aside to* **Guildenstern**]   What say you?

290 **Hamlet**   Nay, then I have an eye of you. If you love me, hold
not off.

Guildenstern   My lord, we were sent for.

Hamlet   I will tell you why; so shall my anticipation prevent
your discovery, and your secrecy to the King and Queen
295   moult no feather. I have of late, but wherefore I know not,
lost all my mirth, forgone all custom of exercise; and indeed
it goes so heavily with my disposition that this goodly frame
the earth seems to me a sterile promontory, this most
excellent canopy the air, look you, this brave o'erhanging
300   firmament, this majestical roof fretted with golden fire, why,
it appeareth nothing to me but a foul and pestilent
congregation of vapours. What a piece of work is a man, how
noble in reason, how infinite in faculties, in form and
moving how express and admirable, in action how like an

Guildenstern   What should we say, my lord?

Hamlet   Why, anything. But give me a straight answer.   [**Rosencrantz** *and* **Guildenstern** *exchange embarrassed looks*]   You were sent for. There's a kind of confession in your looks that you're too unsophisticated to disguise. I know the good King and Queen have sent for you.

Rosencrantz   For what purpose, my lord?

Hamlet   *That* you must tell me. But let me solemnly entreat you: by the bonds of our fellowship; by the comradeship of our youth; by the claims of our longstanding love; and by whatever is more precious that could be proposed – be candid and frank with me as to whether you were sent for or not.

Rosencrantz   [*aside to* **Guildenstern**]   What are you going to say?

Hamlet   Now, I'm watching you. If you love me, don't hang back.

Guildenstern   My lord, we were sent for.

Hamlet   I'll tell you why; that way, you needn't reveal anything, and your oath of secrecy to the King and Queen won't be broken in the slightest. Lately – why I don't know – I have lost my good spirits, dropped all form of exercise. Indeed, I feel so depressed that this beautiful structure the earth seems to me to be a useless lump of rock; this admirable canopy, the air, look you   [*he gestures upwards*] – this splendid overhanging sky – this majestic roof adorned with golden fire – why, it seems nothing to me but a foul and toxic collection of vapors. What a work of art is man: how noble in his ability to reason; how infinite in his abilities; in design and movement, how fitted to his

117

305 angel, in apprehension how like a god: the beauty of the
world, the paragon of animals – and yet, to me, what is this
quintessence of dust? Man delights not me – no, nor woman
neither, though by your smiling you seem to say so.

Rosencrantz   My lord, there was no such stuff in my
310 thoughts.

Hamlet   Why did ye laugh then, when I said man delights
not me?

Rosencrantz   To think, my lord, if you delight not in man,
what Lenten entertainment the players shall receive from
315 you. We coted them on the way, and hither are they coming
to offer you service.

Hamlet   He that plays the King shall be welcome – his
Majesty shall have tribute of me; the adventurous knight
shall use his foil and target; the lover shall not sigh gratis; the
320 humorous man shall end his part in peace; the clown shall
make those laugh whose lungs are tickle a th' sear; and the
lady shall say her mind freely, or the blank verse shall halt
for't. What players are they?

Rosencrantz   Even those you were wont to take such delight
325 in; the tragedians of the city.

Hamlet   How chances it they travel? Their residence, both in
reputation and profit, was better both ways.

Rosencrantz   I think their inhibition comes by the means of
the late innovation.

330 **Hamlet**   Do they hold the same estimation they did when I
was in the city? Are they so followed?

Rosencrantz   No, indeed are they not.

Hamlet   How comes it? Do they grow rusty?

purpose and admirable; in what he does, how like an angel;
in mental perception, how like a god: the world's most
beautiful creature; the supremely perfect animal. And yet, to
me, what is this ultimate refinement of basic matter? Man
gives me no pleasure.   [**Rosencrantz** *and* **Guildenstern**
exchange knowing looks]   No, nor does woman either,
though by your smiles you seem to imply so.

Rosencrantz   My lord I thought no such thing.

Hamlet   Why did you laugh, then, when I said "Man gives me
no pleasure"?

Rosencrantz   To think, my lord, that if you get no pleasure
from man, what a dull reception the actors will receive from
you. We overtook them on the way here, and they are
coming to offer their services.

Hamlet   The one who plays the King will be welcome. I shall
pay him proper tribute. The Wandering Knight will use his
sword and shield. The Lover shall not sigh for nothing. The
Hot-tempered Character will rant on, unchecked. The Clown
will make the ones who laugh at nothing, laugh. The
Leading Lady will speak her mind without restraint – or the
blank verse will sound lame. Which actors are they?

Rosencrantz   The ones you used to like so much. The tragedy
players from the city.

Hamlet   Why are they on tour? Having a home theater was
better for their reputation and their profit.

Rosencrantz   I think they were banned because of the recent
disturbances.

Hamlet   Have they as good a reputation as when I lived in the
city? Are they still popular?

Rosencrantz   No, indeed, they are not.

Hamlet   How's that? Have they gone stale?

119

335 **Rosencrantz**   Nay, their endeavour keeps in the wonted pace;
but there is, sir, an eyrie of children, little eyases, that cry
out on the top of question, and are most tyrannically clapped
for't. These are now the fashion, and so berattle the common
stages – so they call them – that many wearing rapiers are
340 afraid of goose-quills and dare scarce come thither.

Hamlet   What, are they children? Who maintains 'em? How
are they escoted? Will they pursue the quality no longer than
they can sing? Will they not say afterwards, if they should
grow themselves to common players – as it is most like, if
345 their means are no better – their writers do them wrong to
make them exclaim against their own succession?

Rosencrantz   Faith, there has been much to do on both sides;
and the nation holds it no sin to tar them to controversy.
There was for a while no money bid for argument unless the
350 poet and the player went to cuffs in the question.

Hamlet   Is't possible?

Guildenstern   O, there has been much throwing about of
brains.

Hamlet   Do the boys carry it away?

355 **Rosencrantz**   Ay, that they do, my lord; Hercules and his load
too.

Hamlet   It is not very strange; for my uncle is King of
Denmark, and those that would make mouths at him while
my father lived give twenty, forty, fifty, a hundred ducats
360 apiece for his picture in little. 'Sblood, there is something in
this more than natural, if philosophy could find it out.

Rosencrantz No, they've maintained their standards. But there is, sir, a rival nest of child actors, little hawks, who overact in shrill voices and are enthusiastically applauded for it. These are now the fashion, and they attack the "common playhouses" (so they call them) so much that many men wearing swords daren't go there for fear of the playwrights' pens.

Hamlet What, are they children? Who runs them? How are they funded? Will they quit acting when their voices break? If they develop into regular actors (which they probably will as it's all they can do), won't they say that their writers did them an injury by making them denounce their future profession?

Rosencrantz Faith, there's been abuse on both sides. The general public thinks that controversy's a good thing. At one time, nobody would commission a play unless the plot contained a row between the children's writers and the adult actors.

Hamlet Really?

Guildenstern Oh, there has been a great deal of intellectual debate.

Hamlet Do the boys come off best?

Rosencrantz Yes, they certainly do, my lord. Even over the theater whose sign outside shows Hercules carrying the Globe. [*The Globe Theatre was the home of Shakespeare's company*]

Hamlet It's not so strange. My uncle is King of Denmark, and those who used to make faces at him while my father was alive now give twenty, forty, fifty or a hundred ducats apiece for a miniature painting of him. Truly, there's something unnatural in this, if philosophy could discover it.

121

[A flourish of trumpets]

Guildenstern   There are the players.

Hamlet   Gentlemen, you are welcome to Elsinore. Your
hands, come then. The appurtenance of welcome is fashion
365   and ceremony. Let me comply with you in this garb – lest
my extent to the players, which I tell you must show fairly
outwards, should more appear like entertainment than yours.
You are welcome. But my uncle-father and aunt-mother are
deceived.

370   **Guildenstern**   In what, my dear lord?

Hamlet   I am but mad north-north-west. When the wind is
southerly, I know a hawk from a handsaw.

[Enter Polonius]

Polonius   Well be with you, gentlemen.

Hamlet   Hark you, Guildenstern, and you too – at each ear a
375   hearer. That great baby you see there is not yet out of his
swaddling-clouts.

Rosencrantz   Happily he's the second time come to them, for
they say an old man is twice a child.

Hamlet   I will prophesy he comes to tell me of the players.
380   Mark it. You say right, sir, a Monday morning, 'twas then
indeed.

Polonius   My lord, I have news to tell you.

Hamlet   My lord, I have news to tell you. When Roscius was
an actor in Rome –

385   **Polonius**   The actors are come hither, my lord.

[*A flourish of trumpets heralds the arrival of the actors*]

Guildenstern   That will be the players.

Hamlet   Gentlemen, you are welcome to Elsinore.   [*He offers his hand*]   Shake hands; come then. Ceremony is an essential part of welcome. Let me observe the formalties in this way, in case the reception I give the actors – which I warn you will appear very cordial – seems superior to yours. You are welcome. But my uncle-father and my aunt-mother are deceived.

Guildenstern   How, my dear lord?

Hamlet   I'm only mad when the wind's in the wrong direction. When it's southerly, I know a hawk from a handsaw.

[**Polonius** *enters*]

Polonius   Greetings, gentlemen.

Hamlet   Listen, Guildenstern.   [*To* **Rosencrantz**]   And you too. A listener for each ear.   [*Indicating* **Polonius**]   That great baby you see there is not yet out of his diapers.

Rosencrantz   Perhaps it's the second time round. They say an old man is in his second childhood.

Hamlet   I will prophesy that he comes to tell me about the actors. Take note.   [*Pretending to be in a normal conversation with his guests*]   You're right, sir. On Monday morning. It was then indeed . . .

Polonius   My lord, I have news for you.

Hamlet.   My lord, I have news for *you*. When Roscius was an actor in ancient Rome . . .

Polonius   The actors are here, my lord.

123

Hamlet   Buzz, buzz.

Polonius   Upon my honour –

Hamlet   *Then came each actor on his ass –*

Polonius   The best actors in the world, either for tragedy,
390   comedy, history, pastoral, pastoral-comical, historical-
pastoral, tragical-historical, tragical-comical-historical-
pastoral, scene individable, or poem unlimited. Seneca
cannot be too heavy, nor Plautus too light. For the law of
writ, and the liberty, these are the only men.

395   **Hamlet**   *O, Jephthah, judge of Israel, what a treasure hadst
thou!*

Polonius   What a treasure had he, my lord?

Hamlet   Why,

One fair daughter and no more,
400   *The which he loved passing well.*

Polonius   [*aside*]   Still on my daughter.

Hamlet   Am I not i'th'right, old Jephthah?

Polonius   If you call me Jephthah, my lord, I have a daughter
that I love passing well.

405   **Hamlet**   Nay, that follows not.

Polonius   What follows then, my lord?

Hamlet   Why,

As by lot God wot,

And then, you know,

410   *It came to pass, as most like it was.*

Hamlet   [*winking at* **Rosencrantz** *and* **Guildenstern** *to emphasize he has been proved right*]   You don't say!

Polonius   Upon my honor –

Hamlet   [*quoting from an old ballad*]   *Then came each actor on his ass.*

Polonius   They're the world's best actors: either for tragedy, comedy, history, pastoral, pastoral-comical, historical-pastoral, tragical-historical, tragical-comical-historical-pastoral, the unclassifiable, and the totally-comprehensive. Seneca's plays aren't too serious for them, nor are those of Plautus too light. For classical plays and romantic ones, these are the best.

Hamlet   [*quoting another well-known ballad*]   *Oh, Jephthah, judge of Israel, what a treasure you once had!*

Polonius   What treasure *did* he have, my lord?

Hamlet   Why:

> *One fair daughter and no more,*
> *The which he loved exceedingly.*

Polonius   [*aside*]   Always harping on my daughter!

Hamlet   Am I not right, old Jephthah?

Polonius   Since you call me Jephthah, my lord, I *do* have a daughter whom I love exceedingly.

Hamlet   No, that doesn't follow.

Polonius   What does follow, then, my lord?

Hamlet   Why:

> *As, by chance, God knows –*

and then, you know:

> *It happened quite inevitably –*

The first row of the pious chanson will show you more, for
look where my abridgement comes.

[*Enter the Players*]

You are welcome, masters. Welcome, all – I am glad to see
thee well – Welcome, good friends – O, old friend, why
415   thy face is valanced since I saw thee last. Com'st thou to
beard me in Denmark? – What, my young lady and mistress!
By'r lady, your ladyship is nearer to heaven than when I saw
you last by the altitude of a chopine. Pray God your voice,
like a piece of uncurrent gold, be not cracked within the
420   ring. Masters, you are all welcome. We'll e'en to't like
French falconers, fly at anything we see. We'll have a speech
straight. Come, give us a taste of your quality. Come, a
passionate speech.

1st Player   What speech, my good lord?

425 **Hamlet**   I heard thee speak me a speech once, but it was
never acted, or if it was, not above once – for the play, I
remember, pleased not the million, 'twas caviare to the
general. But it was, as I received it – and others, whose
judgments in such matters cried in the top of mine – an
430   excellent play, well digested in the scenes, set down with as
much modesty as cunning. I remember one said there were
no sallets in the lines to make the matter savoury, nor no
matter in the phrase that might indict the author of
affection, but called it an honest method, as wholesome as
435   sweet, and by very much more handsome than fine. One
speech in it I chiefly loved; 'twas Aeneas' tale to Dido; and
thereabout of it especially when he speaks of Priam's
slaughter. If it live in your memory, begin at this line – let

The first verse of the pious ballad will tell you the rest.
See how I'm cut short!

[*The* **Actors** *enter*]

You are welcome, gentlemen. Welcome, all.   [*He greets a particular actor*]   I'm glad to see you well.   [*To the company*]   Welcome, good friends.   [*He goes round the group*]   Oh, old friend, why, you've grown a beard since I last saw you! Have you come to beard me in Denmark?   [*To a young actor who normally would play women's parts*]   What, my young lady! My word, your ladyship has grown since I last saw you, by the height of a high heel! Pray God your voice hasn't broken and put you out of circulation like an underweight gold coin!   [*To everyone*]   Gentlemen you are all welcome! We'll have a go at anything that comes in sight, like French falconers. We'll have a speech right now. Come on, give us a sample of your goods. Come – a passionate speech!

1st Actor   Which speech, my lord?

Hamlet   I heard you deliver a speech once, but it was never acted – or if it was, not above a single performance, because the play, I remember, had no popular appeal. It was for the connoisseur, not the masses. But it was, in my opinion (and that of others whose judgment in such matters is better than mine) an excellent play, well constructed, and written with as much restraint as skill. I remember someone said there were no vulgarities in the lines to give the text spice, nor anything in the expression that could find the author guilty of affectation. He called it an honest style, as wholesome as it was refreshing, and with more naturalism in it than fine phrases. One speech in it I liked above the rest. It was the story Aeneas told to Dido, and the particular bit where he speaks of the slaughter of Priam. If you can still remember it, begin at this line – [*He thinks hard*]   let me

127

me see, let me see –

440 *The rugged Pyrrhus, like th'Hyrcanian beast –*

It is not so. It begins with Pyrrhus –

The rugged Pyrrhus, he whose sable arms,
Black as his purpose, did the night resemble
When he lay couched in the ominous horse,
445 *Hath now this dread and black complexion smear'd*
With heraldry more dismal. Head to foot
Now is he total gules, horridly tricked
With blood of fathers, mothers, daughters, sons,
Baked and impasted with the parching streets,
450 *That lend a tyrannous and a damned light*
To their lord's murder. Roasted in wrath and fire,
And thus o'ersized with coagulate gore,
With eyes like carbuncles, the hellish Pyrrhus
Old grandsire Priam seeks.

455 So proceed you.

Polonius 'Fore God, my lord, well spoken, with good accent
and good discretion.

1st Player   *Anon he finds him,*
Striking too short at Greeks. His antique sword,
460 *Rebellious to his arm, lies where it falls,*
Repugnant to command. Unequal matched,
Pyrrhus at Priam drives, in rage strikes wide;
But with the whiff and wind of his fell sword
Th'unnerved father falls. Then senseless Ilium,
465 *Seeming to feel this blow, with flaming top*
Stoops to his base, and with a hideous crash
Takes prisoner Pyrrhus' ear. For lo, his sword,
Which was declining on the milky head
Of reverend Priam, seemed i'th'air to stick;
470 *So, as a painted tyrant, Pyrrhus stood,*
And like a neutral to his will and matter,

see, let me see . . .

The rugged Pyrrhus, like a tiger from Hyrcania . . .

No, that's not right. It begins with Pyrrhus –

The rugged Pyrrhus, he whose black armor,
Black as his purpose, looked just like the night
When he lay outstretched in the Trojan horse,
Has now this fearful, black appearance smeared
With colors much more sinister. Head to foot,
Now is he all red: horridly painted
With blood of fathers, mothers, daughters, sons,
Baked and encrusted on the sun-drenched streets,
That gives a harsh and damned light
To their lord's murder. Roasted in wrath and fire,
And thus smeared over with congealed blood,
With eyes like carbuncles, the hellish Pyrrhus
Old grandfather Priam seeks.

Go on from there.

Polonius   By God, my lord, well spoken, and with good
delivery and taste!

1st Actor   *Soon he finds him,*
Striking feebly at the Greeks. The sword of his youth,
Too heavy to be used, lies where it falls,
Refusing to take orders. Unequal matched,
Pyrrhus drives at Priam; in rage strikes wide;
But by the draught and wind of his fierce sword
The weakened father falls. Then inanimate Ilium,
The fortress, seeming to feel this blow, its top afire,
Falls to the ground, and with a hideous crash
Deafens the ear of Pyrrhus. For lo! His sword,
Which was descending on the snow-white head
Of respected Priam, seemed to pause in mid-air;
So, like a tyrant in a painting, Pyrrhus stood,
And at a standstill 'twixt the will and deed,

>   *Did nothing.*
>   *But as we often see against some storm*
>   *A silence in the heavens, the rack stand still,*
> 475   *The bold winds speechless, and the orb below*
>   *As hush as death, anon the dreadful thunder*
>   *Doth rend the region; so after Pyrrhus' pause*
>   *Aroused vengeance sets him new awork,*
>   *And never did the Cyclops' hammers fall*
> 480   *On Mars's armour, forged for proof eterne,*
>   *With less remorse than Pyrrhus' bleeding sword*
>   *Now falls on Priam.*
>   *Out, out, thou strumpet Fortune! All you gods*
>   *In general synod take away her power,*
> 485   *Break all the spokes and fellies from her wheel,*
>   *And bowl the round nave down the hill of heaven*
>   *As low as to the fiends.*

Polonius   This is too long.

Hamlet   It shall to the barber's with your beard! Prithee say
490   on. He's for a jig or a tale of bawdry, or he sleeps. Say on,
come to Hecuba.

1st Player   *But who – ah, woe! – had seen the mobled queen –*

Hamlet   *The mobled queen?*

Polonius   That's good.

495 **1st Player**   *Run barefoot up and down, threat'ning the flames*
>   *With bisson rheum, a clout upon that head*
>   *Where late the diadem stood, and, for a robe,*
>   *About her lank and all o'erteemed loins*
>   *A blanket, in th'alarm of fear caught up –*
> 500   *Who this had seen, with tongue in venom steeped,*
>   *'Gainst Fortune's state would treason have pronounced.*

Did nothing.
But as we often see when storms are due
A silence in the heavens; the clouds quite still;
The bold winds silent, and the world below
As calm as death – at last the dreadful thunder
Rends the air. Likewise, after Pyrrhus' pause,
Awakened vengeance sets to work anew;
And never did the Cyclops' hammers fall
On Mars's armor, made for everlasting strength,
With less compassion than the bloody sword of Pyrrhus
Now falls on Priam.
Out, out, oh wanton Fortune! All you gods –
Agree collectively to take away her power!
Break all the spokes and the rim sections of her wheel,
And bowl the round hub down the hill of heaven
As low as to the fiends!

Polonius   This is too long.

Hamlet   It shall go to the barber's, to be trimmed along with
your beard.   [*To the* **Actor**]   Please go on. He's all for a
farce, or a smutty story; otherwise he falls asleep. Say on.
Come to Hecuba.

1st Actor   *But who – ah, woe! – had seen the muffled*
queen –

Hamlet   ''*The muffled queen*''?

Polonius   That's good!

1st Actor   *– Run barefoot up and down, threatening the*
flames
With blinding tears, a rag upon that head
Where late her crown had stood; and for a robe,
Around her thin and weakened loins
A blanket: caught up in the alarm of fear –
Whoever had seen this, his tongue in venom steeped,
Would treason have declared, in protest at her state.

> *But if the gods themselves did see her then,*
> *When she saw Pyrrus make malicious sport*
> *In mincing with his sword her husband's limbs,*
> *The instant burst of clamour that she made,*
> *Unless things mortal move them not at all,*
> *Would have made milch the burning eyes of heaven*
> *And passion in the gods.*

505

Polonius   Look whe'er he has not turned his colour and has
510   tears in's eyes. Prithee no more.

Hamlet   'Tis well. I'll have thee speak out the rest of this
soon. Good my lord, will you see the players well bestowed?
Do you hear, let them be well used, for they are the abstract
and brief chronicles of the time. After your death you were
515   better to have a bad epitaph than their ill report while you
live.

Polonius   My lord, I will use them according to their desert.

Hamlet   God's bodykins, man, much better. Use every man
after his desert, and who shall scape whipping? Use them
520   after your own honour and dignity: the less they deserve, the
more merit is in your bounty. Take them in.

Polonius   Come, sirs.

Hamlet   Follow him, friends. We'll hear a play
tomorrow.   [*To* **1st Player**]   Dost thou hear me, old
525   friend? Can you play *The Murder of Gonzago*?

1st Player   Ay, my lord.

Hamlet   We'll ha't tomorrow night. You could for a need
study a speech of some dozen or sixteen lines, which I would
set down and insert in't, could you not?

530   **1st Player**   Ay, my lord.

But if the gods themselves did see her then,
When she saw Pyrrhus make an evil sport
Of mutilating with his sword her husband's limbs,
Her instant lament howling
(Unless things mortal do not touch their hearts)
Would make the twinkling stars give forth their tears
And stir the feelings of the gods.

Polonius   Look how his color has changed, and there are tears in his eyes. Please, no more.

Hamlet   That's fine. I'll have you recite the rest of this soon.   [*To* **Polonius**]   Good my lord, will you see that the actors are comfortably lodged? Do you hear: they must be well cared for. They are the recorders of the history of our time. After your death, you'd be better with a bad epitaph than unfavorable publicity from them while you are alive.

Polonius   My lord, I shall treat them as they deserve.

Hamlet   By God's dear body, man, much better! Treat everybody, as he deserves and who wouldn't be flogged? Treat them honorably and with dignity as becomes you; the less they deserve, the more your generosity is praiseworthy. Take them in.

Polonius   Come, sirs.

Hamlet   Follow him, friends. We'll hear a play tomorrow.   [*To* **1st Actor**]   A word with you, old friend. Can you perform *The Murder of Gonzago*?

1st Actor   Yes, my lord.

Hamlet   We'll have it tomorrow night. If necessary, you could learn a speech of some dozen or sixteen lines that I'll write down and insert in it, couldn't you?

1st Actor   Yes, my lord.

Hamlet   Very well.   [*To the* **Players**]   Follow that lord, and
   look you mock him not.

Exeunt **Polonius** *and* **Players**]

[*To* **Rosencrantz** *and* **Guildenstern**]   My good friends, I'll
leave you till night. You are welcome to Elsinore.

535 **Rosencrantz**   Good my lord.

[*Exeunt* **Rosencrantz** *and* **Guildenstern**]

Hamlet   Ay, so, God be wi'ye. Now I am alone.
         O, what a rogue and peasant slave am I!
         Is it not monstrous that this player here,
         But in a fiction, in a dream of passion,
540   Could force his soul so to his own conceit
         That from her working all his visage wanned,
         Tears in his eyes, distraction in his aspect,
         A broken voice, and his whole function suiting
         With forms to his conceit? And all for nothing!
545   For Hecuba!
         What's Hecuba to him, or he to Hecuba,
         That he should weep for her? What would he do
         Had he the motive and the cue for passion
         That I have? He would drown the stage with tears,
550   And cleave the general ear with horrid speech,
         Make mad the guilty and appal the free,
         Confound the ignorant, and amaze indeed
         The very faculties of eyes and ears.
         Yet I,
555   A dull and muddy-mettled rascal, peak
         Like John-a-dreams, unpregnant of my cause,
         And can say nothing – no, not for a king,
         Upon whose property and most dear life
         A damned defeat was made. Am I a coward?
560   Who calls me villain, breaks my pate across,

Hamlet   Good.   [*To all the* **Actors**]   Follow that lord – and see you don't make fun of him!

[**Polonius** *and the* **Actors** *leave*]

[*To* **Rosencrantz** *and* **Guildenstern**]   My good friends. I'll leave you till tonight. You are welcome to Elsinore.

Rosencrantz   [*bowing*]   Good my lord.

[**Rosencrantz** *and* **Guildenstern** *leave*]

Hamlet   Indeed so. Goodbye. Now I am alone. Oh, what a villain and a worthless wretch I am! Isn't it astounding that this actor here, in a mere story, in a make-believe of passion, could give such expression to imaginary feelings. That his face turned pale, tears came to his eyes, distress showed in his looks, his voice broke; with his gestures aptly expressing his emotions. And all for nothing! For Hecuba! What does Hecuba care about him, or he care about Hecuba, that he should weep for her? What would he do if he had the motive and the reason for passion that I have? He'd drown the stage with tears; rant and rave; make guilty men insane and terrify the innocent; astonish the ignorant; and throw the faculties of sight and hearing into total confusion. Yet I, a lazy and miserable rascal, mope about like Johnny Daydreams, lacking inspiration for my cause, and unable to say a word – no, not even on behalf of a King who was damnably murdered. Am I a coward? Does anyone call me a villain, hit me over the head, pull out my beard and

Plucks off my beard and blows it in my face,
Tweaks me by the nose, gives me the lie i'th'throat
As deep as to the lungs? Who does me this?
Ha!
565 'Swounds, I should take it; for it cannot be
But I am pigeon-livered and lack gall
To make oppression bitter, or ere this
I should ha' fatted all the region kites
With this slave's offal. Bloody, bawdy villain!
570 Remorseless, treacherous, lecherous, kindless villain!
Why, what an ass am I! This is most brave,
That I, the son of a dear father murdered,
Prompted to my revenge by heaven and hell,
Must like a whore unpack my heart with words
575 And fall a-cursing like a very drab,
A scullion! Fie upon't! Foh!
About, my brains. I have heard
That guilty creatures sitting at a play
Have, by the very cunning of the scene,
580 Been struck so to the soul that presently
They have proclaimed their malefactions.
For murder, though it have no tongue, will speak
With most miraculous organ. I'll have these players
Play something like the murder of my father
585 Before mine uncle. I'll observe his looks;
I'll tent him to the quick. If he but blench,
I know my course. The spirit that I have seen
May be a devil, and the devil hath power
T'assume a pleasing shape, yea, and perhaps,
590 Out of my weakness and my melancholy,
As he is very potent with such spirits,
Abuses me to damn me. I'll have grounds
More relative than this. The play's the thing
Wherein I'll catch the conscience of the King.

[*Exit*]

blow it in my face, tell me I'm a dirty liar? Does anyone?
Pah! Truly, I'd take it. I must surely be chicken-livered,
lacking the guts to resent abuse: otherwise, before this I
would have fattened all the vultures in creation with this
wretch's entrails. Bloody, bawdy, villain! Pitiless,
treacherous, lecherous, unnatural villain!   [*He takes a grip
of himself*] Why, what an idiot I am! How very admirable:
that I, the son of a beloved, murdered father – stirred to my
revenge by both heaven and hell – should express myself in
words like a foul-mouthed whore, and fall to cursing like a
common slut! It's too much! Ugh!   [*He pauses, recov-
ering*]   I must think. Hmm . . . [*An idea occurs*]   I've heard
that guilty persons, while attending a play, have been so
affected by the realism of the performance that they have
immediately confessed their crimes: because murder,
though it's mute, will speak out with most miraculous
power. I'll get these actors to perform something that
resembles the murder of my father, with my uncle present.
I'll observe his looks. I'll scrutinize him minutely. If he reacts,
I know what to do. The ghost I've seen may be a devil, and
the devil has the power to appear in attractive forms: yes,
and perhaps, out of my weakness and my melancholy – as
he is very powerful in such circumstances – he's deluding
me to damn me. I'll have better proof than this. The play's
the way I'll entrap the conscience of the King!

[*He leaves*]

Act three

Scene 1

Enter **King, Queen, Polonius, Ophelia, Rosencrantz, Guildenstern.**

King And can you by no drift of conference
Get from him why he puts on this confusion,
Grating so harshly all his days of quiet
With turbulent and dangerous lunacy?

5 **Rosencrantz** He does confess he feels himself distracted,
But from what cause he will by no means speak.

Guildenstern Nor do we find him forward to be sounded,
But with a crafty madness keeps aloof
When we would bring him on to some confession
10 Of his true state.

Queen Did he receive you well?

Rosencrantz Most like a gentleman.

Guildenstern But with much forcing of his disposition.

Rosencrantz Niggard of question, but of our demands
15 Most free in his reply.

Queen Did you assay him
To any pastime?

Rosencrantz Madam, it so fell out that certain players
We o'erraught on the way. Of these we told him,
20 And there did seem in him a kind of joy

Act three

Scene 1

The King's apartments in the castle. Enter the **King,** *the* **Queen, Polonius, Ophelia, Rosencrantz** *and* **Guildenstern.**

King [*to* **Rosencrantz** *and* **Guildenstern**]   And cannot you discover by talking with him the reason why he acts in this confused way, disturbing his calm of mind with wild and dangerous lunacy?

Rosencrantz   He admits he feels deranged, but he won't under any circumstances say why.

Guildenstern   Nor have we found him eager to be questioned. He cunningly avoids the issue when we sound him out.

Queen   Did he welcome you?

Rosencrantz   Most politely.

Guildenstern   But with a great effort.

Rosencrantz   He was somewhat reticent, but he answered our inquiries freely.

Queen   Did you check his interest in any entertainment?

Rosencrantz   Madam, it so happened that we overtook some actors on our way there. We told him of them, and he seemed quite pleased to hear the news. They are here at

To hear of it. They are here about the court,
And, as I think, they have already order
This night to play before him.

Polonius   'Tis most true,
25   And he beseeched me to entreat your Majesties
To hear and see the matter.

King   With all my heart; and it doth much content me
To hear him so inclined.
Good gentlemen, give him a further edge,
30   And drive his purpose into these delights.

Rosencrantz   We shall, my lord.

[*Exeunt* **Rosencrantz** *and* **Guildenstern**]

King   Sweet Gertrude, leave us too,
For we have closely sent for Hamlet hither
That he, as 'twere by accident, may here
35   Affront Ophelia.
Her father and myself, lawful espials,
Will so bestow ourselves that, seeing unseen,
We may of their encounter frankly judge,
And gather by him, as he is behaved,
40   If't be th'affliction of his love or no
That thus he suffers for.

Queen   I shall obey you.
And for your part, Ophelia, I do wish
That your good beauties be the happy cause
45   Of Hamlet's wildness; so shall I hope your virtues
Will bring him to his wonted way again,
To both your honours.

Ophelia   Madam, I wish it may.

[*Exit* **Queen**]

court, and I believe they've already been commissioned to perform for him tonight.

Polonius That's right. And he asked me to entreat your majesties to hear and see the play.

King With all my heart. I'm pleased he's so disposed [*To* **Rosencrantz** *and* **Guildenstern**] Gentlemen, encourage him further, and steer him towards these pleasures.

Rosencrantz We will, my lord.

[**Rosencrantz** *and* **Guildenstern** *leave*]

King Gertrude dear, leave us too. We have conspired to send for Hamlet so that he can confront Ophelia here, as if by accident. Her father and I, as legitimate observers, will conceal ourselves so that we can see without being seen, in order to make a frank assessment of their encounter, and deduce from his behavior whether or not he's suffering from lovesickness.

Queen I'll do as you say. As for you, Ophelia, I do hope that your charms are the happy cause of Hamlet's madness, and equally that your attractions will restore him to his right mind again, in both your interests.

Ophelia Madam, I hope so too.

[*The* **Queen** *leaves*]

Polonius   Ophelia, walk you here. Gracious, so please you,
50   We will bestow ourselves. Read on this book,
That show of such an exercise may colour
Your loneliness. We are oft to blame in this,
'Tis too much proved, that with devotion's visage
And pious action we do sugar o'er
55   The devil himself.

King   [*aside*]   O, 'tis too true.
How smart a lash that speech doth give my conscience!
The harlot's cheek, beautied with plast'ring art,
Is not more ugly to the thing that helps it
60   Than is my deed to my most painted word.
O heavy burden!

Polonius   I hear him coming. Let's withdraw, my lord.

[*Exeunt* **King** *and* **Polonius**]

[*Enter* **Hamlet**]

Hamlet   To be, or not to be, that is the question:
Whether 'tis nobler in the mind to suffer
65   The slings and arrows of outrageous fortune,
Or to take arms against a sea of troubles
And by opposing end them. To die – to sleep,
No more; and by a sleep to say we end
The heart-ache and the thousand natural shocks
70   That flesh is heir to: 'tis a consummation
Devoutly to be wished. To die, to sleep;
To sleep, perchance to dream – ay, there's the rub:
For in that sleep of death what dreams may come,
When we have shuffled off this mortal coil,
75   Must give us pause – there's the respect
That makes calamity of so long life.
For who would bear the whips and scorns of time,
The oppressor's wrong, the proud man's contumely,

Polonius Ophelia, walk here. [*To the **King**, indicating a hiding place*] Your majesty, if you would be so good: we'll conceal ourselves. [*To **Ophelia** again, giving her a book*] Read this prayer book, to give authenticity to your being alone. [*To the **King***] We're often guilty in this respect, as we know from experience: we conceal the devil's work by holy looks and pious actions.

King [*to himself*] Oh, true indeed! How that speech agonizes my conscience! The harlot's painted face is not more ugly in its artificiality than my deeds are when related to my bogus words. Oh, it's a heavy burden!

Polonius I hear him coming. Let's hide, my lord.

[*The **King** and **Polonius** conceal themselves*]

[**Hamlet** *enters*]

Hamlet [*to himself*] To live or not to live. That is the issue. Is it more noble to endure the blows of fickle fortune, or to fight against overwhelming odds and overcome them? To die is to sleep: nothing more. And if – by a sleep – we could end the heartaches and the thousand everyday anxieties that humans suffer, it would be an outcome to be cordially welcomed. To die . . . to sleep . . . to sleep and perhaps to dream . . . Yes, there's the catch! Those dreams that we might have during that sleep of death – after we've cast off the hurly-burly of mortal life – must make us hesitate. That's what makes us tolerate suffering so long. Who would bear the torments of the world we live in – the tyrant's injustice, the arrogant man's rudeness, the pangs of

The pangs of despised love, the law's delay,
80   The insolence of office, and the spurns
That patient merit of the unworthy takes,
When he himself might his quietus make
With a bare bodkin? Who would fardels bear,
To grunt and sweat under a weary life,
85   But that the dread of something after death,
The undiscovered country, from whose bourn
No traveller returns, puzzles the will,
And make us rather bear those ills we have
Than fly to others that we know not of?
90   Thus conscience does make cowards of us all,
And thus the native hue of resolution
Is sicklied o'er with the pale cast of thought,
And enterprises of great pitch and moment
With this regard their currents turn awry
95   And lose the name of action. Soft you now,
The fair Ophelia! Nymph, in thy orisons
Be all my sins remembered.

Ophelia   Good my lord,
How does your honour for this many a day?

100 **Hamlet**   I humbly thank you, well.

Ophelia   My lord, I have remembrances of yours
That I have longed long to redeliver.
I pray you now receive them.

Hamlet   No, not I.
105   I never gave you aught.

Ophelia   My honoured lord, you know right well you did,
And with them words of so sweet breath composed
As made the things more rich. Their perfume lost,
Take these again; for to the noble mind
110   Rich gifts wax poor when givers prove unkind.
There, my lord.

unrequited love, the slow process of law, the insolence of persons in authority, and the insults that the humble suffer – when he could settle everything himself with a mere dagger? Who would be a beast of burden, grunting and sweating with fatigue, if it were not that the dread of something after death – the unexplored country from whose territory no traveler returns – makes us ambivalent and makes us choose to bear the troubles that we have, rather than fly to others that we know nothing about. That's why our intelligence makes us all cowards, and why our determination – normally so healthy-looking – takes on a sickly pallor through thinking too much about precise details. This process causes ventures of the highest importance to go astray and lose their impetus.   [*He sees* **Ophelia**]   But hush! The beautiful Ophelia!   [*Speaking to her*]   Young lady: remember all my sins in your prayers.

Ophelia   My lord, how is your honor these days?

Hamlet   I humbly thank you: well.

Ophelia   My lord, I have keepsakes of yours that I have wanted to return to you for a long time. I'd besobliged if you'd take them now.

Hamlet   No. Not I. I have never given you anything.

Ophelia   My honored lord, you know very well that you did, and that you accompanied them with such fragrant sentiments as to make them especially precious. Since their perfume has faded, take these presents back again: to sensitive people, generous gifts are devalued when the givers become uncaring.

Hamlet   Ha, ha! Are you honest?

Ophelia   My lord?

Hamlet   Are you fair?

115 **Ophelia**   What means your lordship?

Hamlet   That if you be honest and fair, your honesty should
admit no discourse to your beauty.

Ophelia   Could beauty, my lord, have better commerce than
with honesty?

120 **Hamlet**   Ay, truly; for the power of beauty will sooner
transform honesty from what it is to a bawd than the force of
honesty can translate beauty into his likeness. This was
sometime a paradox, but now the time gives it proof. I did
love you once.

125 **Ophelia**   Indeed, my lord, you made me believe so.

Hamlet   You should not have believed me; for virtue cannot
so inoculate our old stock but we shall relish of it. I loved
you not.

Ophelia   I was the more deceived.

130 **Hamlet**   Get thee to a nunnery. Why wouldst thou be a
breeder of sinners? I am myself indifferent honest, but yet I
could accuse me of such things that it were better my mother
had not borne me. I am very proud, revengeful, ambitious,
with more offences at my beck than I have thoughts to put
135 them in, imagination to give them shape, or time to act them
in. What should such fellows as I do crawling between earth
and heaven? We are arrant knaves all; believe none of us. Go
thy ways to a nunnery. Where's your father?

Ophelia   At home, my lord.

140 **Hamlet**   Let the doors be shut upon him, that he may play
the fool nowhere but in's own house. Farewell.

146

Hamlet   Oh yes?   [*Looking at her keenly*]   Are you chaste?

Ophelia   [*taken aback*]   My lord?

Hamlet   Are you beautiful?

Ophelia   What does your lordship mean?

Hamlet   That if you are both chaste *and* beautiful, your chastity should protect your beauty.

Ophelia   Could beauty, my lord, have a safer relationship than with chastity?

Hamlet   Yes, indeed! Beauty can more easily corrupt chastity than chastity can turn beauty into a quality like itself. Once upon a time this was unthinkable, but now there's living proof of it. I loved you, once.

Ophelia   Indeed, my lord, you made me believe you did.

Hamlet   You shouldn't have believed me: a leopard cannot change its spots. That wasn't love.

Ophelia   I was certainly taken in.

Hamlet   Become a nun! What, do you want to give birth to sinners? I'm reasonably moral myself, but I could plead guilty to such things that my mother ought never to have had me. I'm very proud, revengeful, ambitious; with more potential for wrongdoing than my thoughts can conceive, my imagination can fill out, or I have time to put into practice. What right have wretches like me to life? We are all out-and-out scoundrels. Don't believe any of us. Take yourself off to a convent. Where's your father?

Ophelia   At home, my lord.

Hamlet   Lock him in, so that he'll act the fool nowhere but in his own house. Goodbye.

Ophelia   O, help him, you sweet heavens!

Hamlet   If thou dost marry, I'll give thee this plague for thy
dowry: be thou as chaste as ice, as pure as snow, thou shalt
145   not escape calumny. Get thee to a nunnery, farewell. Or if
thou wilt needs marry, marry a fool; for wise men know well
enough what monsters you make of them. To a nunnery, go;
and quickly too. Farewell.

Ophelia   Heavenly powers, restore him!

150 **Hamlet**   I have heard of your paintings well enough. God
hath given you one face and you make yourselves another.
You jig, you amble, and you lisp, you nickname God's
creatures, and make your wantonness your ignorance. Go to,
I'll no more on't, it hath made me mad. I say we will have
155   no more marriages. Those that are married already, all but
one, shall live; the rest shall keep as they are. To a nunnery,
go.

                                        [*Exit*]

Ophelia   O, what a noble mind is here o'erthrown!
    The courtier's, soldier's, scholar's, eye, tongue, sword,
160   Th'expectancy and rose of the fair state,
    The glass of fashion and the mould of form,
    Th'observed of all observers, quite, quite down!
    And I, of ladies most deject and wretched,
    That sucked the honey of his music vows,
165   Now see that noble and most sovereign reason
    Like sweet bells jangled out of tune and harsh,
    That unmatched form and feature of blown youth
    Blasted with ecstasy. O woe is me
    T'have seen what I have seen, see what I see.

[*Enter* **King** *and* **Polonius**]

Ophelia   [*distressed at his apparent madness*]   God help him!

Hamlet   If you do marry, I'll give you this unpleasant fact for your dowry: even if you're as chaste as ice, as pure as snow, you won't avoid scandal. Go to a convent. Farewell. Or if you insist on marrying, marry a fool. Intelligent men know well enough what cuckolds you make of them. Go to a convent, and quick about it. Farewell.

Ophelia   May the gods make him well again!

Hamlet   I know all about your cosmetics. God has given you one face, and you make yourselves another. You wiggle and mince, you put on fancy voices, you use fashionable words, and pretend your affectations are natural. Right, I've had enough; it has made me mad. I say we'll have no more marriages. Those who are married already – all except one! – shall be allowed to continue. The rest shall stay as they are. Go to a convent . . .

[*He leaves*]

Ophelia   Oh, what a noble mind has lost its reason! His courtier's looks, his soldier's skill, his scholarly speech; his promise and perfection as a future king; the model and the mold for others to follow; the most honored amongst the honorable – utterly, utterly ruined! And I, the most dejected and wretched of women, who fed upon his honeyed, pleasing words, now see that noble and supremely excellent reason all harshly out of tune, like sweet bells ringing discordantly; that incomparable example of youth in its prime, devastated by insanity. Oh, alas that I should have seen what I have seen; that I can see what I see now!

[*The* **King** *and* **Polonius** *enter*]

170 **King**   Love! His affections do not that way tend,
　　　　　Nor what he spake, though it lacked form a little,
　　　　　Was not like madness. There's something in his soul
　　　　　O'er which his melancholy sits on brood,
　　　　　And I do doubt the hatch and the disclose
175　　　Will be some danger; which for to prevent,
　　　　　I have in quick determination
　　　　　Thus set it down: he shall with speed to England
　　　　　For the demand of our neglected tribute.
　　　　　Haply the seas and countries different,
180　　　With variable objects, shall expel
　　　　　This something-settled matter in his heart,
　　　　　Whereon his brains still beating puts him thus
　　　　　From fashion of himself. What think you on't?

　　　Polonius   It shall do well. But yet do I believe
185　　　The origin and commencement of his grief
　　　　　Sprung from neglected love. How now, Ophelia!
　　　　　You need not tell us what Lord Hamlet said,
　　　　　We heard it all. My lord, do as you please,
　　　　　But if you hold it fit, after the play
190　　　Let his queen-mother all alone entreat him
　　　　　To show his grief: let her be round with him,
　　　　　And I'll be placed, so please you, in the ear
　　　　　Of all their conference. If she find him not,
　　　　　To England send him; or confine him where
195　　　Your wisdom best shall think.

　　　King　　　　　　　　　　　　　It shall be so.
　　　　　Madness in great ones must not unwatched go.

　　　　　　　　　　　　　　　　　　　　　　　[Exeunt]

King Love? He's not inclined that way; nor was what he said indicative of madness, though it *was* a little lacking in coherence. He's brooding about something deep down, and I fear the outcome involves danger. To prevent it, I have just decided this: he shall be sent to England immediately to collect our outstanding protection money. With luck, the sea journey, the change of scenery, and some sightseeing will cure him of this obsession, which is making him act so strangely. What do you think?

Polonius A good idea. But I still think that his grief can be traced back to unrequited love. [*To his daughter, apparently not noticing her distress*] All right, Ophelia. You needn't tell us what Lord Hamlet said. We heard it all. [*To the* **King**] My lord, do what you wish; but if you approve, after the play ends let his mother the Queen persuade him in private to reveal the reasons for his grief. Let her be forthright with him, and with your permission I'll be concealed where I can hear all they say. If she doesn't find out the truth, then send him to England – or lock him up where you in your wisdom think best.

King Agreed. Madness in the great must not go unheeded.

[*They leave*]

Scene 2

Enter **Hamlet** *and the* **Players**.

Hamlet   Speak the speech, I pray you, as I pronounced it to
you, trippingly on the tongue; but if you mouth it as many of
your players do, I had as lief the town-crier spoke my lines.
Nor do not saw the air too much with your hand, thus, but
5   use all gently; for in the very torrent, tempest, and, as I may
say, whirlwind of your passion, you must acquire and beget
a temperance that may give it smoothness. O, it offends me
to the soul to hear a robustious periwig-pated fellow tear a
passion to tatters, to very rags, to split the ears of the
10   groundlings, who for the most part are capable of nothing
but inexplicable dumb-shows and noise. I would have such
a fellow whipped for o'erdoing Termagant. It out-Herods
Herod. Pray you avoid it.

1st Player   I warrant your honour.

15   **Hamlet**   Be not too tame neither, but let your own discretion
be your tutor. Suit the action to the word, the word to the
action, with this special observance, that you o'erstep not the
modesty of nature. For anything so o'erdone is from the
purpose of playing, whose end, both at the first and now,
20   was and is to hold as 'twere the mirror up to nature; to show
virtue her feature, scorn her own image, and the very age
and body of the time his form and pressure. Now this
overdone, or come tardy off, though it makes the unskilful
laugh, cannot but make the judicious grieve, the censure of
25   the which one must in your allowance o'erweigh a whole
theatre of others. O, there be players that I have seen
play – and heard others praise, and that highly – not to
speak it profanely, that neither having th'accent of
Christians, nor the gait of Christian, pagan, nor man, have

Scene 2

Hamlet *enters with three of the* **Actors.** *He is advising them on their acting techniques.*

Hamlet Please speak the speech as I recited it to you, in a natural way. If you overdo it, as many actors do, I'd rather the town crier spoke my lines. And don't saw the air too much with your hand, either, like this [*he demonstrates a histrionic gesture*] but do everything with restraint: because as your passion reaches torrential, tempestuous, and, as it were, whirlwind proportions, you must develop a self-control that will give it a natural ease. Oh, it gets on my nerves to hear a ham actor in a wig tear a passion to shreds – to rags even – just to play to the unsophisticated standees in the pit who for the most part are capable only of appreciating mindless mime-shows and spectaculars. I'd have a fellow like that whipped for overacting the villain's part: a Demon King would seem mild by comparison. Do avoid that, please!

1st Actor Of course, your honor.

Hamlet Don't be too feeble, either. Use your discretion. Make your gestures suit what you say, and vice-versa. One proviso: don't overact. Anything overdone is against the purpose of acting, which was (and still is) to reflect reality: to demonstrate what's virtuous, to expose the deplorable, and to depict faithfully the essential nature of contemporary life. To be larger than life, or to fall short of it, may make the undiscerning laugh, but it makes people with taste groan – and their opinion, you must admit, outweighs an entire theaterful of the others. Oh, I've seen some actors – and heard people praise them, and very highly too – who neither speak like decent, ordinary men, nor move like Christian, pagan or what-have-you. They've

30   so strutted and bellowed that I have thought some of
        Nature's journeymen had made men, and not made them
        well, they imitated humanity so abominably.

1st Player I hope we have reformed that indifferently with
    us, sir.

35 **Hamlet** O reform it altogether. And let those that play your
        clowns speak no more than is set down for them; for there be
        of them that will themselves laugh, to set on some quantity
        of barren spectators to laugh too, though in the meantime
        some necessary question of the play be then to be
40   considered. That's villainous, and shows a most pitiful
        ambition in the fool that uses it. Go make you ready.

[Exeunt **Players**]

[Enter **Polonius, Rosencrantz,** *and* **Guildenstern**]

How now, my lord? Will the King hear this piece of work?

Polonius And the Queen too, and that presently.

Hamlet Bid the players make haste.

[Exit **Polonius**]

45 Will you two help to hasten them?

Rosencrantz Ay, my lord.

[Exeunt **Rosencrantz** *and* **Guildenstern**]

Hamlet What ho, Horatio!

[Enter **Horatio**]

Horatio Here, sweet lord, at your service.

154

strutted about and bellowed so much that I've concluded men must be the product of Nature's shoddy workmanship, so abominably is humanity represented.

1st Actor I hope we've got that under reasonable control in our case.

Hamlet Oh, control it absolutely. And let your comedians stick to their lines. There are some who laugh themselves, to get a number of foolish spectators to laugh too, in the meantime causing some necessary part of the plot to be delayed. That's unforgivable, and demonstrates a contemptible ambition in the comic who indulges in it. Go and get ready.

[*The* **Actors** *leave*]

[**Polonius, Rosencrantz** *and* **Guildenstern** *enter*]

Well now, my lord: will the King hear this play?

Polonius And the Queen too, and right away.

Hamlet Tell the actors to hurry.

[**Polonius** *leaves*]

Will you two help to hurry them on?

Rosencrantz Yes, my lord.

[**Rosencrantz** *and* **Guildenstern** *leave*]

Hamlet Horatio!

[**Horatio** *enters*]

Horatio Here, sweet lord: at your service.

Hamlet   Horatio, thou art e'en as just a man
50   As e'er my conversation coped withal.

Horatio   O my dear lord!

Hamlet   Nay, do not think I flatter,
For what advancement may I hope from thee
That no revenue hast but thy good spirits
55   To feed and clothe thee? Why should the poor be flattered?
No, let the candied tongue lick absurd pomp,
And crook the pregnant hinges of the knee
Where thrift may follow fawning. Dost thou hear?
Since my dear soul was mistress of her choice,
60   And could of men distinguish her election,
Hath sealed thee for herself; for thou hast been
As one, in suff'ring all, that suffers nothing,
A man that Fortune's buffets and rewards
Hast ta'en with equal thanks; and blest are those
65   Whose blood and judgment are so well co-mingled
That they are not a pipe for Fortune's finger
To sound what stop she please. Give me that man
That is not passion's slave, and I will wear him
In my heart's core, ay, in my heart of hearts,
70   As I do thee. Something too much of this.
There is a play tonight before the King:
One scene of it comes near the circumstance
Which I have told thee of my father's death.
I prithee, when thou seest that act afoot,
75   Even with the very comment of thy soul
Observe my uncle. If his occulted guilt
Do not itself unkennel in one speech,
It is a damned ghost that we have seen,
And my imaginations are as foul
80   As Vulcan's stithy. Give him heedful note;
For I mine eyes will rivet to his face,
And after we will both our judgments join
In censure of his seeming.

Hamlet   Horatio, you're as steady a man as I've ever talked to.

Horatio   [*blushing*]   Oh, my dear lord!

Hamlet   No, don't think I'm flattering you; what advantage can I hope for from you, whose only asset is your good spirits? Why should anyone flatter the poor? No, let flatterers keep their sweet talk for the vanity of the great, and bow their ever-willing knees where there's advantage to be gained from fawning. Listen: ever since I could tell one man's qualities from another's, I've singled you out for friendship. You've been the sort of man who has accustomed himself to suffering, having suffered so much; a man who tolerates both good luck and bad: and blessed are they whose temper and self-control are so well balanced that they aren't at Fortune's mercy, doing her bidding. Give me the man who isn't a slave to his emotions, and I'll take him to my heart, the very center of it, as I do you. That's enough of that. There's a play being performed tonight in the presence of the King. One scene in it resembles the circumstances of my father's death, which I've told you about. When you see that part performed, I'd ask you to watch my uncle with the keenest observation you can muster. If his hidden guilt doesn't come out into the open during one particular speech, then it's a *damned* ghost that we have seen, and my suspicions are as foul as hell. Take careful note of him. My eyes will be riveted on his face. Later we'll compare notes in judging his demeanor.

Horatio   Well, my lord.
85   If he steal aught the whilst this play is playing
And scape detecting, I will pay the theft.

Hamlet   They are coming to the play. I must be idle.
Get you a place.

[*Enter* **King, Queen, Polonius, Ophelia, Rosencrantz,
Guildenstern,** *and the other Lords attendant, with the King's
Guard carrying torches*]

King   How fares our cousin Hamlet?

90   **Hamlet**   Excellent, i'faith, of the chameleon's dish. I eat the
air, promise-crammed. You cannot feed capons so.

King   I have nothing with this answer, Hamlet. These words
are not mine.

Hamlet   No, nor mine now. [*To* **Polonius**] My lord, you
95   played once i'th'university, you say?

Polonius   That did I, my lord, and was accounted a good
actor.

Hamlet   What did you enact?

Polonius   I did enact Julius Caesar. I was killed i'th'Capitol.
100   Brutus killed me.

Hamlet   It was a brute part of him to kill so capital a calf
there. Be the players ready?

Rosencrantz   Ay, my lord, they stay upon your patience.

Queen   Come hither, my dear Hamlet, sit by me.

Horatio   Yes indeed, my lord. If he steals anything while this play is being performed, and escapes detection, I'll pay for what is taken.

[*Trumpets and kettledrums are heard approaching*]

Hamlet   They're coming to the play. I must act crazy. Get yourself a seat.

[*The* **King, Queen, Polonius, Ophelia, Rosencrantz, Guildenstern**, *and other Lords and Attendants enter, with* **Guards** *carrying torches*]

King   How is our nephew Hamlet?

Hamlet   Excellent, indeed. Eating the same food as chameleons: fresh air and empty promises. You can't feed chickens like that.

King   I don't follow your answer, Hamlet. These words don't relate to me.

Hamlet   No, or to me either, now.   [*To* **Polonius**]   My lord, you acted once at the University, you say?

Polonius   I certainly did, my lord, and was considered a good actor.

Hamlet   What did you play?

Polonius   I was Julius Caesar. I was killed in the Capitol. Brutus killed me.

Hamlet   What a brute he was, to kill so capital an idiot there! Are the actors ready?

Rosencrantz   Yes, my lord; ready when you are.

Queen   Come here, my dear Hamlet, and sit by me.

105 **Hamlet**   No, good mother, here's metal more attractive.

[*Turns to* **Ophelia**]

Polonius   [*aside to the* **King**]   O ho! Do you mark that?

Hamlet   [*lying down at* **Ophelia's** *feet*]   Lady, shall I lie in
your lap?

Ophelia   No, my lord.

110 **Hamlet**   I mean, my head upon your lap.

Ophelia   Ay, my lord.

Hamlet   Do you think I meant country matters?

Ophelia   I think nothing, my lord.

Hamlet   That's a fair thought to lie between maids' legs.

115 **Ophelia**   What is, my lord?

Hamlet   Nothing.

Ophelia   You are merry, my lord.

Hamlet   Who, I?

Ophelia   Ay, my lord.

120 **Hamlet**   O God, your only jig-maker! What should a man do
but be merry? For look you how cheerfully my mother looks
and my father died within's two hours.

Ophelia   Nay, 'tis twice two months, my lord.

Hamlet   So long? Nay then, let the devil wear black, for I'll
125   have a suit of sables. O heavens, die two months ago and
not forgotten yet! Then there's hope a great man's memory
may outlive his life half a year. But by'r lady he must build

Hamlet   No, good mother. I'm drawn to something more attractive.

[*He turns to* **Ophelia**]

Polonius   [*aside to the* **King**]   Oh, ho! Did you note that?

Hamlet   [*lying down at* **Ophelia**'s *feet*]   Lady, shall I lie in your lap?

Ophelia   [*blushing*]   No, my lord.

Hamlet   I mean, with my *head* upon your lap.

Ophelia   Yes, my lord.

Hamlet   Did you think I meant something naughty?

Ophelia   I thought nothing, my lord.

Hamlet   It's nice to think of that lying between maidens' legs.

Ophelia   What is, my lord?

Hamlet   Nothing . . .

Ophelia   You are merry, my lord.

Hamlet   Who, I?

Ophelia   Yes, my lord.

Hamlet   Oh God – your actual comedy writer! What else should a man be but merry? Look how cheerful my mother looks, and my father dead less than two hours.

Ophelia   No, it's four months, my lord.

Hamlet   So long? In that case, the devil should wear his customary black, and I'll get myself expensive mourning clothes. Imagine! died two months ago and not yet forgotten! So there's some hope that a great man might still be remembered six months after he dies! But by all that's

churches then, or else shall he suffer not thinking on, with
the hobby-horse, whose epitaph is, *For O, for O, the*
130   *hobby-horse is forgot.*

[*The trumpets sound. A dumb-show follows*]

Enter a **King** *and a* **Queen,** *very lovingly, the* **Queen**
*embracing him and he her. She kneels, and makes show of
protestation unto him. He takes her up, and declines his head
upon her neck. He lies him down upon a bank of flowers. She,
seeing him asleep, leaves him. Anon comes in another* **Man,**
*takes off his crown, kisses it, pours poison in the sleeper's ears,
and leaves him. The* **Queen** *returns, finds the* **King** *dead,
makes passionate action. The* **Poisoner** *with some Three or
Four comes in again. They seem to condole with her. The dead
body is carried away. The* **Poisoner** *woos the* **Queen** *with gifts.
She seems harsh awhile, but in the end accepts his love.*

[*Exeunt*]

Ophelia   What means this, my lord?

Hamlet   Marry, this is miching mallecho. It means mischief.

Ophelia   Belike this show imports the argument of the play.

[*Enter* **Prologue**]

Hamlet   We shall know by this fellow. The players cannot
135   keep counsel: they'll tell all.

Ophelia   Will he tell us what this show meant?

Hamlet   Ay, or any show that you will show him. Be not you
ashamed to show, he'll not shame to tell you what it means.

Ophelia   You are naught, you are naught. I'll mark the play.

holy, he'll have to endow churches then, or resign himself to being forgotten, like the hobbyhorses they used to use in morris dances. Their epitaph is in the refrain of an old song: *For oh, for oh, the hobbyhorse is forgotten . . .*

[*The trumpets sound. A play, performed in mime, is presented by the* **Actors***. It opens with the entry of a* **King** *and a* **Queen***, who embrace affectionately. She kneels, expressing her love for him. He helps her up, and bows his head upon her shoulder. Then he lies down on a bank of flowers. Seeing him asleep, she leaves him. Soon, a* **Man** *enters. He removes the* **King***'s crown, kisses it, and then pours poison into the sleeping* **King***'s ears. He departs. The* **Queen** *returns and finds the* **King** *dead. She expresses her grief. The* **Poisoner** *and three or four attendants enter again. They seem to share her grief. The dead body is carried away. The* **Poisoner** *woos the* **Queen** *with gifts. She resists at first, but in the end she accepts his love.*   [*They leave*]

Ophelia   What does this mean, my lord?

Hamlet   This is dirty work at the crossroads. It means mischief.

Ophelia   No doubt this mime depicts the plot of the play.

[*The* **Prologue** *enters*]

Hamlet   This fellow will tell us. The actors can't keep a secret. They'll reveal all.

Ophelia   Will he tell us the meaning of the dumb show?

Hamlet   Yes, or anything you like to show him. If you don't mind letting him see, he won't be too embarrassed to explain what it's for.

Ophelia   You are very naughty, very naughty. I'll watch the play.

140 **Prologue**   *For us and for our tragedy,*
Here stooping to your clemency,
We beg your hearing patiently.   [*Exit*]

Hamlet   Is this a prologue, or the posy of a ring?

Ophelia   'Tis brief, my lord.

145 **Hamlet**   As woman's love.

[*Enter the* **Player King** *and* **Queen**]

Player King   *Full thirty times hath Phoebus' cart gone round*
Neptune's salt wash and Tellus' orbed ground,
And thirty dozen moons with borrowed sheen
About the world have times twelve thirties been
150 *Since love our hearts and Hymen did our hands*
Unite commutual in most sacred bands.

Player Queen   *So many journeys may the sun and moon*
Make us again count o'er ere love be done.
But woe is me, you are so sick of late,
155 *So far from cheer and from your former state,*
That I distrust you. Yet though I distrust,
Discomfort you, my lord, it nothing must;
For women's fear and love hold quantity,
In neither aught, or in extremity.
160 *Now what my love is, proof hath made you know,*
And as my love is sized, my fear is so.
Where love is great, the littlest doubts are fear;
Where little fears grow great, great love grows there.

Player King   *Faith, I must leave thee, love, and shortly too:*
165 *My operant powers their functions leave to do;*
And thou shalt live in this fair world behind,
Honoured, beloved; and haply one as kind
For husband shalt thou –

Prologue   *For us, and for our tragedy,*
We bow in hope of leniency
And beg you'll hear us patiently.   [*The* **Prologue** *leaves*]

Hamlet   Is this a prologue, or the motto inscribed on a ring?

Ophelia   It's brief, my lord.

Hamlet   As the love of a woman . . .

[*The* "**King**" *and* "**Queen**" *previously in the mime reenter*]

"**King**"   *For thirty years the sun has circled round*
The ocean waves, and earth's surrounding ground –
And thirty dozen moons and their reflected light
Have twelve times thirty times shone out at night –
Since we two fell in love. Our troths were plighted,
And so in wedlock were our lives united.

"**Queen**"   *And may the sun and moon continue on*
For just as long ahead before love's done.
But woe is me! You've been so ill of late –
So far from what's your normal, healthy state –
That I'm alarmed. But though I feel distress,
You must not let this spoil your happiness;
For women's fear, and love, go side by side:
There's either far too much, or one's denied.
How much I love you, I have proved to you;
And as my love is, so my fear is too.
Where love is great, small worries lead to fear;
Where little fears grow great, great love grows there.

"**King**"   *'Faith, I must leave you, love, and shortly too.*
My faculties don't work as they should do.
In the fair world, alone, you'll stay behind,
Honored, beloved; with luck, you'll meet as kind
A husband whom you'll –

Player Queen   *O confound the rest.*
170 *Such love must needs be treason in my breast.*
In second husband let me be accurst;
None wed the second but who killed the first.

Hamlet [*aside*] That's wormwood.

Player Queen *The instances that second marriage move*
175 *Are base respects of thrift, but none of love.*
A second time I kill my husband dead,
When second husband kisses me in bed.

Player King *I do believe you think what now you speak;*
But what we do determine, oft we break.
180 *Purpose is but the slave to memory,*
Of violent birth but poor validity,
Which now, the fruit unripe, sticks on the tree,
But fall unshaken when they mellow be.
Most necessary 'tis that we forget
185 *To pay ourselves what to ourselves is debt.*
What to ourselves in passion we propose,
The passion ending, doth the purpose lose.
The violence of either grief or joy
Their own enactures with themselves destroy.
190 *Where joy most revels grief doth most lament;*
Grief joys, joy grieves, on slender accident.
This world is not for aye, nor 'tis not strange
That even our loves should with our fortunes change,
For 'tis a question left us yet to prove,
195 *Whether love lead fortune or else fortune love.*
The great man down, you mark his favourite flies;
The poor advanced makes friends of enemies;
And hitherto doth love on fortune tend:
For who not needs shall never lack a friend,
200 *And who in want a hollow friend doth try*
Directly seasons him his enemy.
But orderly to end where I begun,

"Queen"   *– Oh, don't say the rest!*
Such love as that is treason to my breast!
If I remarried, I would be accursed.
None marry twice except those who killed the first.

Hamlet [*aside*] That has a bitter taste!

"Queen" *The reason why some people marry twice*
Is not that they're in love; greed is the vice.
I'd be killing again the man already dead
If husband number two made love in bed.

"King" *I'm sure that you believe what you say now;*
But though we make a pledge, we break the vow.
Our good intentions need a strong resolve:
Though sincere at first, they soon dissolve;
Like unripe fruit, they're firm upon the tree
Until they mellow. Then they fall quite free.
Inevitably, we all soon forget
To pay ourselves what is a self-owed debt;
We lose our purpose when the blood's not hot.
Both grief and joy, when felt in great excess,
Destroy the power to act or to express.
Where joy is very great, grief shows its might:
Grief and joy change places for a reason slight.
This world is not forever; it's not strange
That our true love should (with our fortunes) change.
It is a matter left for us to prove:
Does love decide our fate, or fate our love?
The great man in decline will lose his friend:
The rising man finds enmities all end.
It seems, therefore, that love on fortune tends:
The well-heeled man will never want for friends;
Yet he who's out of luck, in seeking aid,
Finds his false friend an enemy's been made.
But tidily to end where I began:

> *Our wills and fates do so contrary run*
> *That our devices still are overthrown:*
> 205 *Our thoughts are ours, their ends none of our own.*
> *So think thou wilt no second husband wed,*
> *But die thy thoughts when thy first lord is dead.*

Player Queen   *Nor earth to me give food, nor heaven light,*
Sport and repose lock from me day and night,
210 *To desperation turn my trust and hope,*
An anchor's cheer in prison be my scope,
Each opposite, that blanks the face of joy,
Meet what I would have well and it destroy,
Both here and hence pursue me lasting strife,
215 *If, once a widow, ever I be a wife.*

Hamlet   If she should break it now.

Player King   *'Tis deeply sworn. Sweet, leave me here awhile.*
My spirits grow dull, and fain I would beguile
The tedious day with sleep.

220 **Player Queen**   *Sleep rock thy brain,*
And never come mischance between us twain.

[Exit. He sleeps]

Hamlet   Madam, how like you this play?

Queen   The lady doth protest too much, methinks.

Hamlet   Oh, but she'll keep her word.

225 **King**   Have you heard the argument? Is there no offence in't?

Hamlet   No, no, they do but jest – poison in jest. No offence
i'th'world.

King   What do you call the play?

Hamlet   *The Mousetrap* – marry, how tropically! This play is

THE LOT

7611 Fay Ave, La Jolla, CA. 92037

858 777 0069

www.thelotent.com

La Jolla

Cinema

Why Him?

Seat Row no. D-2

Mon Jan 02, 2017 02:45 PM

ADMITAUD 7 D-2   ADULT   17.50

La Jolla   Cinema

Why Him?   D-2

Mon Jan 02, 2017 02:45 PM

ADMITAUD 7 D-2   ADULT   17.50

CSH 00435586/001/00023359

* T 1 0 0   4 3 5 5 8 6   *

Like us on FaceBook
Download THE LOT Mobile App to purchase
tickets on your phone!!!

Thank you for visiting
THE LOT

For Terms & Conditions please visit
our website: www.thelotent.com

So different are our wants from fate's own plan,
That schemes and plots are always overthrown.
Our thoughts are ours; the outcome's not our own.
You think you will no second husband wed:
Intent will die when your first lord is dead.

"**Queen**"   *May earth deny me food, and heaven light;*
Dull be my days, and sleepless be my night;
To desperation turn my hope and trust;
My comforts not exceed a hermit's crust;
Thwart my desires; frustrate all my joy;
Note my ambition; all my hopes destroy;
Now and hereafter, punish me with strife
If once a widow, ever I be wife.

Hamlet   If she should break such a promise!

"**King**"   *A solemn vow. Sweet, for a time depart.*
I'm feeling tired. It would do my heart
Much good to take a nap.

"**Queen**"   *Sleep come to you.*
And never must ill luck divide us two.

*[She goes. The "***King***" sleeps]*

Hamlet   Madam, what do you think of this play?

Queen   I think the lady is overdoing it.

Hamlet   Oh, but she'll keep her word.

King   Do you know the plot? Is it offensive?

Hamlet   No, no, they're only joking; the poison isn't real. They commit no offense whatsoever.

King   What's the play called?

Hamlet   *The Mousetrap*. What a catching metaphor! This play

230   the image of a murder done in Vienna; Gonzago is the
Duke's name, his wife Baptista; you shall see anon. 'Tis a
knavish piece of work, but what o'that? Your Majesty, and
we that have free souls, it touches us not. Let the galled jade
wince, our withers are unwrung.

[*Enter* **Lucianus**]

235   This is one Lucianus, nephew to the King.

Ophelia   You are as good as a chorus, my lord.

Hamlet   I could interpret between you and your love if I
could see the puppets dallying.

Ophelia   You are keen, my lord, you are keen.

240 **Hamlet**   It would cost you a groaning to take off my edge.

Ophelia   Still better, and worse.

Hamlet   So you must take your husbands. Begin, murderer.
Leave thy damnable faces and begin. Come, the croaking
raven doth bellow for revenge.

245 **Lucianus**   *Thoughts black, hands apt, drugs fit, and time*
agreeing,
Confederate season, else no creature seeing,
Thou mixture rank, of midnight weeds collected,
With Hecate's band thrice blasted, thrice infected,
250   *Thy natural magic and dire property*
On wholesome life usurps immediately.

[*Pours the poison in the sleeper's ears*]

Hamlet   He poisons him i'th'garden for his estate. His name's
Gonzago. The story is extant, and written in very choice

170

is a real-life story about a murder done in Vienna. Gonzago is
the Duke's name. His wife is Baptista. You'll see soon. It's
a provocative sort of play, but who cares? Your majesty,
and those of us with clear consciences – it's nothing to
do with us. It's no skin off our noses.

["**Lucianus**" *enters*]

This is a character called Lucianus, the King's nephew in the
play.

Ophelia   You are as good as a guide, my lord.

Hamlet   I could do a commentary on you and your lover if I
could see you both performing.

Ophelia   You are sharp, my lord; you are sharp.

Hamlet   You'd have your work cut out to take the edge off
me!

Ophelia   Better still! You are getting worse!

Hamlet   "For better, for worse" is how you deceive your
husbands.   [*To* "**Lucianus**"]   Begin, murderer. Stop
making those awful faces and begin. Come on.   [**Hamlet**
misquotes lines from an old play]   *The croaking raven is
bellowing for revenge.*

"**Lucianus**"   *Evil thoughts – skilled hands – poison –
privacy –
All's right: the perfect opportunity!
Vile mixture of rank weeds, midnight collected,
With witch's curse thrice blasted, thrice infected,
Your natural gift and dreadful faculty
Steals worthy life and kills immediately!*

[*He pours poison in the ear of the* "**King**"]

Hamlet   He poisons him in his garden for his money.
   [*Pointing to the corpse*]   His name's Gonzago. The story is

171

Italian. You shall see anon how the murderer gets the love of
255   Gonzago's wife.

Ophelia   The King rises.

Hamlet   What, frighted with false fire?

Queen   How fares my lord?

Polonius   Give o'er the play.

260   **King**   Give me some light. Away.

Polonius   Lights, lights, lights.

[*Exeunt all but* **Hamlet** *and* **Horatio**]

Hamlet   *Why, let the strucken deer go weep,*
                     The hart ungalled play;
                For some must watch while some must sleep,
265   *Thus runs the world away.*

Would not this, sir, and a forest of feathers, if the rest of my
fortunes turn Turk with me, with two Provincial roses on
my razed shoes, get me a fellowship in a cry of players?

Horatio   Half a share.

270   **Hamlet**   A whole one, I.

For thou dost know, Oh Damon dear,
         This realm dismantled was
Of Jove himself, and now reigns here
         A very, very – pajock.

275   **Horatio**   You might have rhymed.

Hamlet   Oh good Horatio, I'll take the ghost's word for a
thousand pound. Didst perceive?

172

in current circulation, and written in very stylish Italian.
You'll see soon how the murderer wins the love of
Gonzago's wife.

Ophelia   The King has risen to his feet.

Hamlet   What, frightened by blank shots?

Queen   [*to her husband*]   How is my lord?

Polonius   Stop the play!

King   Turn on the lights. Let's go!

Polonius   [*to Attendants*]   More lights, more lights!

[*Everyone leaves except* **Hamlet** *and* **Horatio**]

Hamlet   *Why, let the wounded deer go weep;*
            The hart, uninjured, play –
        For some must guard, while some do sleep,
            That is the world's own way.

[*Referring to the play and the words he has written for it*]   If
I struck hard times, wouldn't this get me a place in a
company of actors, sir, with feathers in my hat and big
rose ribbons on my fashion shoes?

Horatio   Half a share in one!

Hamlet   A whole share for me!

            'Cos you must know, my rural lad,
                This kingdom now, alas,
            No longer has Jove as its King.
                Its ruler is – a peacock!

Horatio   You might have rhymed!   [*In which case,* **Hamlet**
would have said "an ass"]

Hamlet   Oh, good Horatio – I'll back the truth of the ghost's
words for a thousand pounds. Did you notice?

Horatio   Very well, my lord.

Hamlet   Upon the talk of the poisoning?

280 **Horatio**   I did very well note him.

Hamlet   Ah ha! Come, some music; come, the recorders.

> *For if the King like not the comedy,*
> *Why then, belike he likes it not, perdie.*

Come, some music.

[*Enter* **Rosencrantz** *and* **Guildenstern**]

285 **Guildenstern**   Good my lord, vouchsafe me a word with you.

Hamlet   Sir, a whole history.

Guildenstern   The King, sir –

Hamlet   Ay, sir, what of him?

Guildenstern   Is in his retirement marvellous distempered.

290 **Hamlet**   With drink, sir?

Guildenstern   No, my lord, with choler.

Hamlet   Your wisdom should show itself more richer to
signify this to the doctor, for, for me to put him to his
purgation would perhaps plunge him into more choler.

295 **Guildenstern**   Good my lord, put your discourse into some
frame, and start not so wildly from my affair.

Hamlet   I am tame, sir. Pronounce.

Guildenstern   The Queen your mother, in most great
affliction of spirit, hath sent me to you.

300 **Hamlet**   You are welcome.

Guildenstern   Nay, good my lord, this courtesy is not of the

Horatio   Very clearly, my lord.

Hamlet   When they talked about poisoning?

Horatio   I watched him closely.

Hamlet   Ah ha! Come, some music! Come, let's have the recorders!

> *For if the King dislikes the comic plot*
> *Why then, by God, it seems he likes it not!*

Come on, some music!

[**Rosencrantz** *and* **Guildenstern** *enter*]

Guildenstern   Good my lord, grant me a word with you.

Hamlet   Sir, a whole history!

Guildenstern   The King, sir –

Hamlet   Yes, sir, what about him?

Guildenstern   He's retired to his room extremely out of sorts.

Hamlet   With drink, sir?

Guildenstern   No, my lord. With anger.

Hamlet   You ought to have more sense than to tell this to the doctor. If it were up to me to cure him, he'd be angrier still.

Guildenstern   Good my lord, do restrain your tongue and don't go off at a tangent.

Hamlet   I've pulled myself together. Speak on.

Guildenstern   Your mother the Queen, in great distress, has sent me to you.

Hamlet   You are welcome.

Guildenstern   Really, my lord, this kind of politeness is not right breed. If it shall please you to make me a wholesome answer, I will do your mother's commandment; if not, your pardon and my return shall be the end of my business.

Hamlet   Sir, I cannot.

305 **Rosencrantz**   What, my lord?

Hamlet   Make you a wholesome answer. My wit's diseased. But sir, such answer as I can make, you shall command – or rather, as you say, my mother. Therefore no more, but to the matter. My mother, you say –

310 **Rosencrantz**   Then thus she says: your behaviour hath struck her into amazement and admiration.

Hamlet   O wonderful son, that can so astonish a mother! But is there no sequel at the heels of this mother's admiration? Impart.

315 **Rosencrantz**   She desires to speak with you in her closet ere you go to bed.

Hamlet   We shall obey, were she ten times our mother. Have you any further trade with us?

Rosencrantz   My lord, you once did love me.

320 **Hamlet**   And do still, by these pickers and stealers.

Rosencrantz   Good my lord, what is your cause of distemper? You do surely bar the door upon your own liberty if you deny your griefs to your friend.

Hamlet   Sir, I lack advancement.

325 **Rosencrantz**   How can that be, when you have the voice of the King himself for your succession in Denmark?

Hamlet   Ay, sir, but while the grass grows – the proverb is something musty.

176

good manners. If you'll be so good as to give me a rational answer, I'll carry out your mother's instructions. If not, your permission to leave and my return to her will conclude my business.

Hamlet   Sir, I cannot.

Rosencrantz   Cannot what, my lord?

Hamlet   Give you a rational answer. My brain is addled. But, sir, such answer as I can give you, is yours – or rather, as you say, my mother's. Therefore, enough said. To resume; my mother, you say –

Rosencrantz   She says this: your behavior has amazed and astonished her.

Hamlet   What a wonderful son, to bewilder his mother! But is there no follow-up to this mother's astonishment? Reveal all!

Rosencrantz   She wishes to speak with you in her room before you go to bed.

Hamlet   We shall obey, even if she were our mother ten times over. Have you any further business with us?

Rosencrantz   My lord, you used to like me.

Hamlet   And still do, by these hands!

Rosencrantz   Good my lord, what's the reason for your malady? You close the door upon your cure if you won't share your troubles with your friend.

Hamlet   Sir, my ambitions are frustrated.

Rosencrantz   How can that be, when you have been named heir to the throne of Denmark by the King himself?

Hamlet   Yes sir, but *while the grass grows the horse starves*, to quote a stale old proverb.

[*Enter the* **Players** *with recorders*]

Oh, the recorders. Let me see one. To withdraw with you,
330   why do you go about to recover the wind of me, as if you
would drive me into a toil?

Guildenstern Oh my lord, if my duty be too bold, my love is
too unmannerly.

Hamlet I do not well understand that. Will you play upon
335   this pipe?

Guildenstern My lord, I cannot.

Hamlet I pray you.

Guildenstern Believe me, I cannot.

Hamlet I do beseech you.

340 **Guildenstern** I know no touch of it, my lord.

Hamlet It is as easy as lying. Govern these ventages with
your fingers and thumb, give it breath with your mouth, and
it will discourse most eloquent music. Look you, these are
the stops.

345 **Guildenstern** But these cannot I command to any utterance
of harmony. I have not the skill.

Hamlet Why, look you now, how unworthy a thing you
make of me. You would play upon me, you would seem to
know my stops, you would pluck out the heart of my
350   mystery, you would sound me from my lowest note to the
top of my compass; and there is much music, excellent voice,
in this little organ, yet cannot you make it speak. Why, do
you think I am easier to be played on than a pipe? Call me
what instrument you will, though you can fret me, you
355   cannot play upon me.

[*Enter* **Polonius**]

God bless you, sir.
178

[*The* **Actors** *enter, carrying recorders*]

Oh, the recorders. Let me see one.   [*An Actor passes one to him*]   Confidentially, why are you maneuvering to get me into a trap?

Guildenstern   Oh, my lord. If I'm too forward, it's my love that's at fault.

Hamlet   I don't follow you.   [*Offering the recorder*]   Will you play something?

Guildenstern   My lord, I can't.

Hamlet   Please?

Guildenstern   Believe me, I can't.

Hamlet   I beg you . . .

Guildenstern   I don't know the fingering.

Hamlet   It's as easy as lying. Cover these holes with your fingers and thumb, blow with your mouth, and it will produce most tuneful music. See, these are the stops.

Guildenstern   But I can't make them sound right. I haven't got the skill.

Hamlet   Why, now look how you belittle me. You want to play me; you seem to know where my stops are; you want to uncover my secrets; you would sound me out from base to treble. And there's a lot of melody, excellent sound, in this little pipe, but you can't bring it out. Why, do you think I am easier to play upon than a recorder? Call me whatever instrument you like; fret me even; you still can't sound me out.

[**Polonius** *enters*]

God bless you, sir.

Polonius   My lord, the Queen would speak with you, and
presently.

Hamlet   Do you see yonder cloud that's almost in shape of a
360   camel?

Polonius   By th'mass and 'tis like a camel indeed.

Hamlet   Methinks it is like a weasel.

Polonius   It is backed like a weasel.

Hamlet   Or like a whale.

365   **Polonius**   Very like a whale.

Hamlet   Then I will come to my mother by and by.   [*Aside*]
They fool me to the top of my bent. I will come by and by.

Polonius   I will say so.

[*Exit* **Polonius**]

Hamlet   'By and by' is easily said. Leave me, friends.

[*Exeunt all but* **Hamlet**]

370   'Tis now the very witching time of night,
When churchyards yawn and hell itself breathes out
Contagion to this world. Now could I drink hot blood,
And do such bitter business as the day
Would quake to look on. Soft, now to my mother.
375   O heart, lose not thy nature. Let not ever
The soul of Nero enter this firm bosom;
Let me be cruel, not unnatural.
I will speak daggers to her, but use none.
My tongue and soul in this be hypocrites:
380   How in my words somever she be shent,
To give them seals never, my soul, consent.

[*Exit*]

Polonius   My lord, the Queen wishes to speak to you, straight away.

Hamlet   Do you see that cloud over there that's shaped almost like a camel?

Polonius   By heaven, so it is. It's like a camel indeed.

Hamlet   I think it's like a weasel.

Polonius   It has a back like a weasel.

Hamlet   Or like a whale.

Polonius   Very like a whale.

Hamlet   Then I'll visit my mother by and by.   [*Aside*]   They mock me past endurance!   [*To* **Polonius**]   I'll come by and by.

Polonius   I'll say so.

[*He goes*]

Hamlet   "By and by" is easily said.   [*To* **Rosencrantz, Guildenstern**, *and the* **Actors**]   Leave me, friends.

[*They leave*]

It's the dead of night, witchcraft time, when graves in churchyards open, and hell itself breathes foul air upon the world. Now I could drink hot blood, and do such ghastly business as would make the day shudder to look at. Right. Now to my mother. Oh, heart, don't lose your natural feelings! The spirit of Nero, that mother-killer, must not influence me. Let me be ruthless, but not unnatural. My tongue will speak daggers, but I'll use none. In this respect I'll speak with a forked tongue. However much I chastise her in words, my soul would never consent to putting them into action.

[*He goes*]

Scene 3

Enter **King, Rosencrantz,** *and* **Guildenstern**.

King   I like him not; nor stands it safe with us
　　To let his madness range. Therefore prepare you.
　　I your commission will forthwith dispatch,
　　And he to England shall along with you.
5　　The terms of our estate may not endure
　　Hazard so near us as doth hourly grow
　　Out of his brows.

Guildenstern　　We will ourselves provide.
　　Most holy and religious fear it is
10　　To keep those many many bodies safe
　　That live and feed upon your Majesty.

Rosencrantz　　The single and peculiar life is bound
　　With all the strength and armour of the mind
　　To keep itself from noyance; but much more
15　　That spirit upon whose weal depends and rests
　　The lives of many. The cease of majesty
　　Dies not alone, but like a gulf doth draw
　　What's near it with it. Or it is a massy wheel
　　Fixed on the summit of the highest mount,
20　　To whose huge spokes ten thousand lesser things
　　Are mortised and adjoined, which when it falls,
　　Each small annexment, petty consequence,
　　Attends the boist'rous ruin. Never alone
　　Did the King sigh, but with a general groan.

25 **King**　Arm you, I pray you, to this speedy voyage,
　　For we will fetters put about this fear
　　Which now goes too free-footed.

Rosencrantz　　　　　　　We will haste us.

Scene 3

Enter the **King, Rosencrantz** *and* **Guildenstern**.

King   I don't like the look of him, nor is it safe for us to give
him his liberty while he's mad. So get yourselves ready. I'll
issue your commission at once, and he must go to England
with you. As King, I can't tolerate the dangers that his
threatening looks increasingly imply.

Guildenstern   We'll make our preparations. It's a sacred duty
to be cautious on behalf of the countless numbers who
depend on your majesty for their livelihood.

Rosencrantz   The individual instinctively protects himself
against aggression: how much more must a sovereign, on
whose welfare the lives of many depend. The death of a
king is not his alone; like a whirlpool, it draws in whatever's
near it. Or it's like a massive wheel fixed at the top of the
highest mountain, to the huge spokes of which ten
thousand inferior things are firmly attached. When it rolls
downhill, every small appendage, each minor part, is
involved in the final catastrophe. The king never sighs alone.
When he does, so does everyone.

King   Get ready then for this hasty voyage. We'll tie this fear
down that's now at liberty.

Rosencrantz   We'll hurry.

[*Exeunt* **Rosencrantz** *and* **Guildenstern**]

[*Enter* **Polonius**]

Polonius   My lord, he's going to his mother's closet.
30   Behind the arras I'll convey myself
To hear the process. I'll warrant she'll tax him home,
And as you said – and wisely was it said –
'Tis meet that some more audience than a mother,
Since nature makes them partial, should o'erhear
35   The speech of vantage. Fare you well, my liege.
I'll call upon you ere you go to bed,
And tell you what I know.

King   Thanks, dear my lord.

[*Exit* **Polonius**]

Oh, my offence is rank, it smells to heaven;
40   It hath the primal eldest curse upon't –
A brother's murder! Pray can I not,
Though inclination be as sharp as will,
My stronger guilt defeats my strong intent,
And, like a man to double business bound,
45   I stand in pause where I shall first begin,
And both neglect. What if this cursed hand
Were thicker than itself with brother's blood,
Is there not rain enough in the sweet heavens
To wash it white as snow? Whereto serves mercy
50   But to confront the visage of offence?
And what's in prayer but this twofold force,
To be forestalled ere we come to fall
Or pardoned being down? Then I'll look up.
My fault is past. But oh, what form of prayer
55   Can serve my turn? 'Forgive me my foul murder'?
That cannot be, since I am still possessed
Of those effects for which I did the murder –

[**Rosencrantz** *and* **Guildenstern** *leave*]

[**Polonius** *enters*]

Polonius   My lord, he's going to his mother's room. I'll hide myself behind the curtain to hear what goes on. I'm certain she'll get to the bottom of it, and as you said – so wisely – it's better that someone other than a mother – since they are naturally biased – should also hear the dialogue. Farewell, my liege. I'll call on you before you go to bed and tell you what I learn.

King   Thanks, my dear lord.

[**Polonius** *goes*]

Oh, my crime is horrible. It smells to heaven. It has Cain's curse upon it – a brother's murder. I cannot pray, much as I earnestly want to; my overpowering sense of guilt defeats my strong inclinations. Like a man with two alternatives, I stand transfixed, not knowing which to do first, and so neglect both. What if this cursed hand of mine were twice as thick with my brother's blood? Surely there is enough rain in the sweet heavens to wash it as white as snow? What is the point of mercy if it isn't to meet sin face to face? And what's in prayer, if it isn't this double power – to prevent us from doing wrong, and to pardon us if we have transgressed? There's hope for me. My sin has been committed; but oh, what kind of prayer would fit my case? "Forgive me my foul murder"? That cannot be, since I still have the possessions for which I did the murder –

My crown, mine own ambition, and my queen.
May one be pardoned and retain th'offence?
60 In the corrupted currents of this world
Offence's gilded hand may shove by justice,
And oft 'tis seen the wicked prize itself
Buys out the law. But 'tis not so above:
There is no shuffling, there the action lies
65 In his true nature, and we ourselves compelled
Even to the teeth and forehead of our faults
To give in evidence. What then? What rests?
Try what repentance can. What can it not?
Yet what can it, when one cannot repent?
70 O wretched state! O bosom black as death!
O limed soul, that struggling to be free
Art more engaged! Help, angels! Make assay.
Bow, stubborn knees; and heart with strings of steel,
Be soft as sinews of the new-born babe.
75 All may be well. [*He kneels*]

[*Enter* **Hamlet**]

Hamlet Now might I do it pat, now he is a-praying.
And now I'll do't. [*Draws his sword*]
                    And so he goes to heaven;
And so am I revenged. That would be scanned:
80 A villain kills my father, and for that
I, his sole son, do this same villain send
To heaven.
Why, this is hire and salary, not revenge.
He took my father grossly, full of bread,
85 With all his crimes broad blown, as flush as May;
And how his audit stands who knows save heaven?
But in our circumstance and course of thought
'Tis heavy with him. And am I then revenged,
To take him in the purging of his soul,

my crown, my own ambition, and my queen. Can one be
pardoned, and yet retain the spoils? In the corrupt
procedures of this world, the wealthy offender can push
justice to one side; frequently the ill-gotten gains are used to
bribe the law. But it's not that way in heaven. There's no
shady dealing there. There the truth's the truth, and we
ourselves are compelled to supply evidence about our faults
in every revealing particular. What else then? What's the
alternative? To see what repentance can do. What can it
not? Yet, what *can* it do, when one *can't* repent? Oh, what
a wretched situation! Oh, my heart is as black as death! Oh,
my soul is trapped; the more it struggles, the more it is
entangled. Help, angels! Do all you can! Stubborn knees,
bow. Heart with strings of steel, be as soft as the sinews of
a newborn baby! All may yet be well.

[*He kneels*]

[**Hamlet** *enters*]

Hamlet   Now I could do it easily, now he's at prayer. And now
I'll do it.   [*He draws his sword*]   And then he would go to
heaven. So much for my revenge! That needs further
thought! A villain kills my father: and because of that, I – his
only son – send this selfsame villain to heaven. Why, this is
a helping hand, not revenge! He killed my father in a state of
sin, not on a fast day, with all his crimes in full bloom, in his
lusty prime. How his reckoning stands in heaven, who
knows but God alone? By our worldly thinking, it looks very
bad. And am I revenged, then, if I kill him while he is purging

90   When he is fit and seasoned for his passage?
     No.
     Up, sword, and know thou a more horrid hent:
     When he is drunk asleep, or in his rage,
     Or in th'incestuous pleasure of his bed,
95   At game a-swearing, or about some act
     That has no relish of salvation in't,
     Then trip him, that his heels may kick at heaven
     And that his soul may be as damned and black
     As hell, whereto it goes. My mother stays.
100 This physic but prolongs thy sickly days.

[*Exit*]

King   My words fly up, my thoughts remain below.
     Words without thoughts never to heaven go.

[*Exit*]

Scene 4

Enter **Queen** *and* **Polonius**.

Polonius   He will come straight. Look you lay home to him,
     Tell him his pranks have been too broad to bear with
     And that your Grace hath screened and stood between
     Much heat and him. I'll silence me even here.
5   Pray you be round.

Queen   I'll warrant you, fear me not.
     Withdraw, I hear him coming.

[**Polonius** *hides behind the arras*]

188

his sins, when he's thoroughly prepared for his judgment?
No. So I'll sheath my sword till a more sinful occasion turns
up: when he is in a drunken sleep; in a rage; in bed indulging
in incestuous pleasures; blaspheming while playing a game;
or involved in some activity that has no trace of God's
salvation in it. Then I'd trip him – his soul would be as
damned and as black as hell, where he'd be bound to go,
head first. My mother is waiting for me. This praying merely
prolongs your wretched life.

[*He goes*]

King   [*rising to his feet*]   My words rise upward, but my
thoughts remain here below. Words without sincerity never
reach heaven.

[*He leaves*]

Scene 4

Enter the **Queen** *and* **Polonius**.

Polonius   He's on his way. See you don't mince words. Tell
him his pranks have been too outrageous to be tolerated,
and that your Grace has protected him from a lot of heated
criticism.   [*Pulling back the tapestry that lines the wall*]   I'll
hide here silently. Be direct with him!

Queen   Trust me. Never fear. Hide: I can hear him coming.

[**Polonius** *hides behind the tapestry*]

[*Enter* **Hamlet**]

Hamlet   Now, mother, what's the matter?

Queen   Hamlet, thou hast thy father much offended.

10 **Hamlet**   Mother, you have my father much offended.

Queen   Come, come, you answer with an idle tongue.

Hamlet   Go, go, you question with a wicked tongue.

Queen   Why, how now, Hamlet?

Hamlet   What's the matter now?

15 **Queen**   Have you forgot me?

Hamlet   No, by the rood, not so.
You are the Queen, your husband's brother's wife,
And, would it were not so, you are my mother.

Queen   Nay, then I'll set those to you that can speak.

20 **Hamlet**   Come, come, and sit you down, you shall not budge.
You go not till I set you up a glass
Where you may see the inmost part of you.

Queen   What wilt thou do? Thou wilt not murder me?
Help, ho!

25 **Polonius**   [*behind the arras*]   What ho! Help!

Hamlet   How now? A rat! Dead for a ducat, dead.

[*He thrusts his rapier through the arras*]

Polonius   [*behind*]   Oh, I am slain.

Queen   O me, what hast thou done?

[**Hamlet** *enters*]

Hamlet Now, mother. What's the matter?

Queen Hamlet, you have deeply offended your father. [*She means King Claudius*]

Hamlet Mother, you have deeply offended my father. [*He means the late King Hamlet*]

Queen Come, come. You answer me foolishly.

Hamlet Go, go. You question me wickedly.

Queen Now really, Hamlet . . .

Hamlet What's the matter now?

Queen Have you forgotten who I am?

Hamlet No, by the cross, not at all. You are the Queen, your husband's brother's wife. And – would it were otherwise! – you are my mother.

Queen Right, then. I'll send people to you to do the talking. [*She gets up to leave*]

Hamlet [*preventing her*] Come, come. Sit yourself down. You're not moving. You're not going till I've set up a mirror for you to see your inner self. [*He pushes her back into her seat*]

Queen What are you going to do? You don't intend to murder me? [*She panics*] Help, help!

Polonius [*from behind the tapestry*] Help, help I say!

Hamlet [*spinning round*] What! A rat? [*He draws his rapier and thrusts through the tapestry*] I'll kill it cheap! Dead!

Polonius [*behind the tapestry*] Oh, he's killed me!

Queen Oh heavens, what have you done?

Hamlet   Nay, I know not.
30   Is it the King?

[*He lifts up the arras and discovers* **Polonius**, *dead*]

Queen   Oh what a rash and bloody deed is this!

Hamlet   A bloody deed. Almost as bad, good mother,
As kill a king and marry with his brother.

Queen   As kill a king?

35 **Hamlet**   Ay, lady, it was my word.
Thou wretched, rash, intruding fool, farewell.
I took thee for thy better. Take thy fortune:
Thou find'st to be too busy is some danger.
Leave wringing of your hands. Peace, sit you down,
40   And let me wring your heart; for so I shall
If it be made of penetrable stuff,
If damned custom have not brazed it so,
That it be proof and bulwark against sense.

Queen   What have I done, that thou dar'st wag thy tongue
45   In noise so rude against me?

Hamlet   Such an act
That blurs the grace and blush of modesty,
Calls virtue hypocrite, takes off the rose
From the fair forehead of an innocent love
50   And sets a blister there, makes marriage vows
As false as dicers' oaths. O, such a deed
As from the body of contraction plucks
The very soul, and sweet religion makes
A rhapsody of words. Heaven's face does glow
55   O'er this solidity and compound mass
With tristful visage, as against the doom,
Is thought-sick at the act.

Hamlet   Really, I've no idea. Is it the King?   [*He lifts up the tapestry and discovers* **Polonius** *lying dead behind it*]

Queen   Oh, what an impetuous and murderous deed this is!

Hamlet   A murderous deed! Almost as bad, good mother, as to kill a king, and marry his brother . . .

Queen   As kill a king?

Hamlet   Yes, lady, that's what I said.   [*To the body of* **Polonius**]   You wretched, rash, intruding fool – farewell. I thought you were the King. Accept your bad luck. You've learned that to be too inquisitive puts you in danger.   [*To the* **Queen**]   Stop wringing your hands. Quiet. Sit yourself down, and let me wring your heart. And that I surely will, if it's not impregnable, and so brazen from habitual wickedness that it's beyond all appeals to reason.

Queen   What have I done, that you dare to wag your tongue so loudly and offensively against me?

Hamlet   Such conduct as puts innocence to shame, abuses virtue, turns ideal love to harlotry, makes marriage vows as false as gamblers' promises – oh, such a deed as voids all solemn pledges, and turns sweet religion into a string of meaningless words! God's face blushes over the world with sadness, anticipating judgment day: sickened at the thought of what you've done.

Queen   Ay me, what act
       That roars so loud and thunders in the index?

60 **Hamlet**   Look here upon this picture, and on this,
       The counterfeit presentment of two brothers.
       See what a grace was seated on this brow;
       Hyperion's curls, the front of Jove himself,
       An eye like Mars, to threaten and command,
65   A station like the herald Mercury
       New-lighted on a heaven-kissing hill;
       A combination and a form indeed
       Where every god did seem to set his seal
       To give the world assurance of a man.
70   This was your husband. Look you now what follows.
       Here is your husband, like a mildewed ear
       Blasting his wholesome brother. Have you eyes?
       Could you on this fair mountain leave to feed
       And batten on this moor? Ha, have you eyes?
75   You cannot call it love; for at your age
       The heyday in the blood is tame, it's humble,
       And waits upon the judgment, and what judgment
       Would step from this to this? Sense sure you have,
       Else could you not have motion; but sure that sense
80   Is apoplexed, for madness would not err,
       Nor sense to ecstasy was ne'er so thralled
       But it reserved some quantity of choice
       To serve in such a difference. What devil was't
       That thus hath cozened you at hoodman-blind?
85   Eyes without feeling, feeling without sight,
       Ears without hands or eyes, smelling sans all,
       Or but a sickly part of one true sense
       Could not so mope. Oh shame, where is thy blush?
       Rebellious hell,
90   If thou canst mutine in a matron's bones,
       To flaming youth let virtue be as wax
       And melt in her own fire; proclaim no shame

Queen   Wretched me: what have I done that's so outrageous?

Hamlet   Look here at this picture   [*he indicates a miniature he is wearing on a chain round his neck*]   and at this   [*he grasps a similar one worn by the* **Queen**].   The portraits of two brothers. See what a godlike presence was evident in these features: the curls of the sun-god Hyperion; the forehead of kingly Jove himself; an eye like that of Mars, god of war, to threaten and command; a bearing like the herald Mercury, newly-alighted on a lofty hill. A combination stamped, indeed, with the impression of all the gods, to give the world a model man. This was your husband. Observe what follows. Here is your husband, like a contaminating growth, infecting his healthy brother. Are you blind? Could you cease to feed on this beautiful mountain   [*pointing to his father's picture*]   and glut yourself on this wasteland   [*indicating his uncle's portrait*]?   Well, are you blind? You cannot call it love. At your age, desire wanes; it's under control, and uses its judgment. What sort of judgment would step from this   [*his father*]   to this?   [*his uncle*].   You've got your faculties, or else you couldn't get about. But surely those faculties are paralyzed. Because madness wouldn't be so stupid – nor would sense be so overruled by fantasy – as not to retain some modicum of choice to fall back on at times of moral dilemma. Which devil was it that tricked you like this at blind man's buff: having sight without touch, or touch without sight, or hearing without touch sight, or smell alone? Why, even a weak flicker of one sound faculty would have made you aware of what you were doing! Where are your shameful blushes? If matrons have no control, what chance has

When the compulsive ardour gives the charge,
Since frost itself as actively doth burn
95   And reason panders will.

Queen   Oh Hamlet, speak no more.
Thou turn'st my eyes into my very soul,
And there I see such black and grained spots
As will not leave their tinct.

100 **Hamlet**   Nay, but to live
In the rank sweat of an enseamed bed,
Stewed in corruption, honeying and making love
Over the nasty sty!

Queen   Oh speak to me no more.
105   These words like daggers enter in my ears.
No more, sweet Hamlet.

Hamlet   A murderer and a villain,
A slave that is not twentieth part the tithe
Of your precedent lord, a vice of kings,
110   A cutpurse of the empire and the rule,
That from a shelf the precious diadem stole
And put it in his pocket –

Queen   No more.

Hamlet   A king of shreds and patches –

[*Enter* **Ghost**]

115   Save me and hover o'er me with your wings,
You heavenly guards! What would your gracious figure?

Queen   Alas, he's mad.

Hamlet   Do you not come your tardy son to chide,
That, lapsed in time and passion, lets go by
120   Th'important acting of your dread command?
Oh say.

morality in hot-blooded youth? Don't censure ardent youth when frosty age is just as dissolute, and reason yields to lust.

Queen   Oh, Hamlet, say no more! You have made me see my inner self, and it's indelibly stained with guilt.

Hamlet   Imagine! Living in the stinking sweat of a greasy bed, wallowing in corruption, flirting and making love in that disgusting pigsty!

Queen   Oh, don't say another word! Your words stab my ears like daggers. Say no more, sweet Hamlet!

Hamlet   A murderer and a villain; a wretch that isn't worth one twentieth of a tenth of your former husband; a monster amongst kings; a usurper, who stole the precious crown from a shelf and put it in his pocket –

Queen   No more!

Hamlet   A king of rags and tatters –

[*The* **Ghost** *enters*]

Save me, and protect me with your wings, you heavenly angels!   [*To the* **Ghost**]   What does your Majesty wish?

Queen   [*to whom the* **Ghost** *is invisible*]   Alas, he's mad!

Hamlet   Have you not come to scold your negligent son, who has failed to carry out your fearful orders, through letting time and fervor slip away? Tell me.

Ghost   Do not forget. This visitation
Is but to whet thy almost blunted purpose.
But look, amazement on thy mother sits.
125   Oh step between her and her fighting soul.
Conceit in weakest bodies strongest works.
Speak to her, Hamlet.

Hamlet   How is it with you, lady?

Queen   Alas, how is't with you,
130   That you do bend your eye on vacancy,
And with th'incorporal air do hold discourse?
Forth at your eyes your spirits wildly peep,
And, as the sleeping soldiers in th'alarm,
Your bedded hair, like life in excrements,
135   Start up and stand on end. Oh gentle son,
Upon the heat and flame of thy distemper
Sprinkle cool patience. Whereon do you look?

Hamlet   On him, on him! Look you how pale he glares.
His form and cause conjoined, preaching to stones,
140   Would make them capable. Do not look upon me,
Lest with this piteous action you convert
My stern effects. Then what I have to do
Will want true colour – tears perchance for blood.

Queen   To whom do you speak this?

145 **Hamlet**   Do you see nothing there?

Queen   Nothing at all; yet all that is I see.

Hamlet   Nor did you nothing hear?

Queen   No, nothing but ourselves.

Hamlet   Why, look you there, look how it steals away.
150   My father, in his habit as he lived!
Look where he goes even now out at the portal.

[*Exit* **Ghost**]

Ghost   Do not forget. This visit is just to sharpen your almost
blunted sense of purpose. But look. Your mother is
bewildered. Help her in her own innermost struggle. Weak
people have the most vivid imaginations. Speak to her,
Hamlet.

Hamlet   How are you, madam?

Queen   Alas, how are *you*? What makes you look at nothing,
and talk to thin air? You stare dementedly, and like soldiers
caught sleeping in a crisis, your smooth hair, shocked,
stands on end as if it were alive. Oh, gentle son, control
yourself. What are you looking at?

Hamlet   At him, at him! See how ashen is his stare! Stones
would be moved by the combined appeal of his looks and his
cause.   [*To the* **Ghost**]   Don't look at me, in case your
pitiful condition puts a different slant on my resolute
intentions: what I have to do will have the wrong
motives – sympathy instead of revenge!

Queen   To whom are you saying this?

Hamlet   Can you see nothing there?

Queen   Nothing at all. All there is to see, I can see.

Hamlet   Did you hear nothing?

Queen   No, nothing but ourselves.

Hamlet   Why, look there! Look how it slips away! My father,
dressed as he used to when alive! Look where he's going
out through the door!

[*The* **Ghost** *leaves*]

199

Queen   This is the very coinage of your brain.
This bodiless creation ecstasy
Is very cunning in.

155 **Hamlet**   Ecstasy?
My pulse as yours doth temperately keep time,
And makes as healthful music. It is not madness
That I have uttered. Bring me to the test,
And I the matter will re-word, which madness
160 Would gambol from. Mother, for love of grace,
Lay not that flattering unction to your soul,
That not your trespass but my madness speaks.
It will but skin and film the ulcerous place,
Whiles rank corruption, mining all within,
165 Infects unseen. Confess yourself to heaven,
Repent what's past, avoid what is to come;
And do not spread the compost on the weeds
To make them ranker. Forgive me this my virtue;
For in the fatness of these pursy times
170 Virtue itself of vice must pardon beg,
Yea, curb and woo for leave to do him good.

Queen   Oh Hamlet, thou hast cleft my heart in twain.

Hamlet   Oh throw away the worser part of it
And live the purer with the other half.
175 Good night. But go not to my uncle's bed.
Assume a virtue if you have it not.
That monster, custom, who all sense doth eat
Of habits devil, is angel yet in this,
That to the use of actions fair and good
180 He likewise gives a frock or livery
That aptly is put on. Refrain tonight,
And that shall lend a kind of easiness
To the next abstinence, the next more easy;
For use almost can change the stamp of nature,
185 And either curb the devil or throw him out

Queen   This is a figment of your imagination. Lunacy is very apt to invent such things.

Hamlet   Lunacy? My pulse is just as steady as yours: its rhythm is just as normal. I'm not talking madness. Put me to the test, and I'll say it all again, something I'd shy away from if I were mad. Mother, for the love of heaven, don't salve your conscience by pretending that it's not your misdeed, but my madness, that is speaking. That will only cover the ulcer with a layer of skin, while the foul corruption will fester away underneath, out of sight. Make confession, repent your past; avoid the punishment to come; and do not make matters worse by adding to your sins. Forgive me my presumption. In the grossness of these self-indulgent times even virtue must beg pardon of vice; indeed, bow and beg for permission to offer a helping hand.

Queen   Oh Hamlet, you have cut my heart in two!

Hamlet   Then throw away the worse part of it, and live all the purer with the half that's left. Good night. But don't go to bed with my uncle. Practise decency, even if you haven't got any. That monster, custom, which eats away one's sense of evil, has this good quality: it also makes the practice of good deeds a habit that becomes natural. Stay away tonight, and that will make the next abstinence somewhat easier; the next more easy still. Repetition can change one's normal nature and either accommodate the devil or throw him out quite effectively. Once again,

With wondrous potency. Once more, good night,
And when you are desirous to be blest,
I'll blessing beg of you. For this same lord
I do repent; but heaven hath pleased it so,
190   To punish me with this and this with me,
That I must be their scourge and minister.
I will bestow him, and will answer well
The death I gave him. So, again, good night.
I must be cruel only to be kind.
195   Thus bad begins, and worse remains behind.
One word more, good lady.

Queen   What shall I do?

Hamlet   Not this, by no means, that I bid you do:
Let the bloat King tempt you again to bed,
200   Pinch wanton on your cheek, call you his mouse,
And let him, for a pair of reechy kisses,
Or paddling in your neck with his damned fingers,
Make you to ravel all this matter out
That I essentially am not in madness,
205   But mad in craft. 'Twere good you let him know,
For who that's but a queen, fair, sober, wise,
Would from a paddock, from a bat, a gib,
Such dear concernings hide? Who would do so?
No, in despite of sense and secrecy,
210   Unpeg the basket on the house's top,
Let the birds fly, and like the famous ape,
To try conclusions, in the basket creep,
And break your own neck down.

Queen   Be thou assured, if words be made of breath,
215   And breath of life, I have no life to breathe
What thou hast said to me.

Hamlet   I must to England, you know that?

good night. And when you seek a blessing for yourself, I'll beg a blessing from you. [*Looking at* **Polonius**] As for this gentleman, I express my sorrow. It has pleased heaven to punish me with this, and this man through me: I must be God's instrument. I'll dispose of his body, and atone for killing him. So again, good night. I must be cruel to be kind. This is a bad beginning, and worse is yet to come. One word more, good lady.

Queen What do you want me to do?

Hamlet Do not, whatever happens, do any of these things: don't let the bloated King tempt you to bed again; pinch your cheek lecherously; call you his mouse; and thereby let him, for a couple of repulsive kisses – or fondling with his damned fingers in your neck – make you explain everything: that in fact I'm not truly mad, but only pretending to be. [*Sarcastically*] You have a duty to tell him. Could a mere queen – beautiful, dignified, and wise – conceal matters of such personal importance from a frog, a bat, a tomcat? Who'd be so naughty? No – contrary to commonsense and caution, let the cat out of the bag; spill the beans; copy the proverbial ape that tried to fly – ruin yourself!

Queen [*interpreting* **Hamlet**'s *ironies*] Be assured, if words are made of breath, and breath is the staff of life, I haven't sufficient life to report what you have said to me.

Hamlet I have to go to England. You know that?

Queen   Alack,
I had forgot. 'Tis so concluded on.

220 **Hamlet**   There's letters sealed, and my two schoolfellows,
Whom I will trust as I will adders fanged –
They bear the mandate, they must sweep my way
And marshal me to knavery. Let it work;
For 'tis the sport to have the engineer
225 Hoist with his own petard, and't shall go hard
But I will delve one yard below their mines
And blow them at the moon. Oh, 'tis most sweet
When in one line two crafts directly meet.
This man shall set me packing.
230 I'll lug the guts into the neighbouring room.
Mother, good night indeed. This counsellor
Is now most still, most secret, and most grave,
Who was in life a foolish prating knave.
Come, sir, to draw toward an end with you.
235 Good night, mother.

[*Exit dragging in* **Polonius.** *The* **Queen** *remains*]

Queen   Alas, I had forgotten. It's been confirmed.

Hamlet   The letters of authority are written, and my two
schoolfellows – whom I trust like I trust snakes – are in
charge; they must escort me, and lead me into some
mischief. So be it. It's fun to see the soldier blown to bits
with his own bomb: and see if I don't dig a yard below their
mines and blow them to smithereens! Oh, it's nice when
two crafty schemes proceed on a collision course!   [*Turning
to* **Polonius**]   This man will get me packed off quickly. I'll
lug the guts into the next room. Mother, a final good night.
This counselor is now very still, very secret, and very grave.
In life he was a foolish, talkative idiot.   [*Seizing* **Polonius***'s
body*]   Come, sir. To finish my business with you.
Good night, mother.

[*He drags* **Polonius** *off. The* **Queen** *remains sighing and
deeply distressed*]

Act four

Scene 1

To the **Queen,** *enter* **King,** *with* **Rosencrantz** *and*
Guildenstern.

King There's matter in these sighs, these profound heaves,
You must translate. 'Tis fit we understand them.
Where is your son?

Queen Bestow this place on us a little while.

> [*Exeunt* **Rosencrantz** *and* **Guildenstern**]

5 Ah, my good lord, what have I seen tonight!

King What, Gertrude, how does Hamlet?

Queen Mad as the sea and wind when both contend
Which is the mightier. In his lawless fit,
Behind the arras hearing something stir,
10 Whips out his rapier, cries 'A rat, a rat,'
And in this brainish apprehension kills
The unseen good old man.

King Oh heavy deed!
It had been so with us had we been there.
15 His liberty is full of threats to all –
To you yourself, to us, to everyone.
Alas, how shall this bloody deed be answered?
It will be laid to us, whose providence
Should have kept short, restrained, and out of haunt
20 This mad young man. But so much was our love,
We would not understand what was most fit,

Act four

Scene 1

The **King** *joins the* **Queen** *in her room.* **Rosencrantz** *and*
Guildenstern *follow him in.*

King   These sighs, these profound shudders, signify
something: you must explain. It's right that we should
know. Where is your son?

Queen   Leave us alone for a while.

> [**Rosencrantz** *and* **Guildenstern** *bow and leave*]

Oh husband – the things I've seen this night!

King   Poor Gertrude. How is Hamlet?

Queen   As mad as the sea and the wind when they brawl to
prove which is the mightier. In his mania, hearing something
move behind the tapestry, he whips out his rapier, crying ''A
rat, a rat!'' In this frenzied delusion he kills the hidden, good
old man.

King   A grievous deed! It would have been my fate had I been
there. His freedom threatens us all: you yourself, me,
everyone. Alas, how shall we explain this bloody deed?
They'll blame me; I ought to have had the foresight to keep
this mad young man on a short rein, under restraint and out
of circulation. I loved him so much that I refused to accept

But like the owner of a foul disease,
To keep it from divulging, let it feed
Even on the pith of life. Where is he gone?

25 **Queen** To draw apart the body he hath killed,
O'er whom his very madness, like some ore
Among a mineral of metals base,
Shows itself pure: he weeps for what is done.

King Oh Gertrude, come away!
30 The sun no sooner shall the mountains touch
But we will ship him hence; and this vile deed
We must with all our majesty and skill
Both countenance and excuse. Ho, Guildenstern!

[*Enter* **Rosencrantz** *and* **Guildenstern**]

Friends both, go join you with some further aid.
35 Hamlet in madness hath Polonius slain,
And from his mother's closet hath he dragged him.
Go seek him out: speak fair, and bring the body
Into the chapel. I pray you haste in this.

[*Exeunt* **Rosencrantz** *and* **Guildenstern**]

Come, Gertrude, we'll call up our wisest friends,
40 And let them know both what we mean to do
And what's untimely done. So, haply, slander,
Whose whisper o'er the world's diameter,
As level as the cannon to his blank,
Transports his poisoned shot, may miss our name
45 And hit the woundless air. O come away,
My soul is full of discord and dismay.

[*Exeunt*]

what was best. Like someone with a foul disease who
wants to keep it from becoming public, it's been allowed to
feed on life itself. Where has he gone?

Queen   To remove the corpse, over which his very madness,
like gold in a mine of base metals, shines out pure: he
weeps for what has happened.

King   Oh, Gertrude, come away. At dusk we'll send him away
by sea. Using all my authority and skill, I must condone and
excuse this vile deed.   [*Calling*]   Guildenstern!

[**Rosencrantz** *and* **Guildenstern** *enter*]

Friends, get others to help you. In his madness Hamlet has
killed Polonius, and has dragged him from his mother's
room. Find him – humor him – and take the body to the
chapel. Hurry, will you?

[**Rosencrantz** *and* **Guildenstern** *leave*]

Come, Gertrude. We'll summon our wisest friends, and tell
them what we intend to do, and what has unfortunately
happened. Hopefully, slanderous talk, whose poisoned shot
usually travels from one side of the world to the other as
straight as a cannon to its target, may miss me and hit the
empty air. Let's go – my soul is full of agitation and fear.

[*They go*]

Scene 2

Enter **Hamlet**.

Hamlet Safely stowed.   [*Calling within*]
What noise? Who calls on Hamlet? Oh, here they come!

[*Enter* **Rosencrantz** *and* **Guildenstern**]

Rosencrantz What have you done, my lord, with the dead
body?

5 **Hamlet** Compounded it with dust, whereto 'tis kin.

Rosencrantz Tell us where 'tis, that we may take it thence
and bear it to the chapel.

Hamlet Do not believe it.

Rosencrantz Believe what?

10 **Hamlet** That I can keep your counsel and not mine own.
Besides, to be demanded of a sponge – what replication
should be made by the son of a king?

Rosencrantz Take you me for a sponge, my lord?

Hamlet Ay, sir, that soaks up the King's countenance, his
15 rewards, his authorities. But such officers do the King best
service in the end: he keeps them, like an ape, in the corner
of his jaw; first mouthed, to be last swallowed. When he
needs what you have gleaned, it is but squeezing you and,
sponge, you shall be dry again.

20 **Rosencrantz** I understand you not, my lord.

Hamlet I am glad of it. A knavish speech sleeps in a foolish
ear.

Scene 2

Hamlet *enters*.

Hamlet   [*referring to the body of* **Polonius**]   Safely stowed
away.   [*Voices are heard calling his name*]   What's that?
Who's calling me? Oh, here they come!

[**Rosencrantz** *and* **Guildenstern** *enter*]

Rosencrantz   My lord, what have you done with the dead
body?

Hamlet   Mixed it with dust, with which it is related.

Rosencrantz   Tell us where it is, so that we can take it from
there and carry it to the chapel.

Hamlet   Don't believe it.

Rosencrantz   Believe what?

Hamlet   That I can keep your secrets and not my own.
Besides, to be cross-examined by a sponge! What reply can
the son of a king give?

Rosencrantz   Do you regard me as a sponge, my lord?

Hamlet   Yes sir, that soaks up the King's favors, his rewards,
his influence. Such officers *do* serve the King best in the
end: although he puts them in his mouth first, he hides them
in a corner to be swallowed last, ape-fashion. When he
wants to know what you have found out, he needs only to
squeeze you and – spongelike – you are bone-dry again.

Rosencrantz   I don't understand you, my lord.

Hamlet   Just as well. Satire is wasted on idiots.

Rosencrantz My lord, you must tell us where the body is and
go with us to the King.

Hamlet The body is with the King, but the King is not with
25 the body. The King is a thing –

Guildenstern A thing, my lord?

Hamlet Of nothing. Bring me to him.

[*Exeunt*]

Scene 3

Enter the **King** *and two or three Lords.*

King I have sent to seek him and to find the body.
How dangerous is it that this man goes loose!
Yet must not we put the strong law on him:
He's loved of the distracted multitude,
5 Who like not in their judgment but their eyes,
And where 'tis so, th'offender's scourge is weighed,
But never the offence. To bear all smooth and even,
This sudden sending him away must seem
Deliberate pause. Diseases desperate grown
10 By desperate appliance are relieved,
Or not at all.

[*Enter* **Rosencrantz, Guildenstern,** *and others*]

How now, what hath befallen?

Rosencrantz   My lord, you must tell us where the body is and
go with us to the King.

Hamlet   The body is with the King   [*he means* **King
Hamlet**]   but the King   [*he means* **Claudius**]   is not with
the body. The King   [*he still refers to his uncle*]   is a
thing –

Guildenstern   A thing, my lord?

Hamlet   Of no consequence. Take me to him.

[*They go*]

Scene 3

The **King** *enters, followed by several Lords.*

King   I've sent them to look for him, and to find the body.
How dangerous it is to have this man at large! But we
mustn't invoke the letter of the law: the common people
love him, and they go by appearances, not reason; that
means the offender's punishment is mulled over, but never
the offense. To keep everything calm, this sudden departure
must seem to be the outcome of careful deliberation.
Desperate illnesses require desperate remedies.

[**Rosencrantz, Guildenstern** *and the search party enter*]

Well, what's happened?

Rosencrantz   Where the dead body is bestowed, my lord,
We cannot get from him.

15 **King**   But where is he?

Rosencrantz   Without, my lord, guarded, to know your
pleasure.

King   Bring him before us.

Rosencrantz   Ho! Bring in the lord.

[*Enter* **Hamlet** *with guards*]

20 **King**   Now, Hamlet, where's Polonius?

Hamlet   At supper.

King   At supper? Where?

Hamlet   Not where he eats, but where he is eaten. A certain
convocation of politic worms are e'en at him. Your worm is
25 your only emperor for diet: we fat all creatures else to fat us,
and we fat ourselves for maggots. Your fat king and your
lean beggar is but variable service – two dishes, but to one
table. That's the end.

King   Alas, alas.

30 **Hamlet**   A man may fish with the worm that hath eat of a
king, and eat of the fish that hath fed of that worm.

King   What dost thou mean by this?

Hamlet   Nothing but to show you how a king may go a
progress through the guts of a beggar.

35 **King**   Where is Polonius?

Hamlet   In heaven. Send thither to see. If your messenger
find him not there, seek him i'th'other place yourself. But if

Rosencrantz   We can't get him to say where he's put the dead body, my lord.

King   But where is he?

Rosencrantz   Outside, my lord, under guard, awaiting your pleasure.

King   Bring him in to me.

Rosencrantz   [*calling*]   Bring in the lord!

[**Hamlet** *is brought in, guarded*]

King   Now, Hamlet: where's Polonius?

Hamlet   At supper.

King   At supper? Where?

Hamlet   Not where he eats, but where he's eaten. A certain committee of wise worms is busy with him at this very moment. Your actual worm is a great eater. We fatten up the animals to make us fat, and we get fat ourselves to feed maggots. Your fat king and your skinny beggar are just alternative menus: two dishes, but served at the same table. That's the end.

King   Alas, alas . . .

Hamlet   A man can go fishing with the worm that fed off a king, and then eat the fish that ate that worm.

King   Meaning?

Hamlet   Nothing – just to show you how a king can make a state journey through the guts of a beggar.

King   Where is Polonius?

Hamlet   In heaven. Send for him there. If your messenger can't find him, search for him in the other place yourself. If

indeed you find him not within this month, you shall nose
him as you go up the stairs into the lobby.

40 **King**   [*to some Attendants*]   Go seek him there.

Hamlet   He will stay till you come.

[*Exeunt Attendants*]

King   Hamlet, this deed, for thine especial safety –
Which we do tender, as we dearly grieve
For that which thou hast done – must send thee hence
45 With fiery quickness. Therefore prepare thyself.
The bark is ready, and the wind at help,
Th'associates tend, and everything is bent
For England.

Hamlet   For England?

50 **King**   Ay, Hamlet.

Hamlet   Good.

King   So is it, if thou knew'st our purposes.

Hamlet   I see a cherub that sees them. But come, for
England. Farewell, dear mother.

55 **King**   Thy loving father, Hamlet.

Hamlet   My mother. Father and mother is man and wife,
man and wife is one flesh; so my mother. Come, for England.

[*Exit*]

King   Follow him at foot. Tempt him with speed aboard,
Delay it not. I'll have him hence tonight.

you don't find him inside a month, you'll smell him as you go up the stairs into the lobby.

King [*to some Attendants*]   Go and look for him there.

Hamlet   He'll wait for you!

[*The Attendants exit*]

King   Hamlet, for your own safety, which we worry about just as we profoundly grieve over what you have done: this deed necessitates your instant departure. Make your preparations. The ship is ready, the wind is in the right direction, the escorts are waiting, and everything is set for England.

Hamlet   For England?

King   Yes, Hamlet.

Hamlet   Good.

King   So it is, if you knew my intentions.

Hamlet   I have my informants. But however: to England! Farewell, dear mother.

King   Your loving *father*, Hamlet.

Hamlet   My mother! Father and mother is man and wife. Man and wife is one flesh. Therefore – my mother. Come on then – to England.

[*He leaves*]

King   [*to Attendants*]   Follow him closely. Get him aboard as quickly as possible. Don't delay: I want him away tonight.

60   Away! For everything is sealed and done
        That else leans on th'affair. Pray you make haste.

                              [*Exeunt all but the* **King**]

        And England, if my love thou hold'st at aught –
        As my great power thereof may give thee sense,
        Since yet thy cicatrice looks raw and red
65   After the Danish sword, and thy free awe
        Pays homage to us – thou mayst not coldly set
        Our sovereign process, which imports at full,
        By letters conjuring to that effect,
        The present death of Hamlet. Do it, England;
70   For like the hectic in my blood he rages,
        And thou must cure me. Till I know 'tis done,
        Howe'er my haps, my joys were ne'er begun.

                                          [*Exit*]

Scene 4

Enter **Fortinbras** *with his army marching over the stage.*

Fortinbras   Go, Captain, from me greet the Danish king.
        Tell him that by his licence Fortinbras
        Craves the conveyance of a promised march
        Over his kingdom. You know the rendezvous.
5   If that his Majesty would aught with us,
        We shall express our duty in his eye;
        And let him know so.

Captain   I will do't, my lord.

Fortinbras   Go softly on.

218

Go – all the relevant documentation has been done. Hurry.

[*Everyone leaves except the* **King**]

King of England: if you value my goodwill – the extent of
which you well know, since you are barely recovered from
our Danish victory over you, and you pay us tribute
money – you cannot lightly disregard my royal wishes,
which are described in letters conveying full instructions for
the immediate death of Hamlet. See that it's done, King. He
disturbs me like a raging fever, and you must cure me of it.
Till I know it's done, whatever my previous good fortune,
my happiness has not yet started.

[*The* **King** *goes*]

Scene 4

Fortinbras, *the King of Norway's nephew, is marching with his
army towards Poland. He halts to give instructions to a*
Captain.

Fortinbras   Captain, go greet the Danish king on my behalf.
Tell him that as agreed, Fortinbras requests safe conduct of
his army through his kingdom. You know our rendezvous. If
his Majesty wants to talk to us, we'll pay our respects to
him personally. Tell him so.

Captain   I'll do so, my lord.

Fortinbras   Advance at slow pace.

[*Exeunt all but the* **Captain**]

[*Enter* **Hamlet, Rosencrantz, Guildenstern** *and others*]

10 **Hamlet**   Good sir, whose powers are these?

Captain   They are of Norway, sir.

Hamlet   How purposed, sir, I pray you?

Captain   Against some part of Poland.

Hamlet   Who commands them, sir?

15 **Captain**   The nephew to old Norway, Fortinbras.

Hamlet   Goes it against the main of Poland, sir,
Or for some frontier?

Captain   Truly to speak, and with no addition,
We go to gain a little patch of ground
20 That hath in it no profit but the name.
To pay five ducats – five – I would not farm it;
Nor will it yield to Norway or the Pole
A ranker rate should it be sold in fee.

Hamlet   Why, then the Polack never will defend it.

25 **Captain**   Yes, it is already garrisoned.

Hamlet   Two thousand souls and twenty thousand ducats
Will not debate the question of this straw!
This is th'imposthume of much wealth and peace,
That inward breaks, and shows no cause without
30 Why the man dies. I humbly thank you, sir.

Captain   God be wi'you, sir.   [*Exit*]

Rosencrantz   Will't please you go, my lord?

[*All go except the* **Captain**]

[**Hamlet, Rosencrantz, Guildenstern,** *and Attendants enter*]

Hamlet   Sir, whose army is this?

Captain   Norwegian, sir.

Hamlet   What's its objective?

Captain   It's against some part of Poland.

Hamlet   Who is in command?

Captain   The nephew of the old King of Norway: Fortinbras.

Hamlet   Is the campaign against Poland as a whole, or some frontier?

Captain   Frankly, and in plain terms, we go to gain a little patch of ground that has no advantage about it except its name. I wouldn't pay five ducats a year − not five − to lease it. It wouldn't raise a penny more for Norway or for Poland if sold outright.

Hamlet   Why, surely the King of Poland will never defend it?

Captain   Yes, it's already garrisoned.

Hamlet   This is a trifling issue that not even two thousand dead and twenty thousand ducats will settle! It's like an abscess that bursts inside a man. It's full of matter − in this case, wealth and soldiers − but externally, you can't tell why he died. My grateful thanks to you, sir.

Captain   God be with you, sir.

[*He leaves*]

Rosencrantz   Are you ready, my lord?

Hamlet   I'll be with you straight. Go a little before.

[*Exeunt all but* **Hamlet**]

How all occasions do inform against me,
35   And spur my dull revenge! What is a man
If his chief good and market of his time
Be but to sleep and feed? A beast, no more.
Sure he that made us with such large discourse,
Looking before and after, gave us not
40   That capability and godlike reason
To fust in us unused. Now whether it be
Bestial oblivion, or some craven scruple
Of thinking too precisely on th'event –
A thought which, quartered, hath but one part wisdom
45   And ever three parts coward – I do not know
Why yet I live to say this thing's to do,
Sith I have cause, and will, and strength, and means
To do't. Examples gross as earth exhort me,
Witness this army of such mass and charge,
50   Led by a delicate and tender prince,
Whose spirit, with divine ambition puffed,
Makes mouths at the invisible event,
Exposing what is mortal and unsure
To all that fortune, death, and danger dare,
55   Even for an eggshell. Rightly to be great
Is not to stir without great argument,
But greatly to find quarrel in a straw
When honour's at the stake. How stand I then,
That have a father killed, a mother stained,
60   Excitements of my reason and my blood,
And let all sleep, while to my shame I see
The imminent death of twenty thousand men
That, for a fantasy and trick of fame,
Go to their graves like beds, fight for a plot
65   Whereon the numbers cannot try the cause,

Hamlet I'll be with you right away. Go on ahead.

[They all leave except **Hamlet**]*

Hamlet How everything pricks my conscience, and spurs me on again to my revenge! What is man, if he merely spends his life sleeping and eating? No better than a beast. Surely the God who gave us the ability to think logically, and to conceive of past and future, didn't endow us with that skill and reasoning power for it to grow moldy in us from disuse. I don't know whether it's brutish ignorance, or some cowardly indecision caused by thinking far too deeply about the consequences (something which always consists of one part wisdom and three parts cowardice!) that makes me put things off. After all, I have the motive, the determination, the strength and the means to do it. There's no shortage of examples to inspire me: witness this large and costly army, led by a sensitive and youthful prince whose courage − inflated with divine ambition − scoffs at danger. He risks his life, exposing himself to chance, death and danger, and all for an empty shell. True greatness lies not in fighting noble causes, but in quibbling over trifles when honor is at stake. What's to be said of me, then? I have a father who has been murdered, a mother who has been defiled, and motives inspired both by reason and passion: yet I've done nothing. To my shame, at the same time I see the imminent deaths of twenty thousand men, who for an illusion, the sham of renown, go to their graves as if to their beds, and fight over a plot of ground not big enough to accommodate the combatants, nor to bury them

Which is not tomb enough and continent
To hide the slain? O, from this time forth
My thoughts be bloody or be nothing worth.

[*Exit*]

Scene 5

Enter **Queen, Horatio,** *and a* **Gentleman**.

Queen   I will not speak with her.

Gentleman   She is importunate,
Indeed distract. Her mood will needs be pitied.

Queen   What would she have?

5 **Gentleman**   She speaks much of her father, says she hears
There's tricks i'th'world, and hems, and beats her heart;
Spurns enviously at straws; speaks things in doubt
That carry but half sense. Her speech is nothing,
Yet the unshaped use of it doth move
10 The hearers to collection. They aim at it,
And botch the words up fit to their own thoughts,
Which, as her winks and nods and gestures yield them,
Indeed would make one think there might be thought,
Though nothing sure, yet much unhappily.

15 **Horatio**   'Twere good she were spoken with, for she may strew
Dangerous conjectures in ill-breeding minds.

Queen   Let her come in.

[*Exit* **Gentleman**]

should they be slain. Oh, from now on my thoughts must
concentrate on vengeance, or they're unworthy!

[*He goes*]

Scene 5

The **Queen** *enters, with* **Horatio** *and a* **Gentleman**.

Queen   I won't speak to her.

Gentleman   She's insistent; out of her mind even. She must
be pitied in her distress.

Queen   What does she want?

Gentleman   She talks a lot about her father; says she's heard
the world's corrupt, and coughs, and beats her breast; takes
offense at every little thing, and speaks foolishly,
half-wittedly. What she says is nonsense, so her listeners
have to infer what she means. They do their best, and piece
the words together by guesswork. Judging by her winks and
nods and gestures one would suppose they had deep
meaning; much appeared indelicate, but one couldn't be
sure.

Horatio   She ought to be talked to, because she might spread
dangerous rumors amongst mischief-makers.

Queen   Let her in.

[*The* **Gentleman** *leaves*]

[*Aside*]   To my sick soul, as sin's true nature is,
20   Each toy seems prologue to some great amiss.
So full of artless jealousy is guilt,
It spills itself in fearing to be spilt.

[*Enter* **Ophelia**]

Ophelia   Where is the beauteous Majesty of Denmark?

Queen   How now, Ophelia?

25 **Ophelia**   [*sings*]   *How should I your true love know*
From another one?
By his cockle hat and staff
And his sandal shoon.

Queen   Alas, sweet lady, what imports this song?

30 **Ophelia**   Say you? Nay, pray you mark.

He is dead and gone, lady,
He is dead and gone;
At his head a grass-green turf,
At his heels a stone.

35   O ho!

Queen   Nay, but Ophelia –

Ophelia   Pray you mark.
[*Sings*]   *White his shroud as the mountain snow –*

[*Enter* **King**]

Queen   Alas, look here, my lord.

40 **Ophelia**   *Larded with sweet flowers*
Which bewept to the grave did not go
With true-love showers.

[*Aside*]   To my heavy conscience, as is always the case with sin, every little incident seems to be the forerunner of some major misfortune. Guilt is so full of fear it gives itself away.

[**Ophelia** *enters*]

Ophelia   Where is the beautiful Queen of Denmark?

Queen   How are you, Ophelia?

Ophelia   [*she sings lines from a popular ballad*]

> How could I a true love know
>   From one untrue?
> By his pilgrim's hat and staff
>   And his sandal shoe.

Queen   Alas, sweet lady, why are you singing this song?

Ophelia   What did you say? Listen:

> He is dead and gone, lady,
>   He is dead and gone,
> At his head is grass-green turf,
>   At his feet a stone.

[*She sighs heavily*]   Oh!

Queen   But Ophelia –

Ophelia   Note this:
[*She sings*]
White was his shroud as the mountain snow –

[*The* **King** *enters*]

Queen   Alas, look at her, my lord!

Ophelia   *Adorned with sweet flowers*
Which tearful to the grave did not go
With true-love showers.

King   How do you, pretty lady?

Ophelia   Well, good 'ild you. They say the owl was a baker's
45   daughter. Lord, we know what we are, but know not what
        we may be. God be at your table.

King   Conceit upon her father.

Ophelia   Pray let's have no words of this, but when they ask
        you what it means, say you this.

50   *Tomorrow is Saint Valentine's day,*
                    All in the morning betime,
                And I a maid at your window,
                    To be your Valentine.
                Then up he rose, and donned his clothes,
55   *And dupped the chamber door,*
                Let in the maid that out a maid
                    Never departed more.

King   Pretty Ophelia –

Ophelia   Indeed, without an oath, I'll make an end on't.

60   *By Gis and by Saint Charity,*
                    Alack and fie for shame!
                Young men will do't if they come to't –
                    By Cock, they are to blame.
                Quoth she, 'Before you tumbled me,
65   *You promised me to wed.'*

        He answers,

                'So would I 'a done, by yonder sun,
                And thou hadst not come to my bed.'

King   How long hath she been thus?

70 **Ophelia**   I hope all will be well. We must be patient. But I
        cannot choose but weep to think they would lay him

King   How are you, pretty lady?

Ophelia   Very well, God bless you. The baker's daughter was turned into an owl.   [*She refers to an old folktale*].   Lord, we know what we are, but not what we are going to be. May God be at your table!

King   She's obsessed with her father.

Ophelia   Don't let's quibble, but when they ask you what it all means, say this:

> *Tomorrow is Saint Valentine's Day,*
> *Early in the morning time;*
> *And I a maid at your window*
> *To be your Valentine.*
> *Then up he rose, and donned his clothes*
> *And opened the bedroom door;*
> *He let in the maid, who out a maid*
> *Never departed more.*

King   Pretty Ophelia –

Ophelia   I'll bring the story to an end without swearing an oath:

> *By jingo, and by charity!*
> *Alas, and oh, for shame!*
> *Young men will take the opportunity*
> *By Cock, they are to blame!*
> *Said she: "Before you slept with me*
> *You promised me to wed –"*

He answers,

> *"By yonder sun, I would have done*
> *If you hadn't come to my bed!"*

King   How long has she been like this?

Ophelia   I hope all will be well. We must be patient. But I can't help crying when I think how they laid him in the cold

i'th'cold ground. My brother shall know of it. And so I
thank you for your good counsel. Come, my coach. Good
night, ladies, good night. Sweet ladies, good night, good

75   night.

[Exit **Ophelia***]*

King   Follow her close; give her good watch, I pray you.

[Exit **Horatio***]*

O, this is the poison of deep grief: it springs
All from her father's death.
O Gertrude, Gertrude,

80   When sorrows come, they come not single spies,
But in battalions. First, her father slain;
Next, your son gone, and he most violent author
Of his own just remove; the people muddied,
Thick and unwholesome in their thoughts and whispers

85   For good Polonius' death – and we have done but greenly
In hugger-mugger to inter him; poor Ophelia
Divided from herself and her fair judgment,
Without the which we are pictures, or mere beasts;
Last, and as much containing as all these,

90   Her brother is in secret come from France,
Feeds on this wonder, keeps himself in clouds,
And wants not buzzers to infect his ear
With pestilent speeches of his father's death;
Wherein necessity, of matter beggared,

95   Will nothing stock our person to arraign
In ear and ear. O my dear Gertrude, this,
Like to a murd'ring-piece, in many places
Gives me superfluous death.   *[A noise within]*
Attend!

100 **Queen**   Alack, what noise is this?

King   Where are my Switzers? Let them guard the door.

[Enter a **Messenger***]*

What is the matter?

ground. My brother will be informed of this! And so I thank
you for your good advice. Come, my coach! Good night,
ladies, good night. Sweet ladies, good night, good night . . .

[*She leaves them*]

King   Follow her. Keep a close eye on her, will you?

[**Horatio** *follows her*]

Oh, this is the poisonous effect of deep grief! It all derives
from the death of her father. Oh Gertrude, Gertrude,
sorrows never come singly, but in battalions. First, her
father murdered. Next, your son gone, the author of his own
just banishment. The people are perplexed; confused and
suspicious in their thoughts and their speculations
concerning the death of good Polonius. I was ill-advised to
bury him secretly. Poor Ophelia, no longer in possession of
her wits, without the which we are shadows, or mere
beasts! Last, but by no means least, her brother has secretly
returned from France. He mulls over these astonishing
events; is full of speculations; and lacks no rumor-mongers
to poison his mind with provocative reports of his father's
death, in respect of which – facts being in short
supply – they do not hesitate to theorize about my
involvement as the rumors spread. Oh, my dear Gertrude,
all this is like grapeshot – I'm killed many times over.

[*A noise is heard outside*]

Queen   Did you hear that?

King   Where are my bodyguards? Guard the door!

[*A* **Messenger** *enters*]

What's going on?

Messenger   Save yourself, my lord.
The ocean, overpeering of his list,
105 Eats not the flats with more impetuous haste
Than young Laertes, in a riotous head,
O'erbears your officers. The rabble call him lord,
And, as the world were now but to begin,
Antiquity forgot, custom not known –
110 The ratifiers and props of every word –
They cry, 'Choose we! Laertes shall be king.'
Caps, hands, and tongues applaud it to the clouds,
'Laertes shall be king, Laertes king.'

Queen   How cheerfully on the false trail they cry.
115 O, this is counter, you false Danish dogs.   [*A noise within*]

King   The doors are broke.

[*Enter* **Laertes** *with Followers*]

Laertes   Where is this King? Sirs, stand you all without.

Followers   No, let's come in.

Laertes   I pray you give me leave.

120 **Followers**   We will, we will.

Laertes   I thank you. Keep the door.

[*Exeunt Followers*]

Oh thou vile King,

Give me my father.

Queen   Calmly, good Laertes.

125 **Laertes**   That drop of blood that's calm proclaims me bastard,
Cries cuckold to my father, brands the harlot
Even here between the chaste unsmirched brow
Of my true mother.

232

Messenger Save yourself, my lord. Not even mountainous
seas flood across the plain with greater violence than young
Laertes sweeps aside your soldiers with his rebel force. The
mob call him ''lord'', and as if the world had just begun and
there were no traditions or established customs – the things
that give society its stability – they cry ''We've made our
choice! Laertes for king!'' Caps, clapping, cheering all reach
for the sky: ''Laertes for king! Laertes king!''

Queen How they bay enthusiastically along false trails: you
are on the wrong track, false Danish dogs! [*A noise
outside*]

King They've broken down the doors!

[**Laertes** *enters with his supporters*]

Laertes Where is this King? [*To his men*] Gentlemen, stay
outside.

Followers No. Let's come in.

Laertes Wait for me there.

Followers We will, we will.

Laertes Thank you. Guard the door.

[*His supporters leave*]

Oh, you vile King! Give me back my father!

Queen [*restraining him*] Calmly, good Laertes!

Laertes If one drop of my blood stays calm, it proves me
illegitimate, makes my father a cuckold, and brands my
faithful mother as a harlot!

233

King   What is the cause, Laertes,
130   That thy rebellion looks so giant-like?
       Let him go, Gertrude. Do not fear our person.
       There's such divinity doth hedge a king
       That treason can but peep to what it would,
       Acts little of his will. Tell me, Laertes,
135   Why thou art thus incensed. Let him go, Gertrude.
       Speak, man.

Laertes   Where is my father?

King   Dead.

Queen   But not by him.

140 **King**   Let him demand his fill.

Laertes   How came he dead? I'll not be juggled with.
       To hell, allegiance! Vows to the blackest devil!
       Conscience and grace, to the profoundest pit!
       I dare damnation. To this point I stand,
145   That both the worlds I give to negligence,
       Let come what comes, only I'll be revenged
       Most throughly for my father's death.

King   Who shall stay you?

Laertes   My will, not all the world's.
150   And for my means, I'll husband them so well,
       They shall go far with little.

King   Good Laertes,
       If you desire to know the certainty
       Of your dear father, is't writ in your revenge
155   That, swoopstake, you will draw both friend and foe,
       Winner and loser?

Laertes   None but his enemies.

King   Will you know them then?

King   Laertes, what has provoked you to a rebellion on this scale? [*To the* **Queen**]   Let him go, Gertrude. Have no fears for my safety. Royalty has such divine protection that treason never gets beyond a glimpse of its objectives. Tell me, Laertes: why are you so incensed? [*Insisting*]   Let him go, Gertrude! [*To* **Laertes**]   Speak up, man!

Laertes   Where is my father?

King   Dead.

Queen   But *he* didn't kill him!

King   Let him ask what he wants.

Laertes   How did he come to die? I want a straight answer. To hell with my allegiance! Satan take my loyalty! To the bottomless pit with conscience and God's grace! I'm not afraid of damnation. I'm not bothered about this world or the next. Come what may, I'm going to be thoroughly revenged for my father's death.

King   Who would hold you back?

Laertes   No one on this earth but myself. As for my means, I'll use what I have to good effect: a little will go a long way.

King   Good Laertes, in wanting to know the facts about your dear father, does your plan for revenge include sweeping the board – making no distinction between friend and foe, and scooping up the lot?

Laertes   Only his enemies.

King   Do you want to know who they are?

Laertes   To his good friends thus wide I'll ope my arms,
160   And, like the kind life-rend'ring pelican,
        Repast them with my blood.

King   Why, now you speak
        Like a good child and a true gentleman.
        That I am guiltless of your father's death
165   And am most sensibly in grief for it,
        It shall as level to your judgment 'pear
        As day does to your eye.

                    [*A noise within.* **Ophelia** *is heard singing*]

                    Let her come in.

Laertes   How now, what noise is that?

[*Enter* **Ophelia**]

170   O heat, dry up my brains! Tears seven times salt
        Burn out the sense and virtue of mine eye.
        By heaven, thy madness shall be paid with weight
        Till our scale turn the beam. O rose of May!
        Dear maid, kind sister, sweet Ophelia!
175   O heavens, is't possible a young maid's wits
        Should be as mortal as an old man's life?
        Nature is fine in love, and where 'tis fine
        It sends some precious instance of itself
        After the thing it loves.

180 **Ophelia**   [*sings*]   *They bore him bare-faced on the bier,*
                            And in his grave rained many a tear –

        Fare you well, my dove.

Laertes   Hadst thou thy wits and didst persuade revenge,
        It could not move thus.

Ophelia   You must sing *A-down a-down,* and you *Call him a-*
185   *down-a.* O, how the wheel becomes it! It is the false steward
        that stole his master's daughter.

Laertes I'll open my arms wide to his good friends, and like the legendary pelican, I'll sustain them with my own blood.

King Why, now you are speaking like a good son and a true gentleman. That I am guiltless of your father's death, and that I'm deeply grieved by it, will be made as clear as daylight to you.

[**Ophelia** *is heard singing outside*]

Let her come in.

Laertes Who's that?

[**Ophelia** *enters*]

Would that I'd lost my reason, and my sight! By heavens, your madness will be outweighed by my revenge! Oh, you rose of May! Dear maid – kind sister – sweet Ophelia! God, is it possible that a young girl's sanity should be as vulnerable as an old man's life? Love is exquisite. It sends a specimen of itself to accompany a loved one who's departed.

Ophelia [*singing*]

> *They bore him, bare-faced, on the bier*
> *And in his grave rained many a tear-*

Farewell, my dove!

Laertes If you were sane and argued for revenge, you couldn't be more persuasive.

Ophelia [*to the* **King**] You must sing *A-down a-down* and [*to the* **Queen**] you *Call him a-down-a*. It's a catchy refrain. The crafty bailiff ran off with the boss's daughter . . .

Laertes   This nothing's more than matter.

Ophelia   There's rosemary, that's for remembrance – pray
you, love, remember. And there is pansies, that's for
190   thoughts.

Laertes   A document in madness: thoughts and remembrance
fitted.

Ophelia   There's fennel for you, and columbines. There's rue
for you. And here's some for me. We may call it herb of
195   grace o' Sundays. You must wear your rue with a difference.
There's a daisy. I would give you some violets, but they
withered all when my father died. They say he made a good
end.

[*Sings*]   *For bonny sweet Robin is all my joy.*

200 **Laertes**   Thought and affliction, passion, hell itself
She turns to favour and to prettiness.

Ophelia   [*sings*]   *And will he not come again?*
        And will he not come again?
          No, no, he is dead,
205   *Go to thy death-bed,*
        He never will come again.

        His beard was as white as snow,
        All flaxen was his poll.
          He is gone, he is gone,
210   *And we cast away moan.*
        God a mercy on his soul.

And of all Christian souls. God be wi' you.

                            [*Exit*]

Laertes   There's meaning in this nonsense . . .

Ophelia   [*distributing flowers from a bunch she is carrying.
She begins with* **Laertes**]   Here's some rosemary. That's for
remembrance. Please, love, remember. And here's some
pansies. They're for thoughts.

Laertes   [*taking them*]   A lesson in madness: thoughts and
remembrance aptly placed.

Ophelia   [*to the* **Queen**]   There's some fennel for you, and
columbines.   [*These plants were identified with
unfaithfulness*].   [*To the* **King**]   There's rue for you.   [*It
signifies repentance*]   And here's some for me.   [*In her
case it signifies sorrow*]   On Sundays it's called "herb
o'grace." You must wear your rue like a coat of
arms.   [*Again to the* **King**]   There's a daisy.   [*The flower
symbolizing unrequited love*]   I'd give you some
violets   [*the flower of faithfulness*]   but they all withered
when my father died. They say he died well.   [*Singing*]   *For
bonny sweet Robin is all my joy.*

Laertes   Sorrow and misfortune; suffering; hell itself – she
makes them charming and delightful.

Ophelia   [*singing*]
    And will he not come again?
    And will he not come again?
      No, no, he is dead.
      Go to your deathbed,
    He never will come again.

    His beard was as white as snow,
    All fair-haired was his head.
      He has gone, he has gone;
      Comfort we have none.
    God have mercy on him, dead.

And on all Christian souls. May God be with you.   [*She goes*]

Laertes   Do you see this, o God?

King   Laertes, I .nust commune with your grief,
215   Or you deny me right. Go but apart,
Make choice of whom your wisest friends you will,
And they shall hear and judge 'twixt you and me.
If by direct or by collateral hand
They find us touched, we will our kingdom give,
220   Our crown, our life, and all that we call ours
To you in satisfaction; but if not,
Be you content to lend your patience to us,
And we shall jointly labour with your soul
To give it due content.

225   **Laertes**   Let this be so.
His means of death, his obscure funeral –
No trophy, sword, nor hatchment o'er his bones,
No noble rite, nor formal ostentation –
Cry to be heard, as 'twere from heaven to earth,
230   That I must call't in question.

King   So you shall.
And where th'offence is, let the great axe fall.
I pray you go with me.

[*Exeunt*]

Scene 6

Enter **Horatio** *and a Servant.*

Horatio   What are they that would speak with me?

Servant   Seafaring men, sir. They say they have letters for
you.

Laertes   Has God seen this?

King   Laertes, respect my right to share your grief. Break off now and choose the wisest friends you have. They shall arbitrate between us. If they find me guilty, either personally or through my agents, then my kingdom, my crown, my life and everything I possess is yours in penalty. If they do not, bear with me patiently and I'll satisfy you absolutely.

Laertes   Agreed. How he died; his secret funeral – with no memorials, no displays of arms, no plaques over his tomb, no rites appropriate to his rank, no formal ceremonies – these all cry out so deafeningly for an explanation that I must question everything.

King   So you shall. And those who are found guilty shall be punished. Come with me.

[*They go*]

Scene 6

Horatio *enters with a* **Servant**.

Horatio   Who are these men who want to speak to me?

Servant   Seafaring men, sir. They say they have letters for you.

Horatio Let them come in. [*Exit Servant*]

5   I do not know from what part of the world
    I should be greeted, if not from Lord Hamlet.

[*Enter* **Sailors**]

1st Sailor God bless you, sir.

Horatio Let him bless thee too.

1st Sailor He shall, sir, and please him. There's a letter for
10   you, sir. It came from th'ambassador that was bound for
    England – if your name be Horatio, as I am let to know it is.

Horatio [*reads the letter*] *Horatio, when thou shalt have
overlooked this, give these fellows some means to the King. They
have letters for him. Ere we were two days old at sea, a pirate of*
15 *very warlike appointment gave us chase. Finding ourselves too
slow of sail, we put on a compelled valour, and in the grapple I
boarded them. On the instant they got clear of our ship, so I
alone became their prisoner. They have dealt with me like
thieves of mercy. But they knew what they did: I am to do a*
20 *turn for them. Let the King have the letters I have sent, and
repair thou to me with as much speed as thou wouldest fly
death. I have words to speak in thine ear will make thee dumb;
yet are they much too light for the bore of the matter. These
good fellows will bring thee where I am. Rosencrantz and*
25 *Guildenstern hold their course for England; of them I have
much to tell thee. Farewell.*

    He that thou knowest thine,
        Hamlet.

  Come, I will give you way for these your letters,
30   And do't the speedier that you may direct me
    To him from whom you brought them.

[*Exeunt*]

Horatio   Let them come in.

[*The* **Servant** *goes*]

Other than Lord Hamlet, I know of no one abroad who would write to me.

[**Sailors** *enter*]

1st Sailor   God bless you, sir.

Horatio   And you too.

1st Sailor   He shall sir, if it's his will.   [*He takes a parchment from his pouch*]   Here's a letter for you, sir. It's from that ambassador who was making for England; I presume your name is Horatio, as I'm led to believe?

Horatio   [*reading the letter*]   *Horatio, when you've read this, arrange for these fellows to meet the King. They have letters for him. Not two days out at sea, a well-armed pirate ship pursued us. Finding we were too slow, we were forced on the attack, and when the two ships were grappled together I boarded them. The next moment they got clear of our ship, so I became their only prisoner. They have treated me with the mercy of canny thieves. They knew what they were about: I am to do them a good turn. Let the King have the letters I have sent, and join me as fast as you would run away from death. You will be dumbstruck by what I have to tell you, but even then I won't do it justice. These good fellows will bring you to where I am. Rosencrantz and Guildenstern are still on course for England. I've a lot to tell you about them. Yours, Hamlet.*

[*To the* **Sailors**]   Come with me. I'll see these letters get through to the King; and as quickly as possible, so that you can take me to their author.

[*They go*]

Scene 7

Enter the **King** *and* **Laertes**.

King   Now must your conscience my acquittance seal,
And you must put me in your heart for friend,
Sith you have heard, and with a knowing ear,
That he which hath your noble father slain
5   Pursued my life.

Laertes   It well appears. But tell me
Why you proceeded not against these feats,
So crimeful and so capital in nature,
As by your safety, wisdom, all things else
10   You mainly were stirred up.

King   O, for two special reasons,
Which may to you perhaps seem much unsinewed,
But yet to me they are strong. The Queen his mother
Lives almost by his looks, and for myself –
15   My virtue or my plague, be it either which –
She's so conjunctive to my life and soul
That, as the star moves not but in his sphere,
I could not but by her. The other motive
Why to a public count I might not go
20   Is the great love the general gender bear him,
Who, dipping all his faults in their affection,
Work like the spring that turneth wood to stone,
Convert his gyves to graces; so that my arrows,
Too slightly timbered for so loud a wind,
25   Would have reverted to my bow again,
But not where I had aimed them.

Laertes   And so have I a noble father lost,
A sister driven into desp'rate terms,
Whose worth, if praises may go back again,

244

Scene 7

*The **King** enters, followed by **Laertes**.*

King   Now you must concede that I'm vindicated. And you must embrace me as a friend, as you have heard and fully understood that the man who killed your noble father also sought my life.

Laertes   It seems so. But tell me why you took no action against these wicked deeds – so criminal and so capital in character – as you were mightily provoked to do on grounds of safety, wisdom and everything else?

King   Oh, for two special reasons, which may perhaps seem to you to be pretty feeble, but nonetheless to me they're strong. The Queen, his mother, dotes on him, and as for myself – to my credit or my misfortune, one or the other – she is so central to my being that, just as a star has a fixed orbit, I am tied to her. The other reason why I couldn't throw this open to the public is the great love the common people have for him. Such is their affection that they overlook all his faults. They act like the mineral spring that turns wood into stone: they convert his shortcomings into virtues. My accusations, too insubstantial for the circumstances, would have been blown back in my face, not reaching their intended target.

Laertes   And therefore I have lost a noble father; and my sister, whose merit was such in former times that she could

30   Stood challenger on mount of all the age
    For her perfections. But my revenge will come.

King   Break not your sleeps for that. You must not think
    That we are made of stuff so flat and dull
    That we can let our beard be shook with danger
35   And think it pastime. You shortly shall hear more.
    I loved your father, and we love ourself,
    And that, I hope, will teach you to imagine –

[*Enter a* **Messenger** *with letters*]

Messenger   These to your Majesty, this to the Queen.

King   From Hamlet! Who brought them?

40 **Messenger**   Sailors, my lord, they say. I saw them not.
    They were given me by Claudio. He received them
    Of him that brought them.

King   Laertes, you shall hear them.
    Leave us.   [*Exit* **Messenger**]

45   [*Reads*] *High and mighty, you shall know I am set naked on*
    your kingdom. Tomorrow shall I beg leave to see your kingly
    eyes, when I shall, first asking your pardon, thereunto recount
    the occasion of my sudden and more strange return.
             Hamlet.

50   What should this mean? Are all the rest come back?
    Or is it some abuse, and no such thing?

Laertes   Know you the hand?

King   'Tis Hamlet's character.
    'Naked' –
55   And in a postscript here he says 'Alone'.
    Can you devise me?

Laertes   I am lost in it, my lord. But let him come.

have stood on a mountain top and challenged the world to better her perfections, is now driven into insanity. But I'll have my revenge.

King Lose no sleep on that account. You mustn't think I'm so gutless that I'll let myself be threatened and treat it as a joke. You'll hear more of this soon. I loved your father, and I love myself: and that, I hope, will give you an idea –

[*A* **Messenger** *enters, with the seafarers' letters*]

Messenger This is for your Majesty. This is to the Queen.

King From Hamlet! Who brought them?

Messenger Sailors, my lord, so they say. I did not see them. They were given to me by Claudio. He got them from the man who brought them.

King Laertes, you shall hear what's in them. [*To the* **Messenger**] Leave us.

[*The* **Messenger** *goes*]

[*Reading*] *Your high and mighty Majesty,*
This is to tell you that I am back in your kingdom, stripped of all my belongings. Tomorrow I beg leave to appear before you, when I shall – first begging your pardon – recount to you the reasons for my sudden and extraordinary return. Hamlet.

What's the meaning of this? Have all the others come back? Or is this some hoax, and quite untrue?

Laertes Do you recognize the handwriting?

King It's Hamlet's. "Stripped of all my belongings" . . . And in a postcript here, he says, "Alone." Can you explain?

Laertes I'm completely lost, my lord. But let him come. It does

It warms the very sickness in my heart
That I shall live and tell him to his teeth,
60   'Thus diest thou.'

King   If it be so, Laertes –
As how should it be so, how otherwise? –
Will you be ruled by me?

Laertes   Ay, my lord,
65   So you will not o'errule me to a peace.

King   To thine own peace. If he be now returned,
As checking at his voyage, and that he means
No more to undertake it, I will work him
To an exploit, now ripe in my device,
70   Under the which he shall not choose but fall;
And for his death no wind of blame shall breathe,
But even his mother shall uncharge the practice
And call it accident.

Laertes   My lord, I will be ruled,
75   The rather if you could devise it so
That I might be the organ.

King   It falls right.
You have been talked of since your travel much,
And that in Hamlet's hearing, for a quality
80   Wherein they say you shine. Your sum of parts
Did not together pluck such envy from him
As did that one, and that, in my regard,
Of the unworthiest siege.

Laertes   What part is that, my lord?

85 **King**   A very riband in the cap of youth –
Yet needful too; for youth no less becomes
The light and careless livery that it wears
Than settled age his sables and his weeds
Importing health and graveness. Two months since

my sick heart good to think I shall live to tell him to his face:
''This is your death.''

King [*indicating the letter*]   If this is correct, Laertes – it
seems very strange, but why shouldn't it be? – will you take
my advice?

Laertes Yes, my lord, provided you don't try to coerce me into
a peacemaking.

King Only with yourself! If he has now returned, cutting his
voyage short, with no intention of resuming it, I'll
manipulate him into a situation for which I have devised a
plot. It will undoubtedly bring about his downfall. His death
will be received without a whisper of blame. Even his
mother will fall for the trick and call it an accident.

Laertes My lord, I'll go along with you, especially if you could
arrange it so that I could be the instrument.

King Just so. There has been a lot of talk since you went
abroad, and in Hamlet's hearing, of a skill they say you shine
in. All your other attributes put together didn't provoke such
envy as that one did, though in my opinion it was not the
worthiest.

Laertes To what are you referring, my lord?

King To a youthful folly – but necessary too. It's no less
appropriate for youth to be frivolous than it is for middle age
to look staid in order to suggest respectability and wisdom.

90   Here was a gentleman of Normandy –
        I have seen myself, and served against, the French,
        And they can well on horseback, but this gallant
        Had witchcraft in't. He grew unto his seat,
        And to such wondrous doing brought his horse
95   As he had been incorpsed and demi-natured
        With the brave beast. So far he topped my thought
        That I in forgery of shapes and tricks
        Come short of what he did.

Laertes   A Norman was't?

100 **King**   A Norman.

Laertes   Upon my life, Lamond.

King   The very same.

Laertes   I know him well. He is the brooch indeed
        And gem of all the nation.

105 **King**   He made confession of you,
        And gave you such a masterly report
        For art and exercise in your defence,
        And for your rapier most especial,
        That he cried out 'twould be a sight indeed
110   If one could match you. The scrimers of their nation
        He swore had neither motion, guard, nor eye,
        If you opposed them. Sir, this report of his
        Did Hamlet so envenom with his envy
        That he could nothing do but wish and beg
115   Your sudden coming o'er, to play with you.
        Now out of this –

Laertes   What out of this, my lord?

King   Laertes, was your father dear to you?
        Or are you like the painting of a sorrow,
120   A face without a heart?

250

Two months ago a gentleman of Normandy was here. I've seen the French myself, and fought against them, and they are good on horseback, but this young fellow was a wizard at it. He was rooted to his saddle, and did such wonderful routines with his horse that he might have been grafted to it, and half-horse himself. He so far exceeded my imagination that any feats of skill I could devise fell short of what he did.

Laertes A Norman, was he?

King A Norman.

Laertes Lamond, for sure!

King The very same.

Laertes I know him well. He's the jewel in his nation's crown.

King He volunteered an assessment of you and gave you such a marvelous report for skill and agility in your swordsmanship – and particularly with the rapier – that he declared it really would be something special if a man could be found to match you. He swore that the French fencers were not up to you in style, defense, or accuracy should you oppose them. Sir, Hamlet was so green with envy at this report that he could not resist wishing and begging for your swift return so that he could fence with you. Now, out of this –

Laertes What can come out of this, my lord?

King Laertes, was your father dear to you? Or are you like a painting of a sorrow? A likeness lacking spirit?

Laertes   Why ask you this?

King   Not that I think you did not love your father,
But that I know love is begun by time,
And that I see, in passages of proof,
125   Time qualifies the spark and fire of it.
There lives within the very flame of love
A kind of wick or snuff that will abate it;
And nothing is at a like goodness still;
For goodness, growing to a pleurisy,
130   Dies in his own too-much. That we would do,
We should do when we would: for this 'would' changes
And hath abatements and delays as many
As there are tongues, are hands, are accidents,
And then this 'should' is like a spendthrift sigh
135   That hurts by easing. But to the quick of th'ulcer:
Hamlet comes back; what would you undertake
To show yourself your father's son in deed
More than in words?

Laertes   To cut his throat i'th'church.

140   **King**   No place indeed should murder sanctuarize;
Revenge should have no bounds. But good Laertes,
Will you do this, keep close within your chamber;
Hamlet, returned, shall know you are come home;
We'll put on those shall praise your excellence,
145   And set a double varnish on the fame
The Frenchman gave you; bring you, in fine, together,
And wager o'er your heads. He, being remiss,
Most generous, and free from all contriving,
Will not peruse the foils, so that with ease –
150   Or with a little shuffling – you may choose
A sword unbated, and in a pass of practice
Requite him for your father.

Laertes   Why do you ask?

King   Not that I think you didn't love your father. It's because I
know love has a time when it begins; experience tells me
time also diminishes the passion of it. Within the very flame
of love there lives a kind of wick or snuff that extinguishes
it. Nothing stays always at the same level of goodness. It
gathers like an inflammation, then dies of its own excess.
What we want to do, we ought to do straight away.
Otherwise resolution changes, and has qualifications and
postponements as numerous as there are words and deeds
and practical reasons for not proceeding. Then this intention
becomes like the sigh of a spendthrift: it gives relief, but it
does more harm than good. But to get to the essential point:
Hamlet has returned. What would you do to show you are
your father's son, in deeds rather than in words?

Laertes   I'd cut his throat in church!

King   Indeed, no place should be a sanctuary against murder;
revenge should know no restraints. Good Laertes, do
this; keep to your room. Hamlet, now returned, shall be
told you have come home. I'll arrange for people to praise
your skill, doubling the reputation given you by the
Frenchman. Eventually, you'll be contestants, with wagers
laid on each side. Being very trusting, generous-minded,
and free from all subterfuge, he won't inspect the foils; so
quite easily, or with a little sleight-of-hand, you can choose a
foil without a button on its tip. Then, with an artful lunge,
you can settle with him for your father.

Laertes   I will do't.
And for that purpose, I'll anoint my sword.
155 I bought an unction of a mountebank
So mortal that but dip a knife in it,
Where it draws blood, no cataplasm so rare,
Collected from all simples that have virtue
Under the moon, can save the thing from death
160 That is but scratched withal. I'll touch my point
With this contagion, that if I gall him slightly,
It may be death.

King   Let's further think of this,
Weigh what convenience both of time and means
165 May fit us to our shape. If this should fail,
And that our drift look through our bad performance,
'Twere better not assayed. Therefore this project
Should have a back or second that might hold
If this did blast in proof. Soft, let me see.
170 We'll make a solemn wager on your cunnings –
I ha't!
When in your motion you are hot and dry –
As make your bouts more violent to that end –
And that he calls for drink, I'll have prepared him
175 A chalice for the nonce, whereon but sipping,
If he by chance escape your venomed stuck,
Our purpose may hold there. But stay; what noise?

[*Enter* **Queen**]

Queen   One woe doth tread upon another's heel,
So fast they follow. Your sister's drowned, Laertes.

180 **Laertes**   Drowned? O, where?

Queen   There is a willow grows aslant the brook
That shows his hoary leaves in the glassy stream.
There with fantastic garlands did she come

Laertes I'll do it. And for that purpose I'll put poison on my sword. I bought an ointment from a quack doctor: it's so lethal that you have only to dip a knife in it, and where it draws blood, no antidote however rare, even if collected from the strongest herbs available, can save the thing from death that's so much as scratched by it. I'll put this poison on the point of my rapier, so that if I graze him only slightly, he's bound to die.

King Let's think further about this, and decide what's the best time and means for us to act our parts. If this should fail, and our real selves show through our bad performances, it would be better not attempted. Therefore this project should have a secondary backup, that should work if this one goes wrong. So let me see. I'll make a solemn wager on your respective skills . . . I've got it! When you become hot and dry through your exertions – so make your bouts all the more violent with that in mind – and when he asks for a drink, I'll have a goblet ready for him for the purpose. He has only to sip it and should he by chance escape your poisoned thrust, we'll achieve our objective that way. [*There is a commotion outside the door*] What's that noise?

[*The* **Queen** *enters in great distress*]

Queen One sorrow follows on the heels of another, they happen so quickly. Your sister is drowned, Laertes!

Laertes Drowned? Oh, where?

Queen There is a willow that leans across the brook. Its silver leaves reflect in still water. There she went with plaited garlands made from buttercups, nettles, daisies, and

Of crow-flowers, nettles, daisies, and long purples,
185   That liberal shepherds give a grosser name,
But our cold maids do dead men's fingers call them.
There on the pendent boughs her coronet weeds
Clamb'ring to hang, an envious sliver broke,
When down her weedy trophies and herself
190   Fell in the weeping brook. Her clothes spread wide,
And mermaid-like awhile they bore her up,
Which time she chanted snatches of old tunes,
As one incapable of her own distress,
Or like a creature native and indued
195   Unto that element. But long it could not be
Till that her garments, heavy with their drink,
Pulled the poor wretch from her melodious lay
To muddy death.

Laertes   Alas, then she is drowned.

200 **Queen** Drowned, drowned.

Laertes   Too much of water hast thou, poor Ophelia,
And therefore I forbid my tears. But yet
It is our trick; nature her custom holds,
Let shame say what it will.   [*Weeps*]   When these are gone,
205   The woman will be out. Adieu, my lord,
I have a speech o'fire that fain would blaze
But that this folly douts it.

                                                              [*Exit*]

King   Let's follow, Gertrude.
How much I had to do to calm his rage.
210   Now fear I this will give it start again.
Therefore, let's follow.

                                                              [*Exeunt*]

long purples, which vulgar shepherds give a more indelicate name, and which our chaste maidens call "dead men's fingers." As she climbed to hang her wreaths on the overhanging boughs, a malicious branch broke off. Down into the weeping brook she and her garlands fell. Her clothes spread out wide, and for a time they held her afloat, mermaidlike, during which time she sang snatches of old tunes, like somebody unaware of her own dangerous predicament, or like a creature accustomed to living in water. But it could not be long before her garments, heavy with water, pulled the poor wretch from her melodious song to a muddy death.

Laertes   Alas, then: she is drowned?

Queen   Drowned, drowned . . .

Laertes   You have had more than your share of water, poor Ophelia, so I'll restrain my tears.   [*He tries hard to control his emotions*]   But it's only human; nature must be obeyed, however shameful it may seem.   [*He is convulsed with sobs*]   When these tears have gone, it will be the last of the woman in me. Farewell, my lord. I have a fiery speech inside me that wants to blaze out, but this crying douses it.

[*He goes*]

King   Let's follow him, Gertrude. How hard I had to work to calm him down. Now I fear this will start it all up again. So let's follow him.

[*They leave*]

Act five

Scene 1

Enter two Clowns – a **Grave-digger** *and* **Another**.

Grave-digger Is she to be buried in Christian burial, when she wilfully seeks her own salvation?

Other I tell thee she is, therefore make her grave straight. The crowner hath sat on her and finds it Christian burial.

5 **Grave-digger** How can that be, unless she drowned herself in her own defence?

Other Why, 'tis found so.

Grave-digger It must be se offendendo, it cannot be else. For here lies the point: if I drown myself wittingly, it argues
10 an act, and an act hath three branches – it is to act, to do, to perform; argal, she drowned herself wittingly.

Other Nay, but hear you, Goodman Delver –

Grave-digger Give me leave. Here lies the water: good. Here stands the man: good. If the man go to this water and drown
15 himself, it is, will he nill he, he goes, mark you that. But if the water come to him and drown him, he drowns not himself. Argal, he that is not guilty of his own death shortens not his own life.

Other But is this law?

Act five

Scene 1

A graveyard. A **Gravedigger** *and his* **Mate** *are at work.*

Gravedigger Is she to have a Christian burial, in spite of being a suicide?

Mate I tell you she is, so get digging. The coroner has sat on her case, and he says it's a Christian burial.

Gravedigger How can that be, unless she drowned herself in self-defense?

Mate Well, that's the verdict.

Gravedigger It must be *se offendendo* [*he means the opposite – se defendendo*]. It couldn't be anything else. This is the point: if I drown myself deliberately, that's an act, and an act has three parts – to act something, to do something, and to perform something. Therefore she drowned herself deliberately.

Mate Yes, but listen, Mister Digger . . .

Gravedigger [*not to be interrupted*] Excuse me. Here lies the water: good. [*He demonstrates on the ground with his shovel*] Here stands the man: good. [*He places his pick near the shovel*] If the man goes to this water and drowns himself, it is, whether he likes it or not, the end of him, note that. But if the water comes to him and drowns him, he doesn't drown himself. Therefore, the man who isn't guilty of his own death can't shorten his own life.

Mate Is this the law?

20 **Grave-digger** Ay, marry is't, crowner's quest law.

Other Will you ha' the truth on't? If this had not been a
gentlewoman, she should have been buried out o' Christian
burial.

Grave-digger Why, there thou say'st. And the more pity
25   that great folk should have countenance in this world to
drown or hang themselves more than their even – Christian.
Come, my spade. There is no ancient gentlemen but
gardeners, ditchers, and grave-makers – they hold up
Adam's profession.   [*He digs*]

30 **Other** Was he a gentleman?

Grave-digger He was the first that ever bore arms.

Other Why, he had none.

Grave-digger What, art a heathen? How dost thou
understand the Scripture? The Scripture says Adam digged.
35   Could he dig without arms? I'll put another question to thee.
If thou answerest me not to the purpose, confess thyself –

Other Go to.

Grave-digger What is he that builds stronger than either the
mason, the shipwright, or the carpenter?

40 **Other** The gallows-maker, for that frame outlives a thousand
tenants.

Grave-digger I like thy wit well in good faith, the gallows
does well. But how does it well? It does well to those that do
ill. Now, thou dost ill to say the gallows is built stronger
45   than the church; argal, the gallows may do well to thee. To't
again, come.

Gravedigger   Certainly it is. Coroner's inquest law.

Mate   Do you want the honest truth? If this hadn't been a gentlewoman, she wouldn't have been given a Christian burial.

Gravedigger   Too true. And the more's the pity that great folk should have permission in this world to drown or hang themselves more than their fellow Christians can. Give me my spade.   [*His* **Mate** *hands it to him*]   There were no gentlemen in ancient times except gardeners, ditchdiggers and gravemakers. They followed Adam's profession.   [*He digs vigorously*]

Mate   Was he a gentleman?

Gravedigger   He was the first who ever had arms.

Mate   Why, he had no arms!   [*He means heraldic arms, the sign of a gentleman*]

Gravedigger   What, are you a heathen? How do you interpret the Bible? The Bible says, ''Adam digged.'' Could he dig without arms? I'll put another question to you. If you don't answer it right, God help you!

Mate   Go on.

Gravedigger   Who builds stronger than either the mason, the shipwright, or the carpenter?

Mate   The gallows maker, because that structure outlives a thousand tenants!

Gravedigger   I like that, I really do. The gallows is a good answer. But how is it good? It's good to those who do evil. Now it's wrong to say the gallows is built stronger than the church: therefore, the gallows might do *you* some good. Try again. Come on.

261

Other   Who builds stronger than a mason, a shipwright, or a
carpenter?

Grave-digger   Ay, tell me that and unyoke.

50 **Other**   Marry, now I can tell.

Grave-digger   To't.

Other   Mass, I cannot tell.

Grave-digger   Cudgel thy brains no more about it, for your
dull ass will not mend his pace with beating. And when you
55 are asked this question next, say, 'A grave-maker.' The
houses he makes lasts till doomsday. Go, get thee to
Yaughan; fetch me a stoup of liquor.

[*Exit the* **Other Clown.** *The* **Grave-digger** *continues digging*]

[*Sings*]   *In youth when I did love, did love,*
                Methought it was very sweet:
60   *To contract – O – the time for – a –*
                my behove,
                O methought there – a – was
                nothing – a – meet.

[*While he is singing, enter* **Hamlet** *and* **Horatio**]

Hamlet   Has this fellow no feeling of his business that he
65 sings in grave-making?

Horatio   Custom hath made it in him a property of easiness.

Hamlet   'Tis e'en so, the hand of little employment hath the
daintier sense.

Grave-digger   *But age with his stealing steps*
70   *Hath clawed me in his clutch,*
                And hath shipped me intil the land,
                As if I had never been such.

[*He throws up a skull*]

Mate   [*thinking hard*]   Who builds stronger than a mason, a shipwright or a carpenter?

Gravedigger   Yes, tell me that and have done with it.

Mate   Oh, now I know!

Gravedigger   Go on.

Mate   [*subsiding*]   Drat. I dunno.

Gravedigger   Don't cudgel your brains about it any more. You can't make a stupid ass walk quicker by beating it. When you are next asked this question, say "a gravemaker". The houses he makes last till doomsday! Off you go to Yaughan's tavern. Get me some whiskey.

[*The* **Gravedigger's Mate** *leaves; the* **Gravedigger** *gets down to his work, singing and grunting as he labors*]

> *In youth, when I did love, did love,*
>   *I thought it was very sweet:*
> *To shorten (oh!) the time of (ah!) my delight*
> *I thought there (ah!) was no greater (ah!) treat!*

[**Hamlet** *and* **Horatio** *enter in the middle of his song, the words of which suggest a bad memory*]

Hamlet   Has this fellow no sensitivity about his job that he can sing while he's gravedigging?

Horatio   He's so used to it that he doesn't give it a thought.

Hamlet   Quite so. Delicate feelings are the privilege of the idle.

Gravedigger   *But age creeps on apace*
>   *And has me old and worn.*
> *It takes me back to earth*
>   *As if I'd never been born.*

[*He hits a skull with his spade and throws it to the surface*]

263

Hamlet   That skull had a tongue in it, and could sing once.
How the knave jowls it to the ground, as if 'twere Cain's
75 jawbone, that did the first murder! This might be the pate of
a politician which this ass now o'er-reaches, one that would
circumvent God, might it not?

Horatio   It might, my lord.

Hamlet   Or of a courtier, which could say, 'Good morrow,
80 sweet lord. How dost thou, sweet lord?' This might be my
Lord Such-a-one, that praised my Lord Such-a-one's horse
when he meant to beg it, might it not?

Horatio   Ay, my lord.

Hamlet   Why, e'en so, and now my Lady Worm's, chopless,
85 and knocked about the mazard with a sexton's spade. Here's
fine revolution and we had the trick to see't. Did these bones
cost no more the breeding but to play at loggats with 'em?
Mine ache to think on't.

Grave-digger   *A pickaxe and a spade, a spade,*
90   *For and a shrouding-sheet,*
                 O a pit of clay for to be made
                 For such a guest is meet.

[*Throws up another skull*]

Hamlet   There's another. Why, may not that be the skull of a
lawyer? Where be his quiddities now, his quillities, his cases,
95 his tenures, and his tricks? Why does he suffer this rude
knave now to knock him about the sconce with a dirty
shovel, and will not tell him of his action of battery? Hum!
This fellow might be in's time a great buyer of land, with his
statutes, his recognizances, his fines, his double vouchers,
100 his recoveries. Is this the fine of his fines and the recovery of

Hamlet   That skull had a tongue in it, and could sing once. How the rascal hurls it to the ground as if it were the jawbone of Cain, who committed the first murder.   [*He picks it up*]   This might be the head of a crafty intriguer, whom this ass now has the better of – the sort who'd try to outwit God, might it not?

Horatio   It might, my lord.

Hamlet   Or of some courtier, who could say, ''Good morning, my dear lord. How are you, my good lord?'' This might be my Lord So-and-so, who praised my Lord So-and-so's horse, when he really meant to borrow it, might it not?

Horatio   Yes, my lord.

Hamlet   Why yes, indeed: and now he's food for worms; his jaw gone, and knocked about the noddle with a sexton's spade. Here's a fine example of the wheel of fortune, if we had the wit to see it. Were these bones begotten for no better purpose than to be used for playing games? My bones ache to think about it.

Gravedigger   *A pickaxe and a spade, a spade,*
            A shroud to be enwrapped
            (Oh!) A hole of clay that's specially
                made
            For such a guest is apt.

[*He throws up a second skull*]

Hamlet   There's another. Mightn't that be the skull of a lawyer? Where are his objections now, his subtleties, his lawsuits, his title deeds, and his clever tricks? Why does he let this coarse knave knock him about the head with a dirty shovel, and not threaten him with a court case for grievous bodily harm? Hm, this fellow might in his time have been a great buyer of land, what with his mortgages, his bonds, his fines, his guarantors, and his possession orders. Is this the

his recoveries, to have his fine pate full of fine dirt? Will his
vouchers vouch him no more of his purchases, and double
ones too, than the length and breadth of a pair of indentures?
The very conveyances of his lands will hardly lie in this box,
105 and must th'inheritor himself have no more, ha?

Horatio   Not a jot more, my lord.

Hamlet   Is not parchment made of sheepskins?

Horatio   Ay, my lord, and of calves' skins too.

Hamlet   There are sheep and calves which seek out assurance
110 in that. I will speak to this fellow. Whose grave's this,
sirrah?

Grave-digger   Mine, sir.

[*Sings*]   *Oh a pit of clay for to be made* –

Hamlet   I think it be thine indeed, for thou liest in't.

115 **Grave-digger**   You lie out on't, sir, and therefore 'tis not
yours. For my part, I do not lie in't, and yet it is mine.

Hamlet   Thou dost lie in't, to be in't and say 'tis thine. 'Tis
for the dead, not for the quick: therefore thou liest.

Grave-digger   'Tis a quick lie, sir, 'twill away again from me
120 to you.

Hamlet   What man dost thou dig it for?

Grave-digger   For no man, sir.

Hamlet   What woman then?

Grave-digger   For none neither.

125 **Hamlet**   Who is to be buried in't?

Grave-digger   One that was a woman, sir; but rest her soul,
she's dead.

final outcome of his fines, the gain he got from his
possession orders – to have his fine head full of fine dirt?
Will his guarantors – even when there's two of them –
refuse to guarantee him any more than the length and
breadth of a parchment deed? The legal conveyances
themselves would just about fit into this box [*he points to
the grave*].   Must the purchaser himself have no more, eh?

Horatio Not an inch more, my lord.

Hamlet Isn't parchment made of sheepskins?

Horatio Yes, my lord, and of calfskin, too.

Hamlet People are no better than sheep or calves if they think
a legal document gives you any security. I'll speak to this
fellow. Whose grave is this, man?

Gravedigger Mine, sir.
    [*Singing*] *A hole of clay that's specially made* –

Hamlet I believe it really is yours, because you are lying in it!

Gravedigger You are lying out of it, sir, and therefore it's not
yours. As for me, I don't lie in it, but nevertheless it's mine.

Hamlet You *are* lying in it. You are in it, and you claim it's
yours. It's for the dead, not for the living. Therefore you are
lying . . .

Gravedigger It's a living lie, sir. If I'm lying, so are you.

Hamlet Who is the man you are digging it for?

Gravedigger Not for any man, sir.

Hamlet What woman then?

Gravedigger No woman either.

Hamlet Who is to be buried in it?

Gravedigger Someone who *was* a woman sir; but God rest
her soul, she's dead.

Hamlet   How absolute the knave is. We must speak by the
card or equivocation will undo us. By the Lord, Horatio,
130   these three years I have taken note of it, the age is grown so
picked that the toe of the peasant comes so near the heel of
the courtier he galls his kibe. How long hast thou been a
grave-maker?

Grave-digger   Of all the days i'th'year I came to't that day
135   that our last King Hamlet o'ercame Fortinbras.

Hamlet   How long is that since?

Grave-digger   Cannot you tell that? Every fool can tell that.
It was the very day that young Hamlet was born – he that is
mad and sent to England.

140   **Hamlet**   Ay, marry. Why was he sent into England?

Grave-digger   Why, because he was mad. He shall recover
his wits there. Or if he do not, 'tis no great matter there.

Hamlet   Why?

Grave-digger   'Twill not be seen in him there. There the
145   men are as mad as he.

Hamlet   How came he mad?

Grave-digger   Very strangely, they say.

Hamlet   How 'strangely'?

Grave-digger   Faith, e'en with losing his wits.

150   **Hamlet**   Upon what ground?

Grave-digger   Why, here in Denmark. I have been sexton
here, man and boy, thirty years.

Hamlet   How long will a man lie i'th'earth ere he rot?

Grave-digger   Faith, if he be not rotten before he die – as we
155   have many pocky corses nowadays that will scarce hold the

268

Hamlet   How literal the rogue is! We must speak with absolute
precision or nit-picking will be the ruin of us. By heavens,
Horatio: these last three years I've noticed we have become
excessively refined. Peasants are so hard on the heels of
courtiers they rub against their foot sores.   [*To the*
Gravedigger]   How long have you been a gravedigger?

Gravedigger   I started on the day that our last King Hamlet
defeated Fortinbras.

Hamlet   How long ago is that?

Gravedigger   Don't you know that? Every fool knows that. It
was on the very same day that young Hamlet was
born – the one who's mad and been sent to England.

Hamlet   Yes, of course. Why was he sent to England?

Gravedigger   Why, because he was mad. He'll recover his
wits there. If he doesn't, it won't matter much there.

Hamlet   Why?

Gravedigger   They won't notice it there. There, the men are
as mad as he is.

Hamlet   How did he come to go mad?

Gravedigger   Very strangely, they say.

Hamlet   How do you mean, ''strangely''?

Gravedigger   Truly, it was caused by losing his wits.

Hamlet   On what ground?

Gravedigger   Why, here in Denmark. I've been sexton here,
man and boy, for thirty years.

Hamlet   How long does a man lie buried before he rots?

Gravedigger   Truly, if he isn't rotten before he dies – and
we have many pocky corpses nowadays that scarcely last till

269

laying in – he will last you some eight year or nine year. A
tanner will last you nine year.

Hamlet   Why he more than another?

Grave-digger   Why, sir, his hide is so tanned with his trade
160   that he will keep out water a great while, and your water is a
sore decayer of your whoreson dead body. Here's a skull now
hath lien you i'th'earth three and twenty years.

Hamlet   Whose was it?

Grave-digger   A whoreson mad fellow's it was. Whose do
165   you think it was?

Hamlet   Nay, I know not.

Grave-digger   A pestilence on him for a mad rogue! He
poured a flagon of Rhenish on my head once. This same
skull, sir, was Yorick's skull, the King's jester.

170 **Hamlet**   This?   [*Takes the skull*]

Grave-digger   E'en that.

Hamlet   Alas, poor Yorick! I knew him, Horatio: a fellow of
infinite jest, of most excellent fancy. He hath borne me on
his back a thousand times. And now, how abhorred in my
175   imagination it is! My gorge rises at it. Here hung those lips
that I have kissed I know not how oft. Where be your gibes
now, your gambols, your songs, your flashes of merriment,
that were wont to set the table on a roar? Not one now to
mock your own grinning? Quite chop-fallen? Now get you to
180   my lady's chamber and tell her, let her paint an inch thick,
to this favour she must come. Make her laugh at that.
Prithee, Horatio, tell me one thing.

Horatio   What's that, my lord?

they're underground – he'll last you about eight or nine years. A tanner will last you nine years.

Hamlet   Why a tanner longer than others?

Gravedigger   Because, sir, his hide is so tanned with his trade that he'll keep water out a long time; and your water is a notorious decayer of your good old dead body.   [*Picking up another skull from his digging*]   Now here's a skull that's been lying in the earth for twenty-three years.

Hamlet   Whose was it?

Gravedigger   A rascally mad fellow it was. Whose do you think it was?

Hamlet   I don't know.

Gravedigger   What a truly mad rogue he was! He poured a pitcher of Rhenish wine over my head once. This same skull, sir, was Yorick's skull – the King's jester!

Hamlet   [*taking it*]   This?

Gravedigger   That very one.

Hamlet   Alas, poor Yorick! I knew him, Horatio. He was a fellow of irrepressible humor, of delightful absurdity. He carried me on his back a thousand times, and now – how abhorrent it is to think about it! My gorge rises at the thought. Here those lips hung that I kissed I don't know how often. Where are your shafts of wit now, your playful tricks, your songs, your quick-witted quips that used to set everyone roaring at table? Not one left to mock at your own grinning? Down-in-the-mouth, are you? Go to my ladyship's room right now, and tell her that however thickly she paints her face, she'll be like you in the end. Make her laugh at that. Horatio: tell me one thing.

Horatio   What's that, my lord?

271

Hamlet   Dost thou think Alexander looked o' this fashion
185   i'th'earth?

Horatio   E'en so.

Hamlet   And smelt so? Pah!   [*Throws down the skull*]

Horatio   E'en so, my lord.

Hamlet   To what base uses we may return, Horatio! Why,
190   may not imagination trace the noble dust of Alexander till he
find it stopping a bung-hole?

Horatio   'Twere to consider too curiously to consider so.

Hamlet   No, faith, not a jot, but to follow him thither with
modesty enough, and likelihood to lead it. Alexander died,
195   Alexander was buried, Alexander returneth to dust, the dust
is earth, of earth we make loam, and why of that loam
whereto he was converted might they not stop a beer-barrel?

> *Imperial Caesar, dead and turned to clay,*
> *Might stop a hole to keep the wind away.*
> 200   *O that that earth which kept the world in awe*
> *Should patch a wall t'expel the winter's flaw.*

But soft, but soft awhile. Here comes the King,
The Queen, the courtiers.

[*Enter a* **Priest, King, Queen, Laertes,** *and a coffin, with
Lords attendant*]

                    Who is this they follow?
205   And with such maimed rites? This doth betoken
The corse they follow did with desp'rate hand
Fordo its own life. 'Twas of some estate.

Laertes   What ceremony else?

Hamlet   That is Laertes, a very noble youth. Mark.

Hamlet   Do you think Alexander the Great looked like this in the earth?

Horatio   Just the same.

Hamlet   And smelled so?   Ugh! [*He puts Yorick's skull down*]

Horatio   Exactly, my lord.

Hamlet   How we are recycled, Horatio, to perform humble tasks! Isn't it conceivable that the noble dust of Alexander could end up as a stopper for a beer barrel?

Horatio   That's carrying things too far.

Hamlet   No, indeed, not one jot. It's a matter of following him step-by-step, guided by what's probable. Alexander died; Alexander was buried; Alexander returned to dust; the dust is earth; of earth we make loam; and why shouldn't they stop up a beer barrel with that very loam into which he was converted?
  Imperial Caesar, dead and turned to clay,
  Might fill a hole to keep the wind away.
  Oh that that earth – which kept the world in thrall –
  Should patch a wall to keep out winter's squall.
But that's enough for now. Here comes the King, the Queen, and members of the court.

[*Bearers enter carrying a coffin, followed by a* **Priest**, *the* **King**, *the* **Queen**, **Laertes**, *Lords, and Attendants*]

Whom are they mourning? And with such scant rites? This suggests that the deceased had committed suicide. It was of high rank. Let us conceal ourselves and watch.

Laertes   What other ceremonies?

Hamlet   That's Laertes, a very noble youth. Note what he says.

210 **Laertes**   What ceremony else?

Priest   Her obsequies have been as far enlarged
As we have warranty. Her death was doubtful;
And but that great command o'ersways the order,
She should in ground unsanctified have lodged
215 Till the last trumpet: for charitable prayers,
Shards, flints, and pebbles should be thrown on her.
Yet here she is allowed her virgin crants,
Her maiden strewments, and the bringing home
Of bell and burial.

220 **Laertes**   Must there no more be done?

Priest   No more be done.
We should profane the service of the dead
To sing sage requiem and such rest to her
As to peace-parted souls.

225 **Laertes**   Lay her i'th'earth,
And from her fair and unpolluted flesh
May violets spring. I tell thee, churlish priest,
A minist'ring angel shall my sister be
When thou liest howling.

230 **Hamlet**   What, the fair Ophelia!

Queen   [*scatters flowers*]   Sweets to the sweet. Farewell.
I hoped thou shouldst have been my Hamlet's wife:
I thought thy bride-bed to have decked, sweet maid,
And not have strewed thy grave.

235 **Laertes**   Oh, treble woe
Fall ten times treble on that cursed head
Whose wicked deed thy most ingenious sense
Deprived thee of. Hold off the earth awhile,
Till I have caught her once more in mine arms.

[*Leaps in the grave*]

Laertes   What other ceremonies?

Priest   Her funeral rites have gone as far as we have sanction. The cause of her death was open to question, and if it were not that higher authority overrules normal practice, she ought to have been buried in unsanctified ground till doomsday. Fragments of pottery, flints, and pebbles should have been thrown on her in place of sympathetic prayers. Here, she is allowed her virgin's funeral garland, her flowers of chastity, and the use of bell and burial rites to bury her.

Laertes   Must that be all?

Priest   No more can be done. We would profane the Service of the Dead if we sang a solemn requiem and put her to rest like those souls that died naturally.

Laertes   Lay her in the earth, and from her fair and virginal flesh may violets grow. I tell you, ungracious priest: my sister will be a ministering angel when you lie howling in hell!

Hamlet   [*shocked*]   What? The beautiful Ophelia?

Queen   [*scattering flowers*]   Sweets to the sweet. Farewell. I hoped you would have been my Hamlet's wife. I thought I would have decorated your bridal bed with flowers, sweet maid, not spread them on your grave.

Laertes   May countless sorrows fall upon that cursed head whose wicked deed deprived you of your reason! Don't bury her yet: not till I have held her once more in my arms.

[*He leaps into the grave*]

240 Now pile your dust upon the quick and dead,
Till of this flat a mountain you have made
To o'ertop old Pelion or the skyish head
Of blue Olympus.

Hamlet   What is he whose grief
245 Bears such an emphasis, whose phrase of sorrow
Conjures the wand'ring stars and makes them stand
Like wonder-wounded hearers? This is I,
Hamlet the Dane.

Laertes [*grappling with him*]   The devil take thy soul!

250 **Hamlet**   Thou pray'st not well.
I prithee take thy fingers from my throat,
For though I am not splenitive and rash,
Yet have I in me something dangerous,
Which let thy wisdom fear. Hold off thy hand.

255 **King**   Pluck them asunder.

Queen   Hamlet! Hamlet!

All   Gentlemen!

Horatio   Good my lord, be quiet.

Hamlet   Why, I will fight with him upon this theme
260 Until my eyelids will no longer wag.

Queen   O my son, what theme?

Hamlet   I loved Ophelia. Forty thousand brothers
Could not with all their quantity of love
Make up my sum. What wilt thou do for her?

265 **King**   O, he is mad, Laertes.

Queen   For love of God forbear him.

Hamlet   'Swounds, show me what thou't do.
Woo't weep, woo't fight, woo't fast, woo't tear thyself,

276

Now pile your earth upon the living and the dead, till you
have made a mountain of this flat ground higher than Mount
Pelion, or the blue-topped Mount Olympus, with its lofty
peak.

Hamlet [*coming forward*] Who's this who rants his grief?
Whose words of sorrow transfix with wonder the wandering
planets? This is I – Hamlet the Dane!

Laertes [*wrestling with him*] The devil take your soul!

Hamlet An unseemly prayer! Take your fingers off my throat,
will you? Though I'm not hot-tempered and rash, there's a
dangerous streak in me which you'd be wise to fear. Take
your hand away!

King Pull them apart. [*Attendants try to separate them*]

Queen Hamlet, Hamlet!

All Gentlemen!

Horatio Good my lord, contain yourself!

Hamlet Why, I'll fight him on this issue till the last flicker of
my life!

Queen Oh, my son: what issue?

Hamlet I loved Ophelia. Forty thousand brothers could not,
with all their lightweight love, equal the sum total of mine.
What will you do for her?

King Oh, he is mad, Laertes!

Queen For the love of God, leave him alone!

Hamlet Confound it – show me what you'll do! Will you
weep, will you fight, will you fast, will you wound yourself,

Woo't drink up eisel, eat a crocodile?
270   I'll do't. Dost come here to whine,
To outface me with leaping in her grave?
Be buried quick with her, and so will I.
And if thou prate of mountains, let them throw
Millions of acres on us, till our ground,
275   Singeing his pate against the burning zone,
Make Ossa like a wart! Nay, and thou'lt mouth,
I'll rant as well as thou.

Queen   This is mere madness,
And thus awhile the fit will work on him.
280   Anon, as patient as the female dove
When that her golden couplets are disclosed,
His silence will sit drooping.

Hamlet   Hear you, sir,
What is the reason that you use me thus?
285   I loved you ever. But it is no matter.
Let Hercules himself do what he may,
The cat will mew, and dog will have his day.

[Exit]

King   I pray, thee, good Horatio, wait upon him.

[Exit **Horatio***]*

[To **Laertes***]*   Strengthen your patience in our last night's
290   speech;
We'll put the matter to the present push.
Good Gertrude, set some watch over your son.
This grave shall have a living monument.
An hour of quiet shortly shall we see;
295   Till then in patience our proceeding be.

[Exeunt]

will you drink vinegar, eat a crocodile? I'll do it. Have you
come here to whine, to upstage me with leaping into her
grave? Be buried alive with her and so will I! And if you
prattle on about mountains, let them throw millions of acres
over us, till the ground beneath us singes its head against
the earth's hot core, making Mount Ossa look like a wart. If
you're going to bluster, I'll rant as loud as you.

Queen   This is sheer madness. He'll be in this fit for a while.
Then he'll be as meek as a mother dove when her eggs have
hatched, sitting in dejected silence.

Hamlet   Listen, sir: why are you treating me like this? I always
liked you. But that's of no consequence. Not even Hercules
can stop a cat from mewing, or the dog from having its day.

[*He runs off*]

King   Good Horatio, look after him will you?

[**Horatio** *follows* **Hamlet**]

[*To* **Laertes**]   Be patient with the thought of our discussion
last night. We'll put things in hand immediately. Good
Gertrude, see your son is guarded. This grave will have a
lasting monument. We'll break off for a quiet hour; we must
bide our time till then.

[*They all leave*]

Scene 2

Enter **Hamlet** *and* **Horatio**.

Hamlet   So much for this, sir. Now shall you see the other.
You do remember all the circumstance?

Horatio   Remember it, my lord!

Hamlet   Sir, in my heart there was a kind of fighting
5   That would not let me sleep. Methought I lay
Worse than the mutines in the bilboes. Rashly –
And praised be rashness for it: let us know
Our indiscretion sometimes serves us well
When our deep plots do pall; and that should teach us
10   There's a divinity that shapes our ends,
Rough-hew them how we will.

Horatio   That is most certain.

Hamlet   Up from my cabin,
My sea-gown scarfed about me, in the dark
15   Groped I to find out them; had my desire,
Fingered their packet, and in fine withdrew
To mine own room again, making so bold,
My fears forgetting manners, to unseal
Their grand commission; where I found, Horatio –
20   Ah, royal knavery! – an exact command,
Larded with many several sorts of reasons
Importing Denmark's health, and England's too,
With ho! such bugs and goblins in my life,
That on the supervise, no leisure bated,
25   No, not to stay the grinding of the axe,
My head should be struck off.

Horatio   Is't possible?

Scene 2

Hamlet *and* **Horatio** *enter.*

Hamlet   [*Indicating the letter he sent to* **Horatio**]   So much for this, sir. Now for the rest.   [*He means what happened to* **Rosencrantz** *and* **Guildenstern**]   You remember all the circumstances?

Horatio   I remember, my lord!

Hamlet   Sir, I couldn't sleep for the turmoil within me. I lay there feeling worse than mutineers in chains. Impulsively – and all praise to impulse for it: note that our instinct some-times helps us out when our careful schemes go wrong; which should teach us that however much we plan, there is a God who decides the outcome –

Horatio   That's for certain.

Hamlet   – I got up from my cabin, wrapped my sailor's coat round me, and groped my way to find them, which I did. I stole their documents, and finally I withdrew to my own room again. I made so bold as to open their official papers, my fears making me forget my manners. In them I found – oh, such royal wickedness! – a precise order, embroidered with a variety of reasons concerning the King of Denmark's welfare, and the King of England's too – with, oh, such blood-curdling reasons for fear! – that on scanning the letter, without a moment's delay – no, not even to sharpen the axe – my head should be cut off!

Horatio   Surely not?

Hamlet   Here's the commission, read it at more leisure.
30   But wilt thou hear now how I did proceed?

Horatio   I beseech you.

Hamlet   Being thus benetted round with villainies –
Ere I could make a prologue to my brains,
They had begun the play – I sat me down,
35   Devised a new commission, wrote it fair –
I once did hold it, as our statists do,
A baseness to write fair, and laboured much
How to forget that learning, but, sir, now
It did me yeoman's service. Wilt thou know
40   Th'effect of what I wrote?

Horatio   Ay, good my lord.

Hamlet   An earnest conjuration from the King,
As England was his faithful tributary,
As love between them like the palm might flourish,
45   As peace should still her wheaten garland wear
And stand a comma 'tween their amities,
And many such-like 'as'es of great charge,
That on the view and knowing of these contents,
Without debatement further more or less,
50   He should those bearers put to sudden death,
Not shriving-time allowed.

Horatio   How was this sealed?

Hamlet   Why, even in that was heaven ordinant.
I had my father's signet in my purse,
55   Which was the model of that Danish seal;
Folded the writ up in the form of th'other,
Subscribed it, gave't th'impression, placed it safely,
The changeling never known. Now the next day
Was our sea-fight, and what to this was sequent
60   Thou knowest already.

Hamlet   Here's the authority for it. Read it at your leisure. Would you like to hear how I dealt with it?

Horatio   Please tell me.

Hamlet   Being caught like that in a villainous net, I began to act before I'd worked out the plot. I sat down, devised a new set of orders, and wrote them out in official hand-writing. I once used to believe, as our business people do, that it's vulgar to write that way, and tried hard to unlearn the art. But now, sir, it did me an invaluable service. Do you want to know what I said?

Horatio   Yes, my good lord.

Hamlet   I made an earnest plea from the Danish King: as the King of England was his faithful dependent; as the love between them should flourish like the biblical palm tree; as peace should be maintained between them and bond them in their friendship – and many more similar as–es of great significance – that on seeing and digesting the contents of the letter, he should put the bearers immediately to death, without further argument or the slightest variation, giving them no time for absolution.

Horatio   What did you do about an official seal?

Hamlet   Why, even there heaven led the way. I had my father's signet ring in my pouch, and it was identical to the King's seal. I folded the forgery up like the real letter, signed it, sealed it and replaced it safely, the switch being undetected. The next day was our fight at sea, and what happened after that you already know.

ACT FIVE   Scene 2

Horatio   So Guildenstern and Rosencrantz go to't.

Hamlet   Why, man, they did make love to this employment.
They are not near my conscience, their defeat
Does by their own insinuation grow.

65 'Tis dangerous when the baser nature comes
Between the pass and fell incensed points
Of mighty opposites.

Horatio   Why, what a king is this!

Hamlet   Does it not, think thee, stand me now upon –

70 He that hath killed my King and whored my mother,
Popped in between th'election and my hopes,
Thrown out his angle for my proper life,
And with such cozenage – is't not perfect conscience
To quit him with this arm? And is't not to be damned

75 To let this canker of our nature come
In further evil?

Horatio   It must be shortly known to him from England
What is the issue of the business there.

Hamlet   It will be short. The interim is mine.

80 And a man's life's no more than to say 'one'.
But I am very sorry, good Horatio,
That to Laertes I forgot myself;
For by the image of my cause I see
The portraiture of his. I'll court his favours.

85 But sure the bravery of his grief did put me
Into a towering passion.

Horatio   Peace, who comes here?

[*Enter* **Osric,** *a Courtier*]

Osric   Your lordship is right welcome back to Denmark.

Hamlet   I humbly thank you sir. Dost know this water-fly?

Horatio So Guildenstern and Rosencrantz went to their deaths?

Hamlet Why, man, they loved their work. They're not on my conscience. Their downfall was the result of their own attempts to ingratiate themselves. When lesser mortals come between the sword points of the great, it's risky.

Horatio What sort of king is this!

Hamlet Isn't it – don't you think – now up to me? He killed the King my father, debauched my mother, came between me and my expectation of succession, and had a treacherous stab at taking my life. Wouldn't it be poetic justice if I dispatched him myself? Wouldn't it be damnable to let this maggot do more evil harm?

Horatio He'll soon learn from the English King what happened there.

Hamlet Very shortly. The interval is at my disposal. It doesn't take long to end a man's life. But I'm very sorry, good Horatio, that I lost control of myself with Laertes. In looking at my own cause I see the mirror image of his. I'll make it up to him. It was just that the pretentiousness of his grief put me into a towering rage.

Horatio Now who is this?

[**Horatio** *has observed the approach of* **Osric**, *a young courtier fashionable in dress and manner of speech*]

Osric [*bowing very elaborately*] Your lordship is very welcome back to Denmark!

Hamlet [*dryly*] I humbly thank you, sir. [*To* **Horatio**] Do you know this pretty dragonfly?

90 **Horatio**   No, my good lord.

Hamlet   Thy state is the more gracious, for 'tis a vice to know him. He hath much land and fertile. Let a beast be lord of beasts and his crib shall stand at the king's mess. 'Tis a chough, but, as I say, spacious in the possession of dirt.

95 **Osric**   Sweet lord, if your lordship were at leisure, I should impart a thing to you from his Majesty.

Hamlet   I will receive it, sir, with all diligence of spirit. Put your bonnet to his right use: 'tis for the head.

Osric   I thank your lordship, it is very hot.

100 **Hamlet**   No, believe me, 'tis very cold, the wind is northerly.

Osric   It is indifferent cold, my lord, indeed.

Hamlet   But yet methinks it is very sultry and hot for my complexion.

Osric   Exceedingly, my lord, it is very sultry – as 'twere – I
105 cannot tell how. My lord, his Majesty bade me signify to you that he has laid a great wager on your head. Sir, this is the matter –

Hamlet   [*signing to him to put on his hat*]   I beseech you remember –

110 **Osric**   Nay, good my lord, for my ease, in good faith. Sir, here is newly come to court Laertes; believe me an absolute gentleman, full of most excellent differences, of very soft society and great showing. Indeed, to speak feelingly of him, he is the card or calendar of gentry; for you shall find in him
115 the continent of what part a gentleman would see.

Horatio No, my good lord.

Hamlet What a blessing: it's a vice to know him! He has large, fertile estates. Let one dumb animal own lots of other dumb animals, and the King will invite him to eat at his table. He's a crow, but as I say, he owns a lot of soil.

Osric [*bowing elaborately, his hat sweeping the ground*] Sweet lord, if your lordship is not otherwise engaged, I would convey a message to you from his Majesty . . .

Hamlet [*replying in the same manner*] I will receive it, sir, most attentively. Put your hat to its right use: it's for your head.

Osric I thank your lordship. It's very hot.

Hamlet No, take my word for it: it's very cold. The wind is northerly.

Osric It *is* rather cold, my lord, yes.

Hamlet But nevertheless, it's very sultry and hot for my kind of constitution.

Osric Exceedingly so, my lord. It *is* very sultry – as if it were – there's no word for it. My lord, his Majesty asked me to indicate to you that he has laid a large wager on your head. Sir, the situation is this –

Hamlet [*gesturing to him to put on his hat*] Your hat, if you would –

Osric Really, my lord, if you'll allow me, with respect – [*He fans himself with his hat as he speaks*] Sir, Laertes has just returned to court. He is, believe me, a perfect gentleman: unusually gifted, of pleasing manners, and distinguished appearance. Indeed, to do him full credit, he is the ideal or model of good breeding. He epitomizes what one gentleman admires in another.

Hamlet   Sir, his definement suffers no perdition in you;
though I know to divide him inventorially would dozy
th'arithmetic of memory, and yet but yaw neither, in respect
of his quick sail. But, in the verity of extolment, I take him
120   to be a soul of great article and his infusion of such dearth
and rareness as, to make true diction of him, his semblable is
his mirror and who else would trace him his umbrage,
nothing more.

Osric   Your lordship speaks most infallibly of him.

125   **Hamlet**   The concernancy, sir? Why do we wrap the
gentleman in our more rawer breath?

Osric   Sir?

Horatio   Is't not possible to understand in another tongue?
You will do't, sir, really.

130   **Hamlet**   What imports the nomination of this gentleman?

Osric   Of Laertes?

Horatio   His purse is empty already, all's golden words are
spent.

Hamlet   Of him, sir.

135   **Osric**   I know you are not ignorant –

Hamlet   I would you did, sir. Yet in faith if you did, it would
not much approve me. Well, sir?

Osric   You are not ignorant of what excellence Laertes is –

Hamlet   I dare not confess that, lest I should compare with
140   him in excellence; but to know a man well were to know
himself.

Osric   I mean, sir, for his weapon; but in the imputation laid
on him, by them in his meed, he's unfellowed.

Hamlet   What's his weapon?

288

Hamlet [*still mocking* **Osric**'*s speech*]   Sir, your description
does him full justice, though I know that to catalog his
qualities would tax the mind, and would be extremely
difficult, as he's so gifted. But to do him the fullest justice, I
take him to be well worth evaluating. His qualities are so
rare that, to describe him adequately, the only one like him is
the reflection in his mirror. Anyone trying to match him
would be his shadow, nothing more.

Osric   Your lordship speaks most flawlessly of him.

Hamlet   The relevancy, sir? Why are we gasping with
admiration for this gentleman?

Osric   Sir?

Horatio   [*to* **Osric**]   Can't we speak more simply? You'll try,
I'm sure.

Hamlet   Why speak about him at all?

Osric   About Laertes?

Horatio   He's bankrupt already. No more golden words left!

Hamlet   About him, sir.

Osric   I know you are not ignorant –

Hamlet   I wish you did, sir. But even if you did, it wouldn't do
me much credit. Well, sir?

Osric   You are not ignorant of Laertes' excellence –

Hamlet   I daren't admit to that, or I'd be assuming my own
excellence. However, to know another man well one has to
know oneself well first.

Osric   I mean, sir, excellence with his weapon. According to
his reputation amongst those in his service, he has no equal.

Hamlet   What *is* his weapon?

145   **Osric**   Rapier and dagger.

Hamlet   That's two of his weapons. But well.

Osric   The King, sir, hath wagered with him six Barbary
horses, against the which he has impawned, as I take it, six
French rapiers and poniards, with their assigns, as girdle,
150   hanger, and so. Three of the carriages, in faith, are very dear
to fancy, very responsive to the hilts, most delicate carriages,
and of very liberal conceit.

Hamlet   What call you the carriages?

Horatio   I knew you must be edified by the margin ere you
155   had done.

Osric   The carriages, sir, are the hangers.

Hamlet   The phrase would be more german to the matter if
we could carry a cannon by our sides. I would it might be
hangers till then. But on. Six Barbary horses against six
160   French swords, their assigns, and three liberal-conceited
carriages; that's the French bet against the Danish. Why is
this – impawned, as you call it?

Osric   The King, sir, hath laid, sir, that in a dozen passes
between yourself and him he shall not exceed you three hits;
165   he hath laid on twelve for nine. And it would come to
immediate trial if your lordship would vouchsafe the answer.

Hamlet   How if I answer no?

Osric   I mean, my lord, the opposition of your person in trial.

Hamlet   Sir, I will walk here in the hall. If it please his
170   Majesty, it is the breathing time of day with me. Let the
foils be brought, the gentleman willing, and the King hold
his purpose, I will win for him an I can; if not, I will gain
nothing but my shame and the odd hits.

Osric Rapier and dagger.

Hamlet That's two of his weapons, but still . . .

Osric The King, sir, has wagered six Barbary horses, against
which Laertes had staked, I believe, six French rapiers and
daggers, with their accessories – such as belts, straps, and
so on. Three of the carriages indeed, are in very pleasing
taste, very well matched with the sword hilts; very
finely wrought carriages, and ingeniously executed.

Hamlet What are these "carriages" you speak of?

Horatio I knew you'd need footnotes in the end!

Osric The carriages, sir, are the straps.

Hamlet The word would be more appropriate if we were
mounting cannon at our sides; till we're talking about
gun carriages, I'd prefer to call them straps. But carry on.
Six Barbary horses against six French swords, their
accessories, and three fancifully named "carriages." That's
the French bet against the Danish. Why is this "staked," as
you call it?

Osric The King, sir, has wagered, sir, that in a dozen bouts
between you and Laertes, he will not win three more than
you. Laertes wagered he'll score nine hits out of the twelve.
It could be settled immediately if your lordship would deign
to grant an answer.

Hamlet What if I answer "no"?

Osric I mean, my lord, "accept the challenge."

Hamlet Sir, I will take a walk here in the hall. It's my exercise
time, if that's all right with his Majesty. If the foils are
brought, the gentleman is willing, and the King hasn't
changed his mind, I'll win for him if I can. If not, I'll gain
nothing but my own shame and the odd hits.

Osric Shall I deliver you so?

175 **Hamlet** To this effect, sir, after what flourish your nature will.

Osric I commend my duty to your lordship.

Hamlet Yours.

[*Exit* **Osric**]

He does well to commend it himself, there are no tongues
180 else for's turn.

Horatio This lapwing runs away with the shell on his head.

Hamlet He did comply with his dug before he sucked it.
Thus has he – and many more of the same bevy that I know
the drossy age dotes on – only got the tune of the time and
185 outward habit of encounter, a kind of yeasty collection,
which carries them through and through the most fanned
and winnowed opinions; and do but blow them to their trial,
the bubbles are out.

[*Enter a* **Lord**]

Lord My lord, his Majesty commended him to you by young
190 Osric, who brings back to him that you attend him in the
hall. He sends to know if your pleasure hold to play with
Laertes or that you will take longer time.

Hamlet I am constant to my purposes, they follow the King's
pleasure. If his fitness speaks, mine is ready. Now or
195 whensoever, provided I be so able as now.

Lord The King and Queen and all are coming down.

Hamlet In happy time.

Lord The Queen desires you to use some gentle entertainment to Laertes before you fall to play.

Osric   Shall I quote you thus?

Hamlet   To that effect sir, using whatever rhetoric comes naturally to you.

Osric   [*bowing affectedly*]   At your lordship's service, if I may so recommend.

[**Osric** *leaves*]

Hamlet   [*dryly*]   Yours.   [*To* **Horatio**]   He does well to recommend himself. Nobody would do it for him.

Horatio   [*observing* **Osric** *has at last replaced his hat*]   This shrill young bird flies off with his shell stuck to his head!

Hamlet   He curtsied before his mother's nipple before he sucked it. Like many more of his sort that I know are fashionable in these frivolous days, he's only capable of platitudes and small talk. It's a kind of trendy vocabulary which enables them to hold their own with cultured persons. Put them to any real test, and their bubbles are burst.

[*A* **Lord** *enters*]

Lord   My lord, his Majesty approached you via young Osric, who returned with the message that you await his Majesty in the hall. He would like to know if you are ready to compete with Laertes now, or whether you wish to do so later.

Hamlet   I haven't changed my mind. I'm at the King's service. If he's ready, so am I. Now or whenever, provided I'm as fit as I am now.

Lord   The King and Queen, and the court, are all on their way down.

Hamlet   Well timed.

Lord   The Queen would like you to show courtesy to Laertes before you begin.

200   **Hamlet**   She well instructs me.

[*Exit* **Lord**]

Horatio   You will lose this wager, my lord.

Hamlet   I do not think so. Since he went into France, I have
been in continual practice. I shall win at the odds. Thou
wouldst not think how ill all's here about my heart; but it is
205   no matter.

Horatio   Nay, good my lord.

Hamlet   It is but foolery, but it is such a kind of gaingiving as
would perhaps trouble a woman.

Horatio   If your mind dislike anything, obey it. I will forestall
210   their repair hither and say you are not fit.

Hamlet   Not a whit. We defy augury. There is a special
providence in the fall of a sparrow. If it be now, 'tis not to
come; if it be not to come, it will be now; if it be not now, yet
it will come. The readiness is all. Since no man of aught he
215   leaves, knows aught, what is't to leave betimes? Let be.

[*A table prepared. Trumpets, Drums, and Officers with
cushions. Enter* **King, Queen, Laertes, Osric,** *and all the
State, and Attendants with foils and daggers.*]

King   Come, Hamlet, come, and take this hand from me.

[*Puts* **Laertes'** *hand into* **Hamlet's**]

Hamlet   Give me your pardon, sir. I have done you wrong;
But pardon't as you are a gentleman.
This presence knows, and you must needs have heard,
220   How I am punished with a sore distraction.
What I have done

294

Hamlet   I accept her advice.

[The **Lord** *leaves]*

Horatio   You will lose, my lord.

Hamlet   I don't think so. Since he went to France, I've been in continual practice. At the odds laid, I shall win. You wouldn't believe how uneasy I feel, but that's of no consequence.

Horatio   But my good lord –

Hamlet   It's silly: the kind of misgiving that might perhaps trouble a woman.

Horatio   If your mind tells you something's wrong, don't ignore it. I'll stop them coming here, and say you aren't well.

Hamlet   Not at all. We must disregard premonitions. Everything is carefully preordained. If death comes now, it won't come in the future. If not in the future, then now. If not now, then sometime, for certain. Being prepared for it is what matters. Since no man knows what he will be missing, what's so bad about an early death? Enough of that!

[A table is set out by Attendants. Trumpets and drums herald the entrance of Officers with cushions, who are followed by the **King**, *and* **Queen**, **Laertes**, *members of the Court, and more Attendants with foils and daggers]*

King   Come, Hamlet, come – and take Laertes' hand.   *[He puts* **Laertes'** *hand into* **Hamlet's**]*

Hamlet   Your pardon, sir. I have done you wrong. Forgive me, as you are a gentleman. This eminent assembly knows, and you must surely have heard, that I've been suffering badly from insanity. Whatever I've done to provoke you, in terms

That might your nature, honour, and exception
Roughly awake, I here proclaim was madness.
Was't Hamlet wronged Laertes? Never Hamlet.
225   If Hamlet from himself be ta'en away,
And when he's not himself does wrong Laertes,
Then Hamlet does it not, Hamlet denies it.
Who does it then? His madness. If't be so,
Hamlet is of the faction that is wronged;
230   His madness is poor Hamlet's enemy.
Sir, in this audience,
Let my disclaiming from a purposed evil
Free me so far in your most generous thoughts
That I have shot my arrow o'er the house
235   And hurt my brother.

Laertes   I am satisfied in nature,
Whose motive in this case should stir me most
To my revenge; but in my terms of honour
I stand aloof, and will no reconcilement
240   Till by some elder masters of known honour
I have a voice and precedent of peace
To keep my name ungored. But till that time
I do receive your offered love like love
And will not wrong it.

245 **Hamlet**   I embrace it freely,
And will this brother's wager frankly play.
Give us the foils.

Laertes   Come, one for me.

Hamlet   I'll be your foil, Laertes. In mine ignorance
250   Your skill shall like a star i'th'darkest night
Stick fiery off indeed.

Laertes   You mock me, sir.

Hamlet   No, by this hand.

of your filial affection, your honor or your sense of
grievance, I here proclaim was madness. Was it Hamlet who
wronged Laertes? No, not Hamlet. If the real Hamlet is
displaced, and when he is not himself does some wrong to
Laertes, then Hamlet doesn't do it: Hamlet denies it. Who
does it then? His madness. If that is so, Hamlet is the party
who's aggrieved. His madness is poor Hamlet's enemy. Sir,
before this audience: let my denial that I acted with
deliberate malice allow you in your generosity to accept that
I hurt you accidentally.

Laertes   I am satisfied with regard to my natural feelings,
which of all things should stir me to revenge. In respect of
honor, I reserve judgment, and to keep my good name
intact will not consider a reconciliation till more experienced
experts in the field have judged in favor of it. Till such
time, I accept your offered love at its face value, and will not
spurn it.

Hamlet   I welcome it wholeheartedly, and will take part in this
wager between brothers with a free mind.   [*To the
Attendants*]   Give us the foils.

Laertes   Come, one for me.

Hamlet   I'll be *your* foil, Laertes! My clumsiness will make your
skill shine very brightly indeed, like a star in the darkest of
nights!

Laertes   You are mocking me, sir.

Hamlet   No, I swear it.

King Give them the foils, young Osric. Cousin Hamlet,
255 You know the wager?

Hamlet   Very well, my lord.
Your Grace has laid the odds o'th'weaker side.

King I do not fear it. I have seen you both,
But since he is bettered, we have therefore odds.

260 **Laertes** This is too heavy. Let me see another.

Hamlet This likes me well. These foils have all a length?

Osric Ay, my good lord. [*They prepare to play*]

[*Enter Servants with flagons of wine*]

King Set me the stoups of wine upon that table.
If Hamlet give the first or second hit,
265 Or quit in answer of the third exchange,
Let all the battlements their ordnance fire:
The King shall drink to Hamlet's better breath,
And in the cup an union shall he throw
Richer than that which four successive kings
270 In Denmark's crown have worn. Give me the cups –
And let the kettle to the trumpet speak,
The trumpet to the cannoneer without,
The cannons to the heavens, the heavens to earth,
'Now the King drinks to Hamlet.' Come, begin.
275 And you, the judges, bear a wary eye.

Hamlet Come on, sir.

Laertes Come, my lord. [*They play*]

Hamlet One.

King   Give them the foils, young Osric. Cousin Hamlet: you
know the wager?

Hamlet   Very well, my lord. Your Grace has backed the
weaker side.

King   I'm not worried. I have seen you both, and because he is
in better form, he has a handicap.   [**Hamlet** *is given a
three-hit start, according to the terms conveyed by* **Osric**]

Laertes   [*finding he has not been given the poisoned
rapier*]   This is too heavy. Let me see another.

Hamlet   [*swishing his*]   I like this one. These foils are all the
same length?

Osric   Yes, my good lord.

[*They prepare to duel. Servants enter with pitchers of wine*]

King   Put the wine on that table. If Hamlet wins the first or
second hit, or draws level in the third bout, let all the
battlements fire their cannon. The King will drink to
Hamlet's continued success, and he'll throw into the
drinking cup a pearl more valuable than the one worn by
four successive Kings of Denmark in their crown. Give me
the cups! And to mark the occasion, let kettle drums signal
to the trumpets, the trumpets to the artillerymen outside,
the cannons to the heavens, the heavens to the earth – signifying: "Now the King drinks to Hamlet." Come, begin!
And you, the judges, keep a watchful eye.

Hamlet   Come on, sir.

Laertes   Come on, my lord.

[**Hamlet** *and* **Laertes** *play their first bout.*]

Hamlet   One!

Laertes   No.

280 **Hamlet**   Judgment.

Osric   A hit, a very palpable hit.

Laertes   Well, again.

King   Stay, give me drink. Hamlet this pearl is thine.
Here's to thy health.

[*Drums; trumpets; and shot goes off*]

285   Give him the cup.

Hamlet   I'll play this bout first. Set it by awhile.
Come   [*They play again*]
Another hit. What say you?

Laertes   A touch, a touch I do confess.

290 **King**   Our son shall win.

Queen   He's fat and scant of breath.
Here, Hamlet, take my napkin, rub thy brows.
The Queen carouses to thy fortune, Hamlet.

Hamlet   Good madam.

295 **King**   Gertrude, do not drink.

Queen   I will, my lord, I pray you pardon me.

[*She drinks and offers the cup to* **Hamlet**]

King   [*aside*] It is the poisoned cup. It is too late.

Hamlet   I dare not drink yet, madam; by and by.

Laertes   No!

Hamlet   A ruling!

Osric   A hit, a very definite hit.

Laertes   Well, again – [*He makes to resume*]

King   Hold. Give me a drink.   [*He takes a long quaff*]
   Hamlet, this pearl is yours! Here's to your health!   [*He drops
   the poison into the cup, and raises it as the drums, the
   trumpets, and the cannon obey his earlier instructions*]
   Give him the cup.

Hamlet   I'll play this bout first. Set it aside a moment. Come.

   [*They play again*]

   Another hit. Agreed?

Laertes   A touch, a touch, I must admit.

King   Our son will win!

Queen   He's not at his fittest, and short of breath. Here,
   Hamlet: take my handkerchief and wipe your brow. The
   Queen drinks to your good fortune, Hamlet!

   [*She picks up the poisoned cup and raises it to her lips*]

Hamlet   [*acknowledging the compliment*]   Good madam.

King   Gertrude – do not drink!

Queen   I shall, my lord. Pardon me, if you will.

   [*She drinks, then offers the cup to* **Hamlet**]

King   [*aside*]   It's the poisoned cup! It's too late!

Hamlet   I dare not drink yet, madam. By and by.

Queen   Come, let me wipe thy face.

300 **Laertes**   My lord, I'll hit him now.

King   I do not think't.

Laertes   [*aside*]   And yet it is almost against my conscience.

Hamlet   Come for the third, Laertes. You do but dally.
I pray you pass with your best violence.
305   I am afeard you make a wanton of me.

Laertes   Say you so? Come on.   [*They play*]

Osric   Nothing neither way.

Laertes   Have at you now.

[**Laertes** *wounds* **Hamlet;** *then, scuffling, they change rapiers*]

King   Part them; they are incensed.

310 **Hamlet**   Nay, come again.

[*He wounds* **Laertes**. *The* **Queen** *falls*]

Osric   Look to the Queen there, ho!

Horatio   They bleed on both sides. How is it, my lord?

Queen   Come, let me wipe your face.

Laertes   [*to the* **King**]   My lord, I'll hit him now.

King   I don't think so.

Laertes   [*aside*]   And yet it's almost against my conscience.

Hamlet   Come for the third bout, Laertes! You are wasting time. Thrust with all your power, do. I think you are teasing me.

Laertes   Really? Come on!

[*They play for the third time. They lock swords, and* **Osric** *divides them, judging it a draw*]

Osric   Nothing either way.

[**Laertes** *catches* **Hamlet** *unawares, by slashing at him with his rapier*]

Laertes   Have at you now!

[**Hamlet** *has sustained a cut. Angered, he fights fiercely. The two men lose their self-control, and drop their weapons during a scuffle. They change rapiers when they resume*]

King   Part them: they are incensed!

Hamlet   Right then: come again!

[*He wounds* **Laertes** *with the poisoned weapon. At the same time, the* **Queen** *falls to the ground*]

Osric   Look after the Queen there! Stop the fighting!

Horatio   Both are bleeding.   [*To* **Hamlet**] How are you, my lord?

Osric   How is't, Laertes?

Laertes   Why, as a woodcock to mine own springe, Osric.
315   I am justly killed with mine own treachery.

Hamlet   How does the Queen?

King   She swoons to see them
bleed.

Queen   No, no, the drink, the drink! O my dear Hamlet!
320   The drink, the drink! I am poisoned.   [*Dies*]

Hamlet   O villainy! Ho! Let the door be locked.
Treachery! Seek it out.

[*Exit* **Osric**]

Laertes   It is here, Hamlet. Hamlet thou art slain.
No medicine in the world can do thee good;
325   In thee there is not half an hour of life.
The treacherous instrument is in thy hand,
Unbated and envenomed. The foul practice
Hath turned itself on me. Lo, here I lie,
Never to rise again. Thy mother's poisoned.
330   I can no more. The King – the King's to blame.

Hamlet   The point envenomed too! Then, venom, to thy
work.

[*Stabs the* **King**]

All   Treason! Treason!

King   Oh yet defend me, friends. I am but hurt.

335 **Hamlet**   Here, thou incestuous, murd'rous, damned Dane,
Drink off this potion. Is thy union here?
Follow my mother.

304   [**King** *dies*]

Osric How are you, Laertes?

Laertes Why, like a bird caught in my own trap, Osric. I am justly killed by my own treachery.

Hamlet What is the matter with the Queen?

King She faints at the sight of their blood.

Queen No, no: the drink, the drink! Oh, my dear Hamlet! The drink, the drink! I've been poisoned!

Hamlet Oh, such villainy! Stop! Lock the door! Treachery! Unmask it!

[**Osric** *leaves*]

Laertes It's here, Hamlet. Hamlet, you're doomed. No medicine in the world can save you. You have less than half an hour to live. You are holding the treacherous weapon: it has no button, and it's poisoned. The foul trick has turned itself on me. Look; here I lie, never to rise again. Your mother is poisoned. I can say no more. The King – the King's to blame!

Hamlet The point poisoned too? Then, venom – to your work!

[*He wounds the King*]

All Treason! Treason!

King Defend me still, my friends! I'm only wounded.

Hamlet Here, you incestuous, murderous, damned Dane! Finish this drink! Is your pearl here? Follow my mother!

[*He forces the* **King** *to drink. The* **King** *dies*]

Laertes   He is justly served.
It is a poison tempered by himself.
340   Exchange forgiveness with me, noble Hamlet.
Mine and my father's death come not upon thee,
Nor thine on me.   [*Dies*]

Hamlet   Heaven make thee free of it. I follow thee.
I am dead, Horatio. Wretched Queen, adieu!
345   You that look pale and tremble at this chance,
That are but mutes or audience to this act,
Had I but time – as this fell sergeant, Death,
Is strict in his arrest – O, I could tell you –
But let it be. Horatio, I am dead,
350   Thou livest. Report me and my cause aright
To the unsatisfied.

Horatio   Never believe it.
I am more an antique Roman than a Dane.
Here's yet some liquor left.

355 **Hamlet**   As thou'rt a man
Give me the cup. Let go, by heaven I'll have't.
O God, Horatio, what a wounded name,
Things standing thus unknown, shall I leave behind me.
If thou didst ever hold me in thy heart,
360   Absent thee from felicity awhile,
And in this harsh world draw thy breath in pain
To tell my story.

                        [*A march afar off and shot within*]

              What warlike noise is this?

[*Enter* **Osric**]

Osric   Young Fortinbras, with conquest come from Poland,
365   To the ambassadors of England gives
This warlike volley.

Laertes   It is only justice. It is poison he concocted himself. Exchange forgiveness with me, noble Hamlet. Be cleared of my death and my father's, and I'll not be accused of yours.

[**Laertes** *dies*]

Hamlet   May God acquit you of it. I follow you. I'm a dead man, Horatio. Unhappy Queen, farewell.   [*To the Courtiers*]   You who look pale, and who tremble at this misfortune; who are merely silent onlookers; if only I had the time – since Death's cruel lieutenant is ruthless in making his arrests – oh, I could tell you – but let that be . . . Horatio, I am as good as dead. You are living. To those who do not know the full story, give a just account of me and my motives.

Horatio   Don't you believe it. There's more of the ancient Roman in me than the Dane.   [*Romans chose suicide to dishonor*]   There's still some of the drink left.   [*He picks up the poisoned cup*]

Hamlet   Give me the cup, man!   [*They struggle*]   Let go: by heaven I'll have it!   [*He wrests it from* **Horatio's** *grasp*]   Oh God, Horatio, what a bad name I'd leave behind me if the truth was never told! If you ever held me in affection, don't commit suicide, and suffer the pain of this harsh world to tell my story.

[*Far off can be heard the sound of marching, and the firing of cannon*]

What's that warlike noise?

[**Osric** *enters*]

Osric   Young Fortinbras, returning from his conquests in Poland, fires this warlike volley in honor of the ambassadors from England.

Hamlet   O, I die, Horatio.
The potent poison quite o'ercrows my spirit.
I cannot live to hear the news from England,
370   But I do prophesy th'election lights
On Fortinbras. He has my dying voice.
So tell him, with th'occurrents more and less
Which have solicited – the rest is silence.   [*Dies*]

Horatio   Now cracks a noble heart. Good night, sweet prince,
375   And flights of angels sing thee to thy rest!

[*March within*]

Why does the drum come hither?

[*Enter* **Fortinbras,** *and the* **English Ambassadors,** *and
Soldiers with drum and colours*.]

Fortinbras   Where is this sight?

Horatio   What is it you would see?
If aught of woe or wonder, cease your search.

380   **Fortinbras**   This quarry cries on havoc. O proud Death,
What feast is toward in thine eternal cell,
That thou so many princes at a shot
So bloodily hast struck?

1st Ambass.   The sight is dismal;
385   And our affairs from England come too late.
The ears are senseless that should give us hearing
To tell him his commandment is fulfilled,
That Rosencrantz and Guildenstern are dead.
Where should we have our thanks?

390   **Horatio**   Not from his mouth,
Had it th'ability of life to thank you.
He never gave commandment for their death.

308

Hamlet Oh, I'm dying, Horatio. The powerful poison triumphs over me. I cannot stay alive to hear the news from England, but I prophesy that Fortinbras will be elected King of Denmark. He has my dying support. Tell him so, with the general details that have persuaded me to – [**Hamlet** *cannot finish the sentence*] The rest is silence . . .

[*He means the silence of the grave. The poison takes effect,*
and **Hamlet** *dies*]

Horatio There ends a noble life. Good night, sweet prince: may choirs of angels sing you to your rest.

[*The sound of marching is heard*]

Why does the drum lead them this way?

[**Fortinbras,** *the* **English Ambassadors,** *and Soldiers enter, to the sound of drums*]

Fortinbras Where is this spectacle?

Horatio What do you wish to see? Seek no further if it's something sorrowful and disastrous.

Fortinbras [*looking around*] This heap of dead proclaim a massacre. Oh, proud Death: what feast are you preparing in your eternal haunt, that you have so bloodily claimed so many nobles all at once?

1st Ambass. The sight is appalling, and our news from England comes too late. The ears are forever deaf that should hear of the deaths of Rosencrantz and Guildenstern, in fulfillment of his orders. To whom do we turn for thanks?

Horatio [*pointing to the* **King**] Not from his mouth, even if it could thank you. He didn't order you to kill them. Since,

309

But since, so jump upon this bloody question,
You from the Polack wars, and you from England,
395   Are here arrived, give order that these bodies
High on a stage be placed to the view,
And let me speak to the yet unknowing world
How these things came about. So shall you hear
Of carnal, bloody, and unnatural acts,
400   Of accidental judgments, casual slaughters,
Of deaths put on by cunning and forced cause,
And, in this upshot, purposes mistook
Fallen on th'inventors' heads. All this can I
Truly deliver.

405   **Fortinbras**   Let us haste to hear it,
And call the noblest to the audience.
For me, with sorrow I embrace my fortune.
I have some rights of memory in this kingdom,
Which now to claim my vantage doth invite me.

410   **Horatio**   Of that I shall have also cause to speak,
And from his mouth whose voice will draw on more.
But let this same be presently performed
Even while men's minds are wild, lest more mischance
On plots and errors happen.

415   **Fortinbras**   Let four captains
Bear Hamlet like a soldier to the stage,
For he was likely, had he been put on,
To have proved most royal; and for his passage,
The soldier's music and the rite of war
420   Speak loudly for him.
Take up the bodies. Such a sight as this
Becomes the field, but here shows much amiss.
Go, bid the soldiers shoot.

[*A dead march. Exeunt, bearing off the bodies, after which a peal
of ordnance is shot off*]

310

however, you from the Polish wars [*indicating* **Fortinbras**] and you from the King of England [*indicating the* **Ambassadors**] have arrived here so opportunely at this bloody time, order these bodies to be placed high on a stage for all to see, and I can explain to the uninformed world how these things came about. That way you will hear of incestuous, murderous, and inhuman acts; of divine retribution and accidental killings; of deaths brought about by trickery and contrivance; and, in this particular respect, of bungled plans that backfired on the originators. All this I can vouch for and relate.

Fortinbras Let us hear it immediately, and assemble the nobility. As for me, with sorrow I seize my opportunity. I have some rights to this kingdom which are not forgotten. This is the appropriate time to claim them.

Horatio I shall speak of that, too, as proxy for one whose vote will influence others in the election. [*He means* **Hamlet***'s naming of* **Fortinbras** *as the new King*] But let the aforesaid ceremony take place at once, even while everyone is excited, to make sure that nothing worse can happen.

Fortinbras Four captains shall bear Hamlet like a soldier to the platform. Had he lived to be crowned, he would surely have proved to be truly royal. To mark his passing, martial sounds and military salutes shall speak loudly for him. [*Drums begin to beat in the background*] Raise the bodies. [*The soldiers carry them aloft on their flattened shields*] A sight such as this befits the battlefield. It's not appropriate here. Go: order the soldiers to shoot.

[*A salute of guns is fired. The drums beat louder. Everyone leaves to a slow march behind the bodies as they are taken to the platform*]

Activities

Characters

Search the text to find answers to the following questions. They will help you to form personal opinions about the major characters in the play. *Record any relevant quotations in Shakespeare's own words.*

Hamlet

1 Hamlet is an enigmatic and complex character, the subject of more detailed analysis than any other character in English literature. There are, however, some basic facts. Find confirmation of the following information, which is provided by various witnesses, and Hamlet himself.

    a Until the death of his father, he was a student at Wittenberg and wished to return (Claudius, *Act I Scene 2*).

    b Although seemingly a young man, he is 30 years of age (Gravedigger, *Act V Scene 1*).

    c He is graced with civilized attributes (Ophelia, *Act III Scene 1*).

    d His manner is normally frank and artless (Claudius, *Act IV Scene 7*).

    e He is popular with the people of Denmark (Claudius, *Act IV Scene 7*).

    f He is keenly interested in plays and acting techniques (*Act III Scene 2*).

    g He is fond of fencing and practices regularly (*Act V Scene 2*).

    h He is not afraid of a fight (*Act IV Scene 7*).

i He does not tolerate fools gladly (*Act II Scene 2*) or take kindly to affectation (*Act V Scene 2*).

j He is magnanimous towards a rival (*Act V Scene 2*).

k He recognizes a man to be trusted (*Act III Scene 2*).

l He is shrewd in detecting those who are not to be trusted (*Act II Scene 2*).

m He is a loving and admiring son to his deceased father (*Act I Scene 2*).

n He readily apologizes when he knows he has done wrong (*Act V Scene 2* and *Act III Scene 4*).

2 Some of these traits have their less attractive counterparts. "Though I am not splenitive and rash," he says, "Yet have I in me something dangerous." In the light of this, comment on

  a his punishment of Rosencrantz and Guildenstern (*Act V Scene 2*);

  b his reasons for reprieving Claudius (*Act III Scene 3*);

  c his treatment of Ophelia (*Act III Scene 1*);

  d his killing of Polonius (*Act III Scene 4*);

  e his dispute with Laertes at Ophelia's funeral (*Act V Scene 1*).

How many deaths in the play is he accountable for?

3 We first meet Hamlet shortly after the funeral of his father and remarriage of his mother.

  a What evidence is there in *Act I Scene 2* that he is depressed and melancholic?

  b What do we learn from his first soliloquy of the reason for this mood?

4 His father's ghost appeals to him to "revenge his foul and most unnatural murder." In *Act I Scene 5*

  a he responds with a passionate intensity of purpose. Find the appropriate lines.

313

b he does something after learning of the murder that suggests the scholar rather than the man of action. What is it?

c he decides "to put an antic disposition on." Thereafter, Hamlet's behavior is frequently baffling. Consider the reports and the interpretations of

    i   Polonius (*Act II Scene 2*)

    ii Ophelia (*Act II Scene 1* and *Act III Scene 1*)

    iii Hamlet himself (*Act III Scene 2* and *Act V Scene 2*)

    iv Claudius (*Act III Scene 1* and *Scene 3*)

    v Gertrude (*Act III Scene 4* and *Act IV Scene 1*)

    vi the Gravedigger (*Act V Scene 1*)

and decide whether Hamlet's madness was real, or feigned, or a mixture of both.

5 Hamlet does not "sweep to his revenge." Instead he delays for reasons which have been the subject of unending debate.

a What are his stated reasons for

    i   setting up the performance of *The Mousetrap* (*Act III Scene 2*)?

    ii reprieving Claudius in *Act III Scene 3*?

Might the real reasons be different?

b In *Act III Scene 4*, Hamlet

    i   commits a "rash and bloody deed" and hopes the victim is Claudius;

    ii admits to procrastination and a diminished zeal;

    iii is revisited by the Ghost for a specific purpose.

Find the relevant lines and say how a previous soliloquy (*Act II Scene 2*) and a later one (*Act IV Scene 4*) reveal Hamlet's sense of guilt about his inaction.

6 Further light is shed on Hamlet's character through his relationship with the two women in his life.

a How do we know from what is said in *Act I Scene 2* and *Act III Scene 4* that Hamlet is

    i   shocked by his mother's swift remarriage?

ii revolted by her sexuality?

iii disgusted at what would have been regarded as an incestuous relationship?

iv contemptuous of her choice of a husband?

b i How do we know from *Act I Scene 3* that Hamlet has wooed Ophelia?

ii How do we know from *Act II Scene 2* that he has written love letters to her?

c Hamlet's first act of madness is to visit Ophelia and frighten her. The details are in *Act II Scene 1*.

i Explain how Hamlet behaves.

ii Explain the interpretation Polonius puts upon the episode.

iii Find evidence from *Act II Scene 2* to show that Hamlet feeds Polonius's theory.

iv Decide whether Hamlet's behavior in *Act III Scene 1* is genuine madness, or anger caused by Ophelia's apparent betrayal of him.

v Account for Hamlet's bawdy jocularity in *Act III Scene 2*, during the performance of *The Mousetrap*.

vi Comment on his behavior at the funeral of Ophelia in *Act V Scene 1*.

7 **a** Read Hamlet's words to Horatio in *Act I Scene 4*: "So oft it chances in particular men . . ."

b Then turn to the Textual Questions on page 320 and trace Hamlet's thought processes through his major soliloquies.

c Decide whether Hamlet carries "the stamp of one defect," and if so, identify it.

Claudius

1 Hamlet's view of Claudius is uncomplicated. He says he is (a) a murderer (b) an incestuous adulterer (c) a villain (d) a hypocrite (e) a drunkard (f) his father's inferior.

Find the evidence from the following scenes:

(i) *Act I Scene 2* (ii) *Act I Scene 4* (iii) *Act I Scene 5* (iv) *Act II Scene 2* (v) *Act III Scene 4*.

2 Show from

   a *Act III Scene 1* that Claudius is (i) perceptive (ii) intuitive (iii) decisive

   b *Act IV Scene 5* that he is (i) courageous (ii) persuasive

   c *Act IV Scene 7* that he is (i) ruthless (ii) scheming (iii) cunning

3 To what extent are the following redeeming features?

   a His avowed love for Gertrude (*Act IV Scene 7*).

   b His soliloquy in *Act III Scene 3*?

Gertrude

1 In his first soliloquy in *Act I Scene 2* Hamlet puts the blame for his melancholy squarely on his mother. What does Gertrude say early in *Act II Scene 2* to show that she is aware of this?

2 **a** In *Act III Scene 4*, Hamlet implies that his mother is implicated in his father's murder. Find the line.

   b Her innocence is indicated elsewhere in various ways

      i What does the Ghost say in *Act 1 Scene 5*?

     ii How does she differ from Claudius in her reaction to *The Mousetrap* in *Act III Scene 2*?

3 We can be sure of her love for Hamlet.

   a Find the confirmatory evidence in a speech by Claudius in *Act IV Scene 7*.

   b Whose name is on her lips in her dying moments?

4 It is equally certain that she wished Hamlet and Ophelia to marry.

a Show how this is hinted at in *Act III Scene 1* and

b Confirmed in *Act V Scene 1*.

5 Do you think the Ghost's attitude to Gertrude, as expressed in *Act I Scene 5*, is fitting, and in the circumstances, just?

Polonius

1 In *Act II Scene 2*, Hamlet calls Polonius a "tedious old fool" and "a great baby" that "is not yet out of his swaddling clothes". Where in the same scene does he

a mock him?

b prevent others from mocking him?

How, in *Act III Scene 4*, does he mock him again?

2 Polonius is open to ridicule, though Claudius always treats him with the respect due to his years and his service to the crown (*Act I Scene 2*, *Act II Scene 2*). Find examples to show he is

a	in *Act I Scene 3*	i	given to uttering platitudinous advice
		ii	cynically worldly-wise
b	in *Act II Scene 2*	i	garrulous
		ii	pedantic
		iii	self-conceited
c	in *Act II Scenes 1 & 2*	i	devious
		ii	forgetful
		iii	unscrupulous
d	in *Act III Scenes 3 & 4*		an eavesdropper

3 Trace Polonius's theory that Hamlet's madness is "the very ecstasy of love" from its inception in *Act II Scene 1*, through *Act II Scene 2* and *Act III Scene 1* where it seems to be disproved. What evidence is there in *Act III Scene 2* that Polonius clings to his theory nevertheless?

Laertes

1 Laertes stands in contrast to Hamlet, who says (in *Act V Scene 2*), "I'll be your foil."

   a Both have lived away from home. Hamlet wished to study in Germany. To which country does Laertes seek permission to return?

   b Both are skilled fencers. Find the evidence in *Act IV Scene 7* and *Act V Scene 2*.

   c Both are popular with the common people. How do we know this from *Act IV Scene 5* and *Act IV Scene 7*?

   d Both have a relationship with Ophelia; Hamlet as lover, Laertes as brother.

      i How do their interests conflict in *Act I Scene 3*?

      ii In which scene do the two men first fight?

      iii On this occasion, which man would you say was the man of words, and which the man of physical action?

2 Most important, both have fathers who have been murdered.

   a Show from *Act IV Scene 5* that Laertes is swift in seeking his revenge.

   b Show from *Act IV Scene 7* that Laertes has no scruples in achieving his purpose, at least when his blood is hot.

   c Show from *Act V Scene 2*

      i that his conscience troubles him before the fatal hit

      ii that afterwards he accepts his guilt

      iii that Hamlet recognizes him as a man with a similar grievance to his own.

   d Taking into account the fact that all three members of Polonius's household die as a result of Hamlet's actions, do you agree that Laertes dies honorably?

Ophelia

1 That Hamlet had made loving overtures to Ophelia before the

play begins is well documented: find the evidence in *Act I Scene 3* and *Act II Scene 2*. But the "honey of his music vows" (*Act III Scene 1*) gives Ophelia short-lived pleasure; in all the scenes in which she appears, she suffers for Hamlet's interest in her. In *Act I Scene 3*

a How does Laertes diminish her self-confidence – and offer her five words of worldly advice?

b How does Polonius destroy it even further – and issue an order?

c What frightening experience results from her obeying it?

2 In *Act 3 Scene 1*, acting under orders, she becomes "of ladies most deject and wretched." In what ways is she

a personally humiliated?

b subjected to a vicious verbal tirade?

c treated by her father as though she had no feelings?

3 In *Act III Scene 2*, at the performance of *The Mousetrap*, Ophelia is the butt of Hamlet's bawdy witticisms.

a Almost all her replies are terse and polite. Give examples.

b Do you agree that the dialogue is a painful experience for her? Why?

4 In *Act III Scene 4* Hamlet kills Ophelia's father. By *Act IV Scene 5*, she has gone mad. In *Act IV Scene 7* her death is reported, and in *Act V Scene 1* she is buried as a suicide.

a In her madness, how does she show

   i sexual frustration?

   ii lack of inhibition?

   iii grief?

b In her death, how is the pathos of her ending conveyed in the Queen's description of it?

c At her funeral, how do Laertes and Hamlet each express their love for "poor Ophelia"?

Textual Questions

Read the original Shakespeare and (if necessary) the modern transcriptions, to gain an understanding of Hamlet's six soliloquies. Then concentrate entirely on the originals in answering the questions.

1 *Oh that this too too solid flesh would melt (Act I Scene 2)*

   a The first line is as it is printed in the Folio edition of 1623. The Quartos replace "solid" with *sallied*, which means "assaulted" or "attacked." Some editors believe "sallied" is a variant spelling of *sullied*, meaning "fouled." Consider the merits of each carefully and decide which you think is best.

   b In the first seven lines, how do

      i ejaculations and

      ii adjectives

   convey Hamlet's mental anguish?

   c Explain

      i the gardening metaphor beginning " 'Tis an unweeded garden . . ."

      ii the effectiveness of monosyllables immediately following it.

   d Hamlet's suffering is reflected in his disjointed sentences.

      i Which word causes him to stumble first?

      ii How often is it repeated?

      iii How are the full implications of his suffering emphasized by the use of comparisons?

   e Some editions choose to omit "even she" in the line beginning, "Like Niobe, all tears," because the two words do not appear in the Second Quarto edition. What is gained by including them?

f   How does the soliloquy confirm that Hamlet has "that within which passes show"?

2   *O all you host of heaven! O earth! What else? (Act I Scene 5)*

    a   How do the first lines of this soliloquy contrast with the melancholic tone of the previous one?

    b   How does passion show in

        i   his questions and answers?

        ii   his use of repetition?

    c   Hamlet's first recourse is to his "tables," to "set it down." Explain why, in terms of Hamlet's future behavior, this can be regarded as ominous.

3   *O what a rogue and peasant slave am I! (Act II Scene 2)*

    a   In talking to the Players immediately before this soliloquy, Hamlet has apparently been confident, relaxed, and good humored. As soon as he is alone, he gives utterance to words of self-reproach. How does this juxtaposition of differing moods emphasize his mental stress?

    b   The simulated feelings shown by the Player contrast with Hamlet's real ones.

        i   Why does Shakespeare give "For Hecuba!" a line to itself?

        ii   Would the next line be as effective if the second "Hecuba" were replaced by the pronoun "her," as it is by some editors, who follow the second Quarto edition?

        iii   How does the second short line in the soliloquy relate to the first?

    c   Hamlet says the Player would "make mad the guilty" if he had "the cue for passion" that Hamlet has. How is this a prediction of what actually happens in *Act III Scene 2*?

    d   Disgust at his own inactivity leads Hamlet to scourge himself with words.

    i   Show how rhetorical questions lead to a crescendo of self-reproach.

    ii   Explain how six successive adjectives make Hamlet ashamed of himself.

e Finally, Hamlet calms down.

    i   Which words introduce a passage of reasoned argument?

    ii   Where have we heard of his plan before?

    iii What is Hamlet's excuse for instigating it?

4 *To be or not to be, that is the question (Act III Scene 1)*

  a The first line of Hamlet's most famous soliloquy is capable of a number of interpretations. Here are some of them: consider each carefully and decide which you favor.

    i   he is contemplating suicide

    ii   he is contemplating murder

    iii he is discussing whether life is worthwhile

    iv he is wondering whether or not to continue with his plans

  b Those who say (i) is the answer are probably in the majority, and they say that Hamlet proceeds to discuss whether misfortune should be accepted passively, or actively opposed. From this starting point

    i   Explain the case for death, as Hamlet expresses it.

    ii   Explain the case against it.

  c Hamlet says that dreams during "the sleep of death" must make us hesitate, adding either

    i   that is what makes us endure suffering so long or, possibly,

    ii   that is why long life is a misfortune.

Which do you think Shakespeare intended?

  d i   List the sufferings that humans commonly endure.

    ii Say what the two consequences are of human ability to reason.

    iii Explain how the second fits Hamlet's own situation precisely.

5 *'Tis now the very witching time of night (Act III Scene 2)*

Earlier in this scene, Hamlet is convinced of the King's guilt: "I'll take the Ghost's word for a thousand pound."

a Select the words and phrases in this speech which indicate that Hamlet's "native hue of resolution" (normally red: see the previous soliloquy) is no longer "sicklied o'er" (i.e., pale), suggesting that he is ready at last to take his revenge.

b Is it significant that he visits his mother first? Why?

6 *Now might I do it pat, now he is a-praying (Act III Scene 3)*

a On the way to see his mother, Hamlet encounters Claudius at prayer. Six very short statements, none more than six words long, take him from the start of his speech to the point where his resolution falters.

    i Identify them.

    ii Which word, repeated, suggests that Hamlet is mixing passion with logic?

    iii Which verb confirms that the latter is predominant?

b Deduce from the soliloquy

    i what special wickedness characterized King Hamlet's murder;

    ii what would be Hamlet's most appropriate form of revenge.

c "Flush" means "full of life" as in the expression "the flush of youth" or "the flush of Spring." This is the word used in the Second Quarto version of the play. The 1623 Folio edition prints "fresh."

    i Do you agree that the former is preferable in this context?

ii Explain your reasons for choosing one word rather than the other.

d Find the lines in *Act V Scene 2* where Hamlet commits Rosencrantz and Guildenstern to a death similar to the one he plans for Claudius here.

e Decide whether Hamlet's reasoning here is

i genuine, or

ii an excuse to buy time.

7 *How all occasions do inform against me (Act IV Scene 4)*

a What, according to Hamlet, distinguishes a person from a beast?

b He gives two reasons for delaying his revenge: how does the second relate to his behavior at the end of *Act III Scene 3*?

c In which other soliloquies does Hamlet refer to cowardice, and how is the recurrence of the theme significant?

d Which words are Hamlet's own answer to the question of why he delays?

e Explain why the army of Fortinbras sets Hamlet an example that should "spur" his "dull revenge."

f How does their example provide Hamlet with a scale by which to measure his responsibilities?

g How does the Fortinbras issue

i provide a character contrast?

ii prepare for the way in which the tragedy ends?

h As Hamlet speaks these lines, he is under escort, and en route for England.

i Are they, therefore, empty words?

ii Is there any hint of "bloody thoughts" occupying his mind on his return?

Examination Questions

The following are typical examination questions.

1 "In the rest of the play, Hamlet bewilders us by his varying moods and activities; in the soliloquies, he lays bare his true motives and his true weaknesses." Discuss and illustrate.

2 Why, in your opinion, does Hamlet fail "to sweep to his revenge"?

3 Consider the extent to which Hamlet's character is thrown into greater relief by contrast with the characters of Laertes, Fortinbras, and Horatio.

4 Identify the various comic episodes in *Hamlet* and explain their dramatic significance and effectiveness.

5 Illustrate Shakespeare's dramatic art from any *two* of the following: (a) the opening scene of *Hamlet*, (b) the graveyard scene, (c) the conclusion of the play after Hamlet's death.

6 What light is shed on Hamlet's character and motives by his relations with (a) his mother, (b) Ophelia?

7 What could be learned of Hamlet solely from the speeches of other characters about him? Illustrate.

8 Show how the visit of the Players to Elsinore is used by Hamlet (a) to comment on the nature and purpose of drama and (b) to ascertain the guilt of Claudius.

9 What contribution do Polonius and his family make to *Hamlet*?

10 What part does madness – real or feigned – play in the tragedy of *Hamlet*?

11 What aspects of Hamlet's character are revealed by his encounters with (a) the Ghost, (b) Rosencrantz and Guildenstern, (c) the gravedigger?

12 "In *Hamlet* the sordid realities of domestic crime are successfully reconciled with the demands of tragedy for great and universal issues." Discuss.

13 Show how in Hamlet, Laertes, and Fortinbras, Shakespeare contrasts three kinds of honor.

14 How, in *The Tragical History of Hamlet, Prince of Denmark* is Ophelia a tragic figure in her own right?

15 What is the interest and dramatic significance of the prose scenes in *Hamlet*?

One-word-answer quiz

1   What was the name of Hamlet's university?

2   According to Hamlet, who should not speak "more than is set down for them"?

3   From what kind of tree did Ophelia fall into the stream?

4   Who was "gracious in the possession of dirt"?

5   After how many days at sea did the pirates attack Hamlet's ship?

6   What was the name of the man to whom the sailors delivered Hamlet's message?

7   What was the name of the skilled horseman who praised Laertes' skill as a fencer?

8   What was the horseman's nationality?

9   Who had Hamlet's "dying voice"?

10 What "dulls the edge of husbandry"?

11 What did the King tell Hamlet he would put into his drinking cup?

12 Who was murdered in *The Mousetrap*?

13 What was the name of his nephew?

14 How many Barbary horses did the King wager on Hamlet?

15 Whom does Pyrrhus kill in the story told by the First Player?

16 Who played the part of Julius Caesar when acting at the university?

17 What was the surname of the gravedigger?

18 According to the gravedigger, who was the first gentleman that ever bore arms?

19 For how many years had the gravedigger been digging graves?

20 On how many occasions prior to the beginning of the play had the two guards seen the Ghost?

21 At what hour in the morning was the Ghost seen?

22 Towards which country was Fortinbras marching?

23 To whom was the gravedigger's companion to go for "a stoup of liquor"?

24 At what hour did Barnardo relieve Francisco on guard duty?

25 Whose skull was that of a former King's Jester?

26 For how many years had the Jester been buried?

27 What musical instrument does Hamlet borrow from the Players?

28 What was said to be a baker's daughter?

29 What was the nationality of Claudius's bodyguards?

30 What, according to Claudius, "doth hedge a king" – and also "shape our ends," according to Hamlet?

What's missing?

Complete the following:

1   A little more than kin, . . .
2   Oh that this too too solid flesh would melt . . .
3   The play's the thing . . .
4   There is a special providence in . . .
5   But that I am forbid To tell the secrets of my prison-house . . .
6   Goodnight, sweet prince, . . .
7   What a piece of work is a man, how noble in reason . . .
8   Beware of entrance to a quarrel, but being in . . .
9   There is a willow grows aslant the brook . . .
10 Truly to speak, and with no addition,/We go to gain . . .
11 Now get you to my lady's chamber and tell her . . .
12 Meet it is I set it down . . .
13 No place indeed should murder sanctuarize . . .
14 Oh my offense is rank, it smells to heaven; . . .
15 And let those that play your clowns . . .
16 To die, to sleep;/To sleep, perchance . . .
17 But look, the morn in russet mantle clad . . .
18 The funeral baked meats/Did coldly furnish forth . . .
19 Give me that man/That is not passion's slave . . .
20 What's Hecuba to him, or . . .
21 See what a grace was seated on this brow . . .
22 Though I am native here,/And to the manner born . . .
23 O God, I could be bounded in a nutshell . . .
24 There's such divinity doth hedge a king . . .

Activities

25 That he is mad, 'tis true; . . .

26 'Tis now the very witching time of night,/When . . .

27 Murder most foul, as in the best it is . . .

28 Forty thousand brothers/Could not . . .

29 Rightly to be great/Is not . . .

30 There are more things in heaven and earth, Horatio . . .